"To double business bound"

Also by René Girard

Deceit, Desire, and the Novel
Critique dans un souterrain
Violence and the Sacred
Des Choses cachées depuis la fondation du monde

"To double business bound"

Essays on Literature, Mimesis, and Anthropology

René Girard

The Johns Hopkins University Press
Baltimore and London

This book has been brought to publication with the
generous assistance of the Andrew W. Mellon Foundation.

Manufactured in the United States of America

The Johns Hopkins University Press, Baltimore, Maryland 21218
The Johns Hopkins Press Ltd., London

Library of Congress Catalog Card Number 78-8418
ISBN 0-8018-2114-2

Library of Congress Cataloging in Publication data
will be found on the last printed page of this book.

Contents

Introduction

The present volume deals with subjects usually regarded as pertaining to separate disciplines; nevertheless, it has little to do with the approaches and methodologies that have insured, in recent years, the growth of "interdisciplinary studies." Rather, it involves a certain view of imitation that binds together literary and anthropological questions. The standard view, derived from Plato's *mimesis* via Aristotle's *Poetics*, has always excluded one essential human behavior from the types subject to imitation—namely, desire and, more fundamentally still, appropriation. If one individual imitates another when the latter appropriates some object, the result cannot fail to be rivalry or conflict. Such conflict is observable in animals; beyond a certain intensity of rivalry the antagonists tend to lose sight of their common object and focus on each other, engaging in so-called prestige rivalry. In human beings, the process rapidly tends toward interminable revenge, which should be defined in mimetic or imitative terms.

Not only in philosophy but also in psychology, sociology, and literary criticism a mutilated version of imitation has always prevailed. The divisive and conflictual dimension of mimesis can still be sensed in Plato, where it remains unexplained. After Plato it disappears completely, and mimesis, esthetic and educational, becomes entirely positive. No philosopher or social scientist has ever challenged this strangely one-sided definition of the concept.

My own theory of mimetic desire comes from literary texts. It is not a methodology in the usual sense; it does not appeal to some extraliterary discipline presumed to be particularly "scientific" in order to elevate itself in an a priori fashion above all literary texts. Yet, this theory was not elaborated in a vacuum; its elaboration was literary in the sense that, to my knowledge at least, the only texts that ever discovered mimetic desire and explored some of its consequences are literary texts. I am speaking here not of all literary texts, not of literature per se, but of a relatively small group of works. In these works, human relations conform to the complex process of strategies and conflicts, misunderstandings and delusions that stem from the mimetic nature of human desire. Implicitly and sometimes explicitly, these works reveal the laws of mimetic desire.

I first posited this notion of a mimetic, mediated, or imitated desire in the somewhat misleading context of *Deceit, Desire, and the Novel*. That work did not look beyond the genre to which the examples discussed in its pages formally belonged. As a result, some critics, notably the late and lamented Lucien Goldmann, interpreted mimetic desire as a phenomenon characteristic only of certain social classes and of a single literary genre, the novel. The short essay that opens the present volume was an early reaction against these views. In spite of its obvious limitations, and even though the Paolo and Francesca episode of the *Inferno* illustrates only certain aspects of mimetic desire, it is reprinted here as a prodigious example of Dante's implacable insight in regard to mimetic desire and also of the no less implacable obstinacy of the lesser literary breed when it comes to canceling out the effects of that insight and reinserting literary genius into the mimetic circle it reveals.

As a group, the texts that reveal mimetic desire share none of the characteristics emphasized by the various schools of literary criticism. They do not share the same rhetorical practices; they do not belong to the same literary genres; they were written at different times, in different languages; they cannot be referred to a single intellectual or religious tradition. Most, if not all of them, however, belong to a group of universally acknowledged world masterpieces. Being unable to find any common ground among all the works that compose that group, literary critics now tend to regard its unity as somewhat mythical. The only notion that was ever invoked to justify the alleged superiority of these works—mimesis, once again—is no longer acknowledged as a valid basis for esthetics, and its discredit has reinforced the tendency to regard the presumed superiority of these works as imaginary.

To the estheticians of mimesis the best writers always were imitators, but for a long time the emphasis was on literary models, especially the most perfect works of the greatest ancient writers. Only very late did this emphasis shift to so-called reality, and the best writers became those who were best at "copying" whatever "reality" surrounded them. In a literary world more and more dominated first by the idea of originality and then by such views as the Saussurian theory of the arbitrary sign, all the esthetic uses of mimesis were questioned and rejected. It has now become more or less axiomatic that "words" and "things" must go their separate ways, or at least that they cannot "imitate" each other. In Europe especially, the notion of an esthetic mimesis is now regarded as virtually meaningless.

There is a great deal of truth in this critique, of course, but it does not go to the heart of the matter. The enormous emphasis on mimesis throughout the entire history of Western literature cannot be a mere mistake; there must be some deep-seated reason for it that has never been explained. I personally believe that the great masterpieces of our literature, primarily the dramas and novels, really are "more mimetic" in the sense that they portray human relations and desire as mimetic, and implicitly at least—sometimes even explicitly, as in Shakespeare's *Troilus and Cressida*—they reintroduce into their so-called fictions the conflictual dimension always eliminated from the theoretical definitions of this "faculty."

The great masterpieces are "more mimetic" than other works in a sense richer and more problematic than the mutilated definition inherited from Aristotle. Literary critics have never been able to challenge this definition, but they have continued to use the word *mimesis*; until recently at least they remained fascinated by it, as if they sensed its unexplored potential. And the truth is that in all its successive versions, impoverished as they were in regard to desire, the word nevertheless always tangentially referred to an objective element in the superiority of the works to which it was applied, works, in fact, of mimetic revelation.

Being more mimetic in the richer but still undefined sense of mimetic desire, these works are also more mimetic, as a consequence, in all traditional uses of the word. For instance, it is true that, whether or not they consciously imitate them, these works always somewhat resemble the most perfect of the ancient writers, being related to them by the common nature of their mimetic revelation. It is also true that the writers of these works are "more mimetic" or more "realistic" than other writers: human desire really *is* mimetic, and the texts that portray it as such cannot fail to be more "true-to-life" than other texts; the superiority of these texts is undeniable, but our reluctance to acknowledge its source has deeper roots than our respect for Aristotle and Plato. Or, rather, our respect for Aristotle and Plato and, most important, the seminal failure of these philosophers to encompass the entire range of imitative behavior cannot be unrelated to the dearest of all our illusions, the intimate conviction that our desires are really our own, that they are truly original and spontaneous. Far from combating such an illusion, Freud flattered it enormously when he wrote that the relationship of a person to his desires is really the same as his relationship to his mother.

If we are blind to mimetic desire, we will also be blind to the experience of "disillusionment" that makes its revelation possible and to the unmistakable traces left by that experience, not necessarily in all works of mimetic revelation but primarily in those transitional works

that accomplish the passage from mimetic reflection to mimetic revelation. For the writer himself, this passage necessarily means the shattering of a mimetic reflection that complacently mirrors itself as pure
originality and spontaneity.

How could critical methodologies, traditional and avant-garde, reach
a real understanding of these masterpieces, since they themselves remain faithful to the impoverished version of mimesis secretly challenged and rejected by the mimetic revelation. Even though Freud in
many respects represents an advance and even though he focused upon
significant patterns of dramatic relationships—the "triangular" pattern
of erotic entanglements, for instance—he also represents a great stumbling block because the solutions he propounds falsify, once more, the
true mimetic nature of desire. These solutions nevertheless exert a
powerful influence because for a long time they were the only theoretical solutions available and because they have become almost a second
nature to us. As in a Pavlovian experiment, they immediately come to
mind when we identify those triangular relationships that the writer
himself, we assume, would have interpreted as "oedipal" had he come
up to the level of intuition we can all reach now without difficulty,
thanks to Freud.

As a result, we never realize that the greatest works have their own
version of these triangular relationships, more economical, really, and
more efficient than that of Freud. The progress psychoanalysis has
achieved by focusing on the more significant relationships and by providing the only technical vocabulary we have for discussing them has
been bought at a very dear price; it has made more obscure than ever
before the original solution of at least some writers to the problems
envisaged by Freud. Even those critics who reject psychoanalysis have
become incapable of thinking about desire except in psychoanalytic
terms.

There is a quasitheoretical voice in the writers of mimetic desire, and
it has always been silenced: first by the conception of art as pure
entertainment, then by art for art's sake, and now by critical methodologies that more than ever deny any real investigative power to a literary work. We must unravel the paradoxical but logical network of
mimetic entanglements spun by the great literary works. We must
elaborate a language more faithful to the intuitions of the authors
themselves.

Instead of interpreting the great masterpieces in the light of modern
theories, we must criticize modern theories in the light of these masterpieces, once their theoretical voice has become explicit. Our relationship with the works of mimetic revelation cannot be defined as
"critical" in the usual sense. We have more to learn from them than

they have to learn from us; we must be students in the most literal sense of the word. Our conceptual tools do not come up to their level; instead of "applying" to them our ever changing methodologies, we should try to divest ourselves of our misconceptions in order to reach the superior perspective they embody.

This view should not be confused with some transcendental Romanticism or with the tendency to turn literature into an absolute. During much of this century, literary criticism has been divided between the "reductionists" and the "worshipers of beauty". Behind the opposition of the two schools lies a common belief in the ultimately inconsequential nature of all works of art as far as real knowledge is concerned. The worshipers of beauty have tacitly surrendered to their adversaries a major part of their inheritance, the treatment of human relations. At bottom, they too are awed by the generally spurious claims of contemporary social sciences. They are secretly convinced that these would-be sciences are infinitely wiser and more powerful than even the greatest literary works. They feel that the work must be kept under wraps. Being men of little faith, really, they want to protect that supposedly fragile and evanescent object from the superior insights of the Freudians, the Marxists, the behaviorists, the structuralists, etc. Like the reductionists, therefore, the esthetes put literary works behind bars. The only difference is that the bars of the latter critics are supposed to be protective. However, both groups believe that the type of thinking embodied in literary works is outmoded and irrelevant; it belongs to the concentration camp or the Indian reservation.

The truth, I believe, is that the social sciences, always trapped in a phenomenological or empirical impasse, are impotent. They need the great literary masterpieces to evolve; they need insights into mimetic desire and rivalries. The so-called incompatibility between the humanities and the sciences, at least in the case of the social sciences, is a meaningless academic ritual. Only with close collaboration can real progress become possible once more, both in the social sciences and in literary criticism.

A literary cult that recognizes only dead works, unable to play a vital role in today's world, is really a dead cult. In Europe at least, contemporary criticism has come to resemble a funeral procession more and more. The reductionists and the antireductionists are now marching together behind the hearse, and they confirm by their structuralist and poststructuralist association the vanity of their former opposition. Their common bond lies in the concepts of the inability of language to deal with anything but itself and the absolute irrelevance of all literary works. Concurrently, this criticism has become the last inheritor of "literary life" as a central point of mimetic fascination. Its increasing

vulnerability to the most hysterical fads and fashions involuntarily testifies to the more and more tyrannical grip upon it of a still unacknowledged mimetic desire.

The historical mutilation of mimesis, the suppression of its conflictual
dimension, was no mere oversight, no fortuitous "error." Real awareness of mimetic desire threatens the flattering delusion we entertain not
only about ourselves as individuals but also about the nature and origin
of that collective self we call our society. If mimesis, like all primitive
gods, has two "sides," one that disrupts the community and another
one that holds it together, how do the two sides relate to each other?
How can the conflictual and destructive mimesis turn into the nonconflictual mimesis of training and learning, indispensable to the elaboration and perpetuation of human societies? If mimetic desire and
rivalries are more or less normal human phenomena, how can societal
orders keep back this force of disorder, or, if they are overwhelmed
by it, how can a new order be reborn of such disorder? The very
existence of human society becomes problematic.

In the second half of the present book, an evolution occurs toward
these questions, but not, I believe, away from the literary text that
dominates the first half. There is no shift of interest, but rather a
growing recognition of the broader cultural implications of the mimetic
interferences that were first studied in literary texts because they were
first suggested there. The observer is compelled to broaden the scope
of his investigation; he must turn to the ethnological text, to those
myths and rituals in which the mimetic cycle is constantly represented.
It is the generally accepted view today that these representations—the
"undifferentiation" of ritual—do not correspond to anything real. The
existence of a conflictual mimesis suggests otherwise. If crises of
mimetic rivalry are more or less normal in certain types of human
society, there must be some equally "normal" mechanism to interrupt
and reverse their disruptive effects.

After perusing a great deal of material less outdated than is often
claimed nowadays, Freud presented in *Totem and Taboo* some of the
clues that point to real collective murders as the origin and model of all
rituals. The problematic of conflictual imitation provides an entirely
new context for the interpretation of these clues. All over the world,
sacrificial immolation occurs at the climax and as the conclusion of
mimetic free-for-alls that could be the reenactment of a spontaneously
unanimous victimage. That victimage would terminate a truly disruptive mimetic crisis by reuniting the entire community against a single,
powerless antagonist. "Scapegoat effects" are still observable today, but
only, perhaps, in residual forms not very productive in terms of myth
and ritual. They are productive enough, however, to suggest the pos-

sibility of a primitive cult originating in infinitely more powerful and "convincing" phenomena of a similar kind.

This is a hypothesis. We should not say, I believe, that it is a "mere" hypothesis, or "only" a hypothesis. It is a full-fledged hypothesis in the sense that it is sufficiently distinct from the data to permit significant confrontations. I tried to show, in the rather essayistic *Violence and the Sacred* (Baltimore: The Johns Hopkins University Press, 1977) and more systematically in *Des Choses cachées depuis la fondation du monde* (Paris: Grasset, 1978), written in collaboration with Jean-Michel Oughourlian and Guy Lefort, that this hypothesis stands the test of such confrontations. One can endlessly verify that all variables as well as all constants of religious actions and beliefs do correspond, all over the world, to what can logically be expected from the deluded interpretation of most powerful scapegoat effects, by those who benefit from them.

The objection has been raised that the immense diversity of religious institutions cannot be reduced to a single ritual, that of the scapegoat. This objection takes no account of the all-important difference between a scapegoat *ritual* and a scapegoat *effect*. We must not underestimate the genetic potential of the latter in regard to patterns of significance that cannot fail to reverse, distort, and even eliminate the respective roles of victims and persecutors in the very fashions that are exhibited by religious themes. The victim must be transfigured "for the worse" because of its alleged responsibility in the mimetic disorders and "for the better" because of the reconciliation brought about by its death, a reconciliation that will be imputed to that victim's omnipotence, beyond a certain level of scapegoat delusion. Through such delusion, therefore, the strange combination of transcendental power for both war and peace, disorder and order, or good and evil that is found all over the world in the notion of the sacred and in similar notions can be generated.

It is impossible, I repeat, to object to the hypothesis on the grounds that primitive institutions are too numerous and too different to be forced into a single mold. There is no mold at all, but we fail to realize that fact unless we grasp the element of *interpretation*, of necessarily deluded and therefore infinitely variable interpretation, that intervenes between the de facto reconciliation of unanimous victimage and the religious imperatives that stem from it and that are intended to preserve and revivify this memorable event. It is from such deluded interpretation that the ever changing forms of sacrificial reenactment (ritual) and communal recollection (mythology) are generated, not from the event itself. These episodes of victimage are not reproduced and remembered such as they really happened but such as they must be (mis)understood by the community they reunified. The victim must appear not as a random instrument of a mimetic shift in the collective mood from conflict to peace but as both a troublemaker and then a peacemaker, as an all-powerful manipulator of all human relations inside the community—in other words, a divinity.

No less than the hypothesis itself, the means through which it was reached and the literary problematic that precedes it are likely to arouse the suspicion of those specialists whose territory is unceremoniously invaded. To make matters worse, the first essays were written quite a few years ago, and they bear what Kenneth Burke would call "terministic" traces of some influences really alien to their real thrust; these can be misleading. Since the essays were published separately, each one had to be independently intelligible and the principles underlying the whole had to be enunciated each time, however briefly. Toward the end of the volume, therefore, the victimage theory is repeatedly summarized but never treated as fully as it should be. And, as I write these words, I realize that the present introduction, up to a point, constitutes one more instance of this regrettable practice.

As a result, the reader may be even more tempted than he normally is to substitute familiar ideas for the unfamiliar: Freudian or ego psychology, for instance, in the place of mimetic desire or, perhaps, the old cathartic and functionalist theories of ritual in the place of my genetic mechanism of structural forms. This mechanism is not intrinsically obscure, I believe, but it is paradoxical from the standpoint of established perspectives, being essentially rooted, I repeat, in the delusions of unanimous victimage.

Many things could have been done to minimize the predictable objections and misunderstandings. Two separate volumes could have been published, one focusing on the literary text and the other on the ethnological. This solution, however, would have been untrue to my own experience; it would have weakened the overall argument even if, in the short run, it would have made the following essays more acceptable.

In the end, I decided against almost all changes. The essays originally written in English are reprinted virtually verbatim. For the three that were written in French, complete translations have been provided. The existence of book-length systematizations of the entire theory provided the main excuse for adopting this laissez-faire solution, not merely because those books are available to the baffled readers of this one, but because of the amount of misunderstanding they themselves have generated. It is difficult to believe that further efforts to express the cohesiveness and rigor of my argument, for the time being at least, would be more successful than the earlier ones.

I can vaguely hope, therefore, that instead of further increasing the confusion, as it would be prudent to expect, the very imperfections of this new book, its visible lacunae as well as its repetitions, will spur the reader into active collaboration with the author and improve the channels of communication.

Professional anthropologists are often severe with theorizers, especially amateur theorizers. For the last fifty years, the distinction between the professional and the amateur has been drawn on the criterion of fieldwork. The philosophy behind this is that the more time you spend on fieldwork, the less time you have for rash speculation, so the more of a hearing you deserve. Many people feel entitled to dismiss even the greatest theoreticians of our era simply because they can murmur to each other, "I understand that he has done very little fieldwork." No one wants to minimize the accomplishments of fieldwork. These accomplishments are made even more precious because they can no longer be duplicated. Almost nowhere does primitive cult survive in unadulterated from.

As this situation grows even worse, how long will it be possible to regard fieldwork as the major determinant of competence in all fields of anthropology, including primitive religion? Should we really confer a monopoly on these generally extinct phenomena to the people who have contributed to the growing overpopulation, primarily by anthropologists, of those few and shrinking areas of our globe still available for primitive research, at least in principle? What will happen when the network of superhighways and Holiday Inns has become as dense in these areas as everywhere else? Will the last anthropologist still able to remember them at an earlier stage in their development declare the field officially closed when he retires? Will all further contributions to the subject be thereafter prohibited?

The opposite, we must hope, will happen. Anthropologists are the first to point out that people threatened with unwelcome change tend to make their *rites de passage* more rigid and obsessive, even as these lose their former substance. Far from discouraging all speculation, the complete disappearance of certain religious phenomena should bring back the sense of wonder that obviously accompanied their early discoveries. Great questions were asked at the time and must be asked anew because they have never been answered successfully. If the absence of a convincing answer, even year after year and century after century, sufficed to disprove the validity of a question, the hard sciences would never have seen the light of day.

There are visible objections, I am aware, to a line of investigation that seems to violate even the rules of "interdisciplinary studies." Who knows, however, if this awkward label, "interdisciplinary," does not minimize the formidable upheaval that is now taking place in the sciences of man? All around us, many walls and partitions have crashed to the ground. To pretend that we need a special license to do "interdisciplinary work" is to assume that these walls are still standing and that their official guardians, in their benignity, regard with tolerance if not with approval the would-be acrobats among us who presume to climb over these nonexistent walls, at their own academic risk, of course.

The walls have crumbled because there never was a solid foundation underneath. There is not a single aspect of anthropology today on which a real consensus exists. Of all the words that have to be used in discussing primitive religion there is not a single one whose definition is not in dispute. The conditions are such that no research orientation can be presented as absolutely "authoritative." No research orientation, therefore, can be dismissed a priori. Objections have to be concrete and detailed. The real test of a hypothesis such as mine lies in its ability or inability to account for the phenomena with which it deals, not with the overall impression it makes, however disagreeable. How does the reading of mythology proposed here compare with other readings? On this point, I rest my case with the last of the essays that follow. And I hope for the best.

"To double business bound"

1

The Mimetic Desire
of Paolo and Francesca

Paolo and Francesca, the adulterous lovers of *The Divine Comedy*, enjoyed a very special popularity at the beginning of the nineteenth century. The two young people defy human and divine laws and appear to bring about the triumph of passion, even in the realm of eternity. What does Hell matter to them, since they are there together? In the minds of innumerable readers, in modern times as well as in the Romantic era, the infernal setting, however artistically remarkable it may be, is no more than a deferential nod in the direction of the moral and theological conventions of the time.

Far from unsettling faith in individualism, romantic passion is regarded as being its fulfillment. The lovers give themselves to each other in an act that is utterly spontaneous and that involves only themselves, though it involves them totally. Thus we have a kind of lovers' *cogito ergo sum* on which existence is founded for the couple—the only real existence in their eyes—and that engenders a new being, at once unified and double, absolutely autonomous with regard to God and to men.

It is this image of love that emerges from the commentaries on Dante, just as it emerges from a thousand other literary works of the time. Yet this romantic reading is obviously contrary to the spirit of *The Divine Comedy*. For Dante, Hell is a reality. No true union is possible between the disembodied "doubles" that Paolo and Francesca represent for each other. The lovers' undertaking does indeed have a Promethean aspect, but its defeat is total, and it is this defeat that the romantic reader does not perceive. To reveal the contradiction in its entirety one need only read of the origin of the passion, as described by Francesca herself at Dante's request.

This essay appeared under the title "From 'The Divine Comedy' to the Sociology of the Novel," trans. Petra Morrison, in *Sociology of Literature and Dráma*, ed. Elizabeth Burns and Tom Burns (Harmondsworth, Eng.: Penguin Books, 1973), pp. 101–8.

One day, Paolo and Francesca were quite innocently reading the story of Lancelot together. When they reached the love scene between the knight and Queen Guinevere, Arthur's wife, they became embarrassed and blushed. Then came the first kiss of the legendary lovers. Paolo and Francesca turned toward each other and kissed likewise. Love advances in their souls in step with their own progress through the book. The written word exercises a veritable fascination. It impels the two young lovers to act as if determined by fate; it is a mirror in which they gaze, discovering in themselves the semblances of their brilliant models.

Thus Paolo and Francesca never achieve, even on earth, the coupled solipsism that is the definition of absolute passion; the Other, the book, the model, is present from the beginning; it is the model that originates their future self-absorption. The romantic and individualist reader fails to perceive the role played by bookish imitation precisely because he too believes in absolute passion. Draw the attention of such a reader to the fact of the book and he will reply that it is an unimportant detail; reading it, for him, does no more than uncover desire that existed beforehand. But Dante gives this "detail" an emphasis that renders even more striking the silence of modern commentators on this point. Interpretations that minimize the role of the model are all belied by the conclusion of Francesca's narrative:

> Galeotto fu il libro e chi lo scrisse.
> (Galeotto was both the book and its author).

Galleot (or Galehalt) is the treacherous knight, Arthur's enemy, who sows the seeds of passion in the hearts of Lancelot and Guinevere. It is the book itself, Francesca maintains, that plays the role of the diabolical go-between, the pander, in her life. The young woman curses the romance and its author. There is no question of drawing our attention to any particular writer. Dante is not writing literary history; he is stressing that, whether written or oral, it has to be some person's word that suggests desire. The book occupies in Francesca's fate the place of the Word in the Fourth Gospel: the Word of man becomes the Word of the devil if it usurps the place of the divine Word in our souls.

Paolo and Francesca are the dupes of Lancelot and the queen, who are themselves the dupes of Galleot. And the romantic readers, in their turn, are dupes of Paolo and Francesca. The malignant prompting is a process perpetually renewed without its victims' being aware of it. An identical internal censorship erases any cognizance of the mediator, suppresses all information contrary to the romantic solipsistic *Weltanschauung*. Georges Sand and Alfred de Musset, leaving for Italy, took themselves for Paolo and Francesca but never questioned their own spontaneity. Romanticism turns *The Divine Comedy* into a new novel of chivalry. It is an extremity of blindness that forces into the role of pander the very work that expressly denounces it.

The Francesca who speaks in the poem is no longer a dupe, but she owes her clear-sightedness to death. An imitator of imitators, she knows that the resemblance between her and her model is real (because one always obtains what one desires strongly). However, this resemblance does not consist in the triumph of an absolute passion, as the lovers at first imagined and as the readers imagine still, but in defeat, a defeat already accomplished at that moment when, in the shadow of the Lancelot story, the first kiss was exchanged.

Don Quixote, in his imitation of a chivalric model, courts the same quasidivinity as Paolo and Francesca. Like them, he spreads the evil of which he is a victim. He has his imitators and the novel of which he is the hero had its plagiarists. This fact allowed Cervantes, in the second part, to make his ironic prophecy about the insensate criticism that would rage around it once more with the Romantic period— Umamuno, for instance, was to insult Cervantes, the novelist himself, for exhibiting a "lack of understanding" of his sublimely inspired hero. The individualist is not unaware that there exists a second, and derivative, form of passion, but it is never, for him, "true passion," that is to say, his own or his models. The genius of Dante, like that of Cervantes, is bound up with the abandonment of the preconceptions of individualism. That is why the very essence of their genius has been misunderstood by the Romantics and their successors of today.[1]

Cervantes and Dante discover within the world of literature a whole territory of awareness that includes Shakespeare's "play within a play" and Gide's *mise en abîme.* In connection with modern novels, the same writers also afford us a rendering of unhappy consciousness that differs significantly from that of Hegel.

The hero in the grip of some second-hand desire seeks to conquer the *being*, the essence, of his model by as faithful an imitation as possible. If the hero lived in the same world as the model instead of being forever distanced from him by myth or history, as in the examples above, he would necessarily come to desire the same object. The nearer the mediator, the more does the veneration that he inspires give way to hate and rivalry. Passion is no longer eternal. A Paolo who encountered Lancelot every day would no doubt prefer Queen Guinevere to Francesca unless he managed to link Francesca and his rival, making the rival desire her, so as to desire her the more himself—to desire her *through* him or rather against him, to tear her, in short, from a desire that transfigures her. It is this second possibility that is illustrated in *Don Quixote* by the story of "the inquisitive, impertinent

man" and in Dostoevski by the short story of "The Eternal Husband."
For novelists who write of *internal* mediation, it is envy and morbid
jealousy that triumph. Stendhal speaks of "vanity," Flaubert and his
critics of Bovaryism; Proust reveals the workings of snobbery and of
l'amour-jalousie.

The model in these instances is still an obstacle. At a lower level of
"degradation," every obstacle will serve as a model. Masochism and
sadism are thus degraded forms of mediated desire. When the erotic
attachment is displaced from the object onto the intermediary-rival,
one has the type of homosexuality demonstrated by Marcel Proust. The
divisions and agonies produced by mediation find their climax in the
hallucination of the double, present in the work of numerous Romantic
and modern writers but comprehended only by the greatest as a conflictual structure.

One must treat the great work of fiction as a single entity, a totality.
The individual and collective history of secondhand desire always
moves toward nothingness and death. A faithful description would
elucidate a dynamic structure in the form of a descending spiral.

How is it possible for the novelist to see the structures of desire? The
vision of the totality is simultaneously a vision of the whole and of the
parts, of the detail and of the ensemble. It demands detachment and
anything but detachment at one and the same time. The true novelist is
neither the Olympian, inactive god whom Sartre describes in *Qu'est-ce
que la littérature?* nor the committed man whom Sartre would like to
substitute for the false God. The novelist must be at once committed
and uncommitted. He is the man who has been caught in the structure
of desire and has escaped from it. The Flaubert of *La Première Education sentimentale,* the Proust of *Jean Santeuil,* and Dostoevski before
Notes from Underground present us with all the ambivalences engendered by mediation as objective outcomes of the world. Their
vision remains shot through with Manicheism. All of them were "Romantics" before writing "novels."[2]

This initial captivity of the writer in illusion corresponds, in his
major work, to the illusion, finally revealed as such, of the hero himself.
The hero never frees himself until the end of the novel, through a
conversion in which he rejects mediated desire, i.e., death of the romantic self, and a resurrection in the true world of the novel. This is
why death and disease are always physically present in the conclusion
and why they always have the nature of a happy deliverance. The final
conversion of the hero is a transposition of the novelist's fundamental
experience, of his renunciation of his own idols, of his own spiritual
metamorphosis. In *Le Temps retrouvé,* Marcel Proust makes plain this

reasoning, which is always present but veiled in the work of previous novelists.

The ending that is death for the world is birth for the creative world of the novel. We can verify this fact in quite concrete form in the chapter entitled "Conclusion" in *Contre Sainte-Beuve* and in other writings left by Proust. The preliminary drafts of *Le Temps retrouvé* boil down to a generalized testament of defeat, to an actual and literary despair that existed just before Proust began work on *A la Recherche du temps perdu*.

We must use the same method for endings as for the worlds of the novel: we must envisage them as a single significant totality. What we find this time is not a continuous historical development but a dynamic form always virtually identical, though realized more or less perfectly in the work of individual novelists. The final revelation illuminates, retrospectively, the path traversed. The work is itself retrospective; it is at the same time narrative of and the recompense for spiritual metamorphosis. In the light of this metamorphosis, worldly existence, the spiral descent, appears as a *descent into Hell*, that is, as a necessary ordeal on the way to final revelation. The descending movement finishes by transforming itself into an ascending movement, without there being any going back. It is obvious, I believe, that this forms the structure of *The Divine Comedy*. And doubtless we must look back further still to define the archetype of the novel form—back to the *Confessions* of Saint Augustine, the first work whose genesis is truly inscribed in its form.

These observations emerge not only from theology but from phenomenology of the novel. I am not making any superficial attempt to "Christianize" novelists; and I am virtually saying the same thing as Lucien Goldmann when he writes:

The final conversion of Don Quixote or Julien Sorel is not . . . the attainment of authenticity or transcendence to a higher plane, but simply the recognition of the vanity and degraded character of not only the previous quest, but also of any hope, of any possible quest.[3]

This sentence is even more true of Flaubert than of Stendhal and Cervantes. These novelists mark a "minimal" conversion in contrast with the "maximal" conversion of Dostoevski; but the Dantean and Augustinian archetype remains inscribed in the form of their work. The resort to Christian symbolism in the work of Stendhal or Proust is all the more striking in that it has no religious significance; and their work deliberately excludes all overt imitation of any recognizably Christian form.

The problem that presents itself here is not that of the ultimate meaning of reality but that of the "view of world views." In the *Confessions*, there is this overview of a pagan view that is the Christian view; it is in the transition from one view to the other that the two views become visible. Dante's *Vita Nuova* carries somewhat analogous implications; so does the transition from Romanticism to the novel, which may certainly be defined as "self-realization" but which can hardly be something simple and easy, something that occurs of its own accord, which Lucien Goldmann suggests in the quotation given above. In this regard his interpretation seems to me to be incompatible with his concept of world view and with the stability, the resistance to change that characterizes social and spiritual structures.

It may be argued that the Dantean archetype seems to reappear in works whose contents reflect widely different philosophies. Without wishing to minimize these divergences, we may note that there exist close analogies as well and that these analogies are not confined to novelists. One finds them, for example, in the work of Georg Lukács, whose theory of world views necessarily rests on a view of these world views, that is, on an experience somewhat similar to that of the novelist. There is something Dantean in Lukács's approach. When he describes the degraded quests of fictional heroes as "demonic," is he not giving us the metaphorical equivalent of that Hell where Dante immersed his own heroes? In *The Meaning of Contemporary Realism*, the following expressions often recur to describe the literature of the Western avant-garde: "infernal," "diabolic," "phantasmal," "monstrous," "grimacing," "subterranean powers," and "demonic principle." One can, of course, accuse Lukács of being a little too severe on contemporary literature; but this reproach, however legitimate, and the somewhat facile irony evoked by his theological language must not let us lose sight of the profound intuition that language expresses. Freud, too, uses the term "demonic" to describe the morbidly repetitive nature of neurosis.

True religious thought, the great novels, psychoanalysis, and Marxism have this in common, that they are all opposed to any "idolatry" or "fetishism." We hear on all sides that Marxism is a "religion," but Judaism and primitive Christianity, equally fiercely iconoclastic, appeared to the pagan world to be forms of atheism at first. The accusation of fetishism is turned today against a Christianity that has often deserved it and that deserves it still; but it is this Christianity, it must not be forgotten, that has handed on to us horror of fetishism in all its forms.

The irreplaceable quality of religious language forces us to ask whether the kind of thinking that first animated that language may not be more appropriate for dealing with actuality than is sometimes imagined. No mode of this thought strikes us as more antiquated and meaningless than patristic and medieval allegory. Perhaps the progress of modern thought will oblige us to revise this judgment. It seems that nothing could be further removed from allegorical thought than the connection that Lucien Goldmann establishes between the world of desire in the novel and the market economy:

> In economic life, which constitutes the most important aspect of life in modern society, every genuine relationship with the qualitative aspect of things and of beings tends to disappear—both relationships between men and things as well as between human beings—to be replaced by a mediated and degraded relationship: the purely quantitative relationship of exchange values.[4]

All particular idols are caught up together and engulfed by the supreme idol of the capitalist world: money. There is a "rigorous homology" between every condition of our existence. Our emotional life and even our spiritual life have the same structure as our economic life. The idea seems outrageous to a religious attitude that affirms the autonomy of "spiritual values" merely to provide better cover for mediation and degradation. But the Fathers of the Church—they who made money symbolically analogous to the Holy Ghost and the spiritual life—would have welcomed the Marxist insight. If money is becoming the center of human life it is also becoming the heart of an analogous system that replicates the structure of Christian redemption in reverse; that, in fact plunges us again into the Hell of Dante and the "demoniac" of Lukács and Freud. Allegorical thought may perhaps be something more than a literary game. To recognize the bonds that unite patristic mediation to the most advanced elements of contemporary thought is to discover a paradoxical unity of Western thought beyond the superficial divergences of beliefs and ideologies.

NOTES

1. In the general indifference to mimetic desire, there are some exceptions. In his *Nuovi Studii Danteschi* (Milan: U. Hoepli, 1907), p. 531, Francesco d'Ovidio writes that the line "Galeotto fu il libro e chi lo scrisse" expresses the fear of the poet at the thought that he too might become a Galehalt. More remarkable still is the analysis of the whole episode by Renato Poggioli, in an essay entitled "Tragedy or Romance?: A Reading of the Paolo and Francesca Episode in Dante's *Inferno*" (*PMLA* 72 [June 1957]: 315–58). The author ascribes to Dante's "imagination" the idea of rooting the passion and destruction of the two lovers in the example provided by the romance of Lancelot. Then, he goes on to say:

The real kiss of Paolo and Francesca follows the imaginary kiss of Lancelot and Guinevere, as an imaging reflecting its object in a perspective similar and different at the same time. In brief, the seduction scene fulfills within the entire episode the function of a play within the play, more properly, of a romance within a romance. This creates an effect of parody, or, if we prefer to use a less negative term, something akin to what, in modern times, has been called "romantic irony," which in this case operates in an anti-romantic sense.

I thank John Freccero for drawing my attention to this important essay.

2. This is an untranslatable allusion to *Mensonge romantique et verité romanesque*, the French title of *Deceit, Desire, and the Novel.*

3. Lucien Goldmann, *Pour une sociologie du roman* (Paris: Gallimard, 1964), p. 22.

4. Ibid., p. 25.

2

Camus's Stranger Retried

We have always pictured Meursault as a stranger to the sentiments of other men. Love and hatred, ambition and envy, greed and jealousy are equally foreign to him. He attends the funeral of his mother as impassively as he watches, on the following day, a Fernandel movie. Eventually, Meursault kills a man, but how could we feel that he is a real criminal? How could this man have any motive for murder?

Meursault is the fictional embodiment of the nihilistic individualism expounded in *Le Mythe de Sisyphe* and commonly referred to as *l'absurde*. Meursault is possessed by this *absurde* as others, in a different spiritual context, are possessed by religious grace. But the word *absurde* is not really necessary; the author himself, in his preface to the Brée-Lynes edition of the novel, defines his hero as a man "who does not play the game." Meursault "refuses to lie" and, immediately, "society feels threatened." This hero has a positive significance, therefore; he is not an *épave*, a derelict; "he is a man poor and naked who is in love with the sun."

It is easy to oppose *L'Etranger* to a novel like *Crime and Punishment*. Dostoevski *approves* the sentence that condemns his hero, whereas Camus *disapproves*. *L'Etranger* must be a work of innocence and generosity, soaring above the morass of a guilt-ridden literature. But the problem is not so simple as it looks. Meursault is not the only character in the novel. If he is innocent, the judges who sentence him are guilty. The presentation of the trial as a parody of justice contains at least an implicit indictment of the judges. Many critics have made this indictment explicit and so has Camus himself in the preface to the American edition of *L'Etranger*. After presenting the death of his hero as the evil fruit of an evil collectivity, the author concludes: "In our society, a man who does not cry at the funeral of his mother is likely to be sentenced to death." This striking sentence is really a quotation from an earlier statement; it is labeled "paradoxical," but it is nevertheless repeated with the obvious intent to clear all possible misunder-

This essay first appeared in *PMLA* 79 (December 1964): 519–33.

standing as to an interpretation of *L'Etranger* that, in a sense, is beyond questioning.

La Chute was published in 1956, one year after the American edition of *L'Etranger*. In it, a fashionable Parisian lawyer named Clamence has made a great reputation defending those criminals whom he could, somehow, picture as victims of the "judges." Clamence has a very high opinion of himself because he has always sided with the "underdog" against the iniquitous "judges." One day, however, he discovers that moral heroism is not so easily achieved in deeds as it is in words, and a process of soul searching begins that leads the "generous lawyer" to abandon his successful career and take refuge in Amsterdam. Clamence realizes that mercy, in his hands, was a secret weapon against the unmerciful, a more complex form of self-righteousness. His real desire was not to save his clients but to prove his moral superiority by discrediting the judges. Clamence, in other words, had been the type of lawyer whom Salinger's hero, in *The Catcher in the Rye*, would hate to become:

Lawyers are right . . . if they go around having innocent guys' lives all the time, and like that, but you don't *do* that kind of stuff if you're a lawyer . . . And besides. Even if you *did* go around saving guys' lives, and all, how would you know if you did it because you really *wanted* to save guys' lives, or because what you *really* wanted to do was be a terrific lawyer, with everybody slapping you on the back and congratulating you in court when the goddam trial was over . . . How would you know you weren't being a phony? The trouble is, you *wouldn't*.[1]

The "generous lawyer" wants to be *above* everybody else and to sit in judgment over the judges themselves; he is a judge in disguise. Unlike the ordinary judges who judge directly and openly, he judges indirectly and deviously. When anti-Pharisaism is used as a device to crush the Pharisees, it becomes another and more vicious form of Pharisaism. This point is a pertinent one, especially in our time, but it is not new and it would not be so striking if Camus, in order to make it, did not return to the themes and symbols of his earlier works, in particular those of *L'Etranger*.

In *La Chute* as in *L'Etranger*, there are a court, a trial, the accused, and, of course, the inevitable judges. The only new character is the generous lawyer himself, who defends his "good criminals" just as Camus, the novelist, defended Meursault in *L'Etranger*. The good criminals lose their cases, and so did Meursault, but the loss, in either case, is more than regained in the wider court of public opinion. When we read *L'Etranger*, we feel pity for Meursault and anger with his judges, the very sentiments that the "generous lawyer" is supposed to derive from his practice of the law.

The pre-*Chute* Camus is quite different, of course, from his hero Clamence, but the two have a common trait in their contempt for the "judges." Both of them have built an intellectually complex and socially successful life around this one hallowed principle. The contemporary advocate of literary "revolt" is perpetually challenging social institutions and values, but his challenge, like that of the lawyer, has become a part of the institutions themselves; far from entailing any personal risks, his activities bring fame and comfort in their wake.

If Camus had conceived any doubts as to the validity of his ethical attitude and if he had wanted to express these doubts in another work of fiction, he could not have hit upon a more appropriate theme than that of *La Chute*. All the earlier works of the author are based upon the explicit or implicit tenet that a systematic hostility to all "judges" provides the surest foundation for an "authentic" ethical life. *La Chute* openly derides this tenet. It is natural, therefore, to conclude that the work contains an element of self-criticism.[2] It is no less natural to reject a conclusion that threatens all established ideas concerning Camus, the writer and the man.

We live in an age of middle-class "individualism" in which self-consistency is rated as a major virtue. But a thinker is not bound by the same rules as a statesman or a banker. We do not think less of Goethe because he repudiated *Werther*. We do not blush at the thought of Rimbaud repudiating his whole work or of Kafka refusing to have his manuscripts published at the time of his death. Progress in matters of the spirit is often a form of self-destruction; it may entail a violent reaction against the past. If an artist has to keep admiring his own works at all times in order to remain admirable, Monsieur Joseph Prud'homme, the caricatural French bourgeois, is certainly greater than Pascal, Racine, Chateaubriand, or Claudel.

A writer's creative process has become a major, if not *the* major, literary theme of our time. The lawyer of *La Chute*, like the doctor of *La Peste*, is, at least to a certain extent, an allegory of the creator. Can this assertion be denied on the grounds that it involves a "naive confusion" between the author and his fictional work? Fear of the "biographical fallacy" must not be an excuse to evade the truly significant problems raised by literary creation. This fear is itself naive because it conceives of the rapport between an author and his work as an all-or-nothing proposition. When I say that Clamence *is* Albert Camus, I do not mean that the two are identical in the sense that an original document is identical to its carbon copy or that a traveler is identical to the snapshot that figures on the first page of his passport. When a work is really profound, the existential significance of its characters and situations can never be stated in terms of straight biography, but why should it have to be so stated?

I may admit that Camus's past is present in *La Chute* and still evade the most difficult consequences of this discovery. By placing the emphasis upon the political and social allusions, I may interpret the confession of Clamence as an attack against whatever is implied in the word *engagement*. Camus's quarrel with Sartre as well as his restrained public attitude during the last years of his life could provide some additional evidence for this view. If *La Chute* is a reaction against the recent past only, is it not, as such, a return to the earlier past and a vigorous—if enigmatic—restatement of the positions defended in *Sisyphe* and *L'Etranger*? This minimal interpretation is attractive; unfortunately, it rests not on internal evidence but on the implicit assumption that Camus's entire itinerary can and must be defined in terms of that *engagement/dégagement* polarity that reigned supreme a dozen years ago. The trouble with this polarity is that it excludes the one possibility that is actually realized in *La Chute*, that of a change in vision radical enough to transcend both the *engagement* of *La Peste* and the *dégagement* of *L'Etranger*.

Engagement can rarely be distinguished from the other targets of satire in *La Chute* because, from the standpoint of Clamence, it no longer constitutes a truly autonomous attitude. The first Camus, as well as the later advocate of *engagement*, can fit the description of the "generous lawyer." The only difference is that the "clients" are characters of fiction in the first case and real human beings in the second. From the cynical perspective of Clamence, this difference is unimportant. To the generous lawyer, the clients are never quite real since they are not an end in themselves, but they are never quite fictional since they are a means to discredit the judges. *Engagement* represents only a variation on the theme of "bad faith," one of the many forms that a secretly self-seeking dedication to the downtrodden can assume. Behind the clients, therefore, we can see the characters created by the early Camus, such as Caligula, the two women murderers in *Le Malentendu*, and, preeminently, Meursault no less than the real but shadowy people whose cause a writer is supposed to embrace when he becomes *engagé*.

The passage in which Clamence describes his kindness to old ladies in distress and other such people is probably the one direct reference to *engagement* in *La Chute*. And we may note that this boy-scoutish behavior is presented as nothing more than an extension of the lawyer's professional attitude. Clamence has become so engrossed in his legal self that he goes on playing the part of the generous lawyer outside of the court; the comedy gradually takes over even the most ordinary circumstances of daily life. Literature and life have become one, not because literature imitates life but because life imitates literature. Unity of experience is achieved at the level of an all-pervasive imposture.

La Chute must be read in the right perspective, which is one of humor. The author, tired of his popularity with all the *bien-pensants* of the intellectual élite, found a witty way to deride his quasiprophetic role without scandalizing the pure at heart among the faithful. Allowance must be made for overstatement, but the work cannot be discounted as a joke or safely extolled as art for art's sake. The confession of Clamence is Camus's own, in a broad literary and spiritual sense. To prove this point, I shall turn first to *L'Etranger* and uncover a structural flaw that, to my knowledge, has not been previously detected. The significance of that structural flaw will provide the evidence needed to confirm the reading of *La Chute* as self-criticism.

From a purely textual standpoint, Meursault's condemnation is almost unrelated to his crime. Every detail of the trial adds up to the conclusion that the judges resent the murderer not for what he did but for what he is. The critic Albert Maquet expressed his truth quite well when he wrote: "The murder of the Arab is only a pretext; behind the person of the accused, the judges want to destroy the truth he embodies."

Let there be no murder and a good pretext to get rid of Meursault will, indeed, have been lost, but a pretext should be easy to replace, precisely because it does not have to be good. If society is as eager to annihilate Meursault as it is pictured by Maquet, the remarkable existence of this hero should provide more "pretexts" than will ever be needed to send an innocent to his doom.

Is this assumption well founded? We ask this question in all awareness that we are abandoning, for the time being, pure textual analysis for common sense realism. If we feel, when we are reading the novel, that Meursault lives dangerously, this impression evaporates under examination. The man goes to work regularly; he swims on the beaches of the Mediterranean and he has dates with the girls in the office. He likes the movies but he is not interested in politics. Which of these activities will take him to a police station, let alone the guillotine?

Meursault has no responsibilities, no family, no personal problems; he feels no sympathy for unpopular causes. Apparently he drinks nothing but *café au lait*. He really lives the prudent and peaceful life of a little bureaucrat anywhere and of a French petit bourgeois in the bargain. He carries the foresight of his class so far that he waits the medically recommended number of hours after his noonday meal before he plunges into the Mediterranean. His way of life should constitute a good insurance against nervous breakdowns, mental exhaustion, heart failure, and, *a fortiori*, the guillotine.

Meursault, it is true, does not cry at his mother's funeral, and this is the one action in his life that is likely to be criticized by his neighbors; from such criticism to the scaffold, however, there is a distance that could never be bridged if Meursault did not commit a murder. Even the most ferocious judge could not touch a single hair on his head, had he not killed one of his fellow men.

The murder may be a pretext, but it is the only one available, and upon this unfortunate event, the whole structure of meaning erected by Camus comes to rest. It is very important, therefore, to understand how the murder comes to pass. How can a man commit a murder and not be responsible for it? The obvious answer is that this murder must be an *accident*, and many critics have taken up that answer. Louis Hudon, for instance, says that Meursault is guilty of involuntary manslaughter at worst.[3] How could Meursault premeditate murder, since he cannot premeditate a successful career in Paris or marriage with his mistress? Involuntary manslaughter, as everyone knows, should not send a man to the guillotine. This interpretation seems to clinch Camus's case against the "judges."

There is a difficulty, however. If Meursault must commit a crime, we agree that he must be an involuntary rather than a voluntary criminal, but why should he commit a crime in the first place? Accidents will happen, no doubt, but no general conclusion can be drawn from them, or they cease, quite obviously, to be *accidents*. If the murder is an accident, so is the sentence that condemns Meursault, and *L'Etranger* does not prove that people who do not cry at their mothers' funerals are likely to be sentenced to death. All the novel proves, then, is that these people will be sentenced to death if they also happen to commit involuntary manslaughter, and this *if*, it will be conceded, is a very big one. The accident theory reduces Meursault's case to the proportions of a pathetic but rather insignificant *fait-divers*.

Let a million devotees of *l'absurde* copy Meursault's way of life down to the last dregs of his *café au lait*, let them bury their entire families without shedding a single tear, and not one of them will ever die on the guillotine, for the simple reason that their *imitatio absurdi* will not and should not include the accidental murder of the Arab; this unfortunate happening, in all probability, will never be duplicated.

The accident theory weakens, if it does not destroy, the tragic opposition between Meursault and society. That is why it does not really account for the experience of the reader. Textually speaking, the relationship between Meursault and his murder cannot be expressed in terms of motivation, as would be the case with an ordinary criminal, but it is nevertheless felt to be essential, rather than accidental. From the very beginning of the novel we sense that something frightful is going to happen and that Meursault can do nothing to protect himself. The hero is innocent, no doubt, and this very innocence will bring about his downfall.

The critics who, like Carl Viggiani, have best captured the atmosphere of the murder reject all rational interpretations and attribute this event to that same *Fatum* that presides over the destinies of epic and tragic heroes in ancient and primitive literatures. They point out that the various incidents and objects connected with this episode can be interpreted as symbols of an implacable Nemesis.

We still invoke fate today when we do not want to ascribe an event to chance, even though we cannot account for it. This "explanation" is not meant seriously, however, when we are talking about real happenings taking place in the real world. We feel that this world is essentially rational and that it should be interpreted rationally.

An artist is entitled to disregard rational laws in his search for esthetic effects. No one denies this. If he makes use of this privilege, however, the world he creates is not only fictional but fantastic. If Meursault is sentenced to death in such a fantastic world, my indignation against the iniquitous judges must be fantastic too, and I cannot say, as Camus did in his preface to the Brée-Lynes edition of *L'Etranger*, that, *in our society*, people who behave like Meursault are likely to be sentenced to death. The conclusions that I infer from the novel are valid for this novel only and not for the real world, since the laws of verisimilitude have been violated. Meursault's drama does not give me the right to look with contempt upon real judges operating in a real court. Such contempt must be justified by a perfectly rational sequence of causes or motivations leading from the funeral of the mother to the death of the hero. If, at the most crucial point in this sequence, *Fatum* is suddenly brandished, or some other deity as vague as it is dark, we must note this sudden disregard for the rational course of human affairs and take a very close look at the antisocial message of the novel.

If supernatural necessity is present in *L'Etranger*, why should Meursault alone come under its power? Why should the various characters in the same novel be judged by different yardsticks? If the murderer is not held responsible for his actions, why should the judges be held responsible for theirs? It is possible, of course, to read part of *L'Etranger* as fantasy and the rest as realistic fiction, but the novel thus fragmented presents no unified world view; even from a purely esthetic point of view it is open to criticism.

The fate theory looks satisfactory as long as the episode of the murder remains detached from the novel, but it cannot be integrated with this novel. Sympathy for Meursault is inseparable from resentment against the judges. We cannot do away with that resentment without mutilating our global esthetic experience. This resentment is really generated by the text, and we must somehow account for it even if it is not logically justified.

The search for the significance of Meursault's murderous gesture leads nowhere. The death of the Arab can be neither an accident nor an event inspired from "above," and yet it must be one of these two things if it is not voluntary. It is as difficult to ascribe an "ontological status" to the murder as it is easy to ascertain its function in the story. Meursault, as I have said, could never have been tried, convicted, and sentenced if he had not killed the Arab. But Camus thought otherwise, and he said so in the preface to L'Etranger: "A man who does not cry at the funeral of his mother is likely to be sentenced to death." Is this an a posteriori judgment deduced from the facts of the story, as everybody has always taken for granted, or is it an a priori principle to which the "facts" must somehow be fitted? Everything becomes intelligible if we choose the second solution. Camus needs his "innocent murder" because his a priori principle is blatantly false. The irritating cult of motherhood and the alleged profundities of l'absurde must not obscure the main issue. Let us translate the brilliant paradoxes of the author back into the terms of his story, let us remove the halo of intellectual sophistication that surrounds the novel, and no one will take its message seriously. Do we really believe that the French judicial system is ruthlessly dedicated to the extermination of little bureaucrats addicted to café au lait, Fernandel movies, and casual love affairs with the boss's secretary?

One of the reasons we do not question the tragic ending of L'Etranger is the lowly status of its hero. Little clerks are, indeed, potential and actual victims of our modern societies. Like the other members of his class, Meursault is vulnerable to a multitude of social ills ranging from war to racial and economic discrimination. But this fact, on close examination, has no bearing on Camus's tragedy. The work is not one of social but of individual protest, even though the author welcomes the ambiguity, or at least does nothing to dispel it. The main point is that Meursault is the incarnation of unique qualities rather than the member of a group. The judges are supposed to resent what is most Meursault-like in Meursault. Unfortunately, the alleged uniqueness of this hero has no concrete consequences in his behavior. For all practical purposes, Meursault is a little bureaucrat devoid of ambition and, as such, he cannot be singled out for persecution. The only real threats to his welfare are those he shares with every other little bureaucrat, or with the human race as a whole.

The idea of the novel is incredible; that is why a direct demonstration is unthinkable. The writer wanted to arouse an indignation that he himself felt, and he had to take into account the demands of elementary realism. In order to become a martyr, Meursault had to commit some truly reprehensible action, but in order to retain the sympathy of the readers, he had to remain innocent. His crime had to be involuntary, therefore, but not so involuntary that the essential Meursault, the man who does not cry at his mother's funeral, would remain untouched by the sentence. All the events leading to the actual scene of the shooting, including that scene itself, with its first involuntary shot followed by four voluntary ones, are so devised that they appear to fulfill these two incompatible exigencies. Meursault will die an innocent, and yet his death sentence will be more significant than a mere judicial error.

This solution is really no solution at all. It can only hide, it cannot resolve, the contradiction between the first and the second Meursault, between the peaceful solipsist and the martyr of society; it *is* that contradiction in a nutshell, as revealed by the two conflicting words, "innocent" and "murder," whose combination sounds unusual and interesting, somewhat like a surrealistic image, precisely because they cannot form a real concept and be fused together any more than a surrealistic image can evoke a real object.

The skillful narrative technique makes it very difficult to perceive the logical flaw in the structure of the novel. When an existence as uneventful as that of Meursault is described in minute detail, without any humor, an atmosphere of tense expectation is automatically created. As I read the novel, my attention is focused upon details that are insignificant in themselves but that come to be regarded as portents of doom just because the writer has seen fit to record them. I sense that Meursault is moving toward a tragedy, and this impression, which has nothing to do with the hero's actions, seems to arise from them. Who can see a woman knitting alone in a dark house at the beginning of a mystery story without being led to believe that knitting is a most dangerous occupation?

In the second half of *L'Etranger*, all the incidents recorded in the first half are recalled and used as evidence against Meursault. The aura of fear that surrounds these incidents appears fully justified. We are aware of these trifles as trifles but we have been conditioned to regard them as potentially dangerous to the hero. It is natural, therefore, to consider the attitude of the judges both unfair and inevitable. In a mystery story, the clues ultimately lead to the murderer; in *L'Etranger*, they all lead to the judges. The murder itself is handled in the same casual and fateful manner as the other actions of Meursault. Thus, the gap between this portentous action and an afternoon swim in the Mediterranean or the absorption of a cup of *café au lait* is gradually narrowed, and we are gently led to the incredible conclusion that the hero is sentenced to death not for the crime of which he is accused and that he has really committed, but for his innocence, which this crime has not tarnished and which should remain obvious to all people at all times, as if it were the attribute of a divinity.

L'Etranger was not written for pure art's sake, nor was it written to vindicate the victims of persecution everywhere. Camus set out to prove that the hero according to his heart will necessarily be persecuted by society. He set out to prove, in other words, that "the judges are always in the wrong." The truth deeply buried in *L'Etranger* would have been discovered long before it became explicit in *La Chute* if we had read the tragedy of Meursault with truly critical eyes. A really close reading leads, indeed, to questioning the structure and, beyond it, the "authenticity" of *L'Etranger* in terms identical with those of Clamence's confession. The allegory of the generous lawyer stems from the structural flaw of *L'Etranger*, fully apprehended for the first time and interpreted as the "objective correlative" of the author's "bad faith." Further evidence can be provided by the explication of some obscure passages and apparent contradictions in the text of *La Chute*.

Here is a first example. At one point in the description of his past professional life Clamence remarks: "Je ne me trouvais pas sur la scène du tribunal mais quelque part, dans les cintres, comme ces dieux que, de temps en temps, on descend, au moyen d'une machine, pour transfigurer l'action et lui donner un sens." Readers acquainted with the terminology of postwar French criticism will remember that Sartre and his school accuse novelists of mistaking themselves for "gods" when they warp the destiny of a character and when, consciously or not, they lead him to some preordained conclusion. If we recognize the figure of the writer behind the mask of the lawyer we shall immediately perceive, in this bizarre statement, an allusion, and a very pertinent one, to the wrong kind of novelist. Can this same statement be made meaningful if *La Chute* is not understood as an allegory of the writer's own literary past?

The image of the god is originally Sartrian, but the Greek element brings us back to those critics who have rejected all rational interpretation of the murder. They themselves are solely concerned with problems of esthetic symbolism, but their writings may well have helped

Camus realize what he now implicitly denounces as the "bad faith" of his own creation. The murder of the Arab, in a novel otherwise rational and realistic, is a *deus ex machina*, or rather a *crimen ex machina* that provides the author not with a happy ending but with a tragic one that is really precluded by the character he himself has given to his hero.

Here is a second example. Clamence tells us that he chose his clients "à la seule condition qu'ils fussent de bons meurtriers comme d'autres de bons sauvages." This sentence is absolutely unintelligible in a non-literary context. It is a thinly disguised reference to Meursault, who plays, in his fictional world, a role similar to that of the good savage, a well-known pre-Romantic stranger, in the world of eighteenth-century literature. Here again, the image may have been suggested by Sartre, who, in his *Situations* article, defined *L'Etranger* as a twentieth-century *conte philosophique*.

Like the "bon sauvage," Meursault is supposed to act as a catalyst; his sole presence reveals the arbitrariness of the values that bind the "insiders" together. The *bonté* of this abstract figure is an absolute that no amount of *sauvagerie* can diminish. Meursault's excellence has the same quality. He is no less innocent and the judges no less guilty for punishing him, a confessed criminal, than if no crime had been committed. Innocence and guilt are fixed essences; they cannot be affected by the vicissitudes of existence any more than Ormazd and Ahriman can exchange their roles as the principle of good and the principle of evil.

In *La Chute*, the author questions his own motives for writing fiction within the framework of this fiction itself. Meursault, as a "client" of Clamence, has retreated in the background and become anonymous, but he is still a *dramatis persona*, and the structural incoherence of *L'Etranger* must be expressed primarily in terms of *his* personal motivations. In order to denounce what he now regards as his own moral illusions and creative weakness, Clamence must say, as he does, that *his clients were not so innocent after all.* Their allegedly spontaneous and unmotivated misdeeds were, in fact, premeditated. If Camus is to abide by the rules of the fictional game initiated in the first novel, he must attribute to the hero the "bad faith" that really belongs to his creator, and this is precisely what he does. The "good criminals" killed, not for any of the ordinary reasons, as we are well aware, but because they *wanted* to be tried and sentenced. Clamence tells us that their motives were really the same as his: like so many of our contemporaries, in this anonymous world, they wanted a little publicity.

Meursault, however, is a character of fiction; responsibility for his crime lies, in the last resort, with the creator himself. The present reading would be more convincing if Clamence, instead of placing the blame upon his "clients," had placed it squarely upon himself. But Clamence is already the lawyer; how could he be the instigator of the crime without absurdity? Such transparent allegory would deal the last blow to *La Chute* as art for art's sake and the present exegesis would be pointless. Let me apologize, therefore, for belaboring the obvious since Clamence does, indeed, present himself both as the passionate defender and as the accomplice of his good criminals. He does not hesitate to assume these two incompatible roles. If we reject the obvious implications of this inconsistency, we must dare condemn *La Chute* as an incoherent piece of fiction.

This is a curious lawyer, indeed, who manipulates the court from high above, as he would a puppet show, and who discovers the guilt of his clients *after* they are sentenced, even though he himself had a hand in their crimes. We must observe, on the other hand, that this collusion with the criminals should destroy the image of the generous lawyer as a stuffy, self-righteous, upper-middle-class man if the reader did not realize, subconsciously at least, that these criminals are only paper ones. The account of Clamence's law career is really a collection of metaphors, all pointing to "unauthentic creation," and Camus uses them as he sees fit, tearing as he goes the thin veil of his fiction. Clamence really suggests that the author of *L'Etranger* was not really conscious of his own motivation until he experienced his own *chute*. His purpose, which disguised itself as "generosity," was really identical with egotistical passion. *L'Etranger* must not be read as a *roman à thèse*. The author did not consciously try to deceive his audience, but he succeeded all the better because he managed to deceive himself in the first place. The dichotomy between Meursault and his judges represents the dichotomy between the Self and the Others in a world of intersubjective warfare.

L'Etranger, as the expression of egotistical values and meanings, forms a structure, a relatively stable "world view." Camus "sincerely" believed in his and, consequently, in Meursault's innocence, because he passionately believed in the guilt of the "judges." The incoherence of the plot does not stem from an awkward effort to prove something that was only half believed or not believed at all. On the contrary, the author's conviction that the iniquity of the judges can always be proved was so strong that nothing could shake it. The innocent will inevitably be treated as a criminal. In the process of proving this point, Camus had to turn his innocent into a real criminal, but his faith was such that he did not perceive the tautology. We can understand, now, why the "generous lawyer" is presented to us both as the sincere defender of his clients and as the accomplice of their crimes.

As long as the egotistical Manicheism that produced *L'Etranger* held its sway over him, the author could not perceive the structural flaw of his novel. All illusions are one. They stand together and they fall together as soon as their cause, egotistical passion, is perceived. The confession of Clamence does not lead to a new "interpretation" of *L'Etranger* but to an act of transcendence; the perspective of this first novel is rejected.

The rejection of the world view expressed in *L'Etranger* is not the fruit of an empirical discovery but of an existential conversion, and it is, indeed, such a conversion that is described ironically but unmistakably throughout the novel, in terms of an ego-shattering *chute*. This spiritual metamorphosis is triggered, so to speak, by the incident of the drowning woman but, basically, it has nothing to do with exterior circumstances. Neither can our own reevaluation of *L'Etranger* in the light of *La Chute* rest on external evidence such as scholarly arguments and "explications de textes," however massive the material proof available through these channels. The evidence will not be judged convincing until there is a willingness to go along with the self-critical mood of the creator. I, the reader, must undergo an experience, less profound to be sure, but somewhat analogous to that of this creator. The true critic must not remain superbly and coldly objective; he is the one most profoundly affected and transformed by the work of art; he truly *sympathizes*, suffers with the author. I, too, must fall from my pedestal; as an admirer of *L'Etranger*, I must accept the risk of an exegetical *chute*.

A refusal to probe the confession of Clamence must not be rationalized on the grounds that it makes the literary reputation of Camus more secure. It is the reverse that is true. The fact that *La Chute* transcends the perspective of *L'Etranger* does not mean that, in a comparison with other works of recent fiction, the earlier work ranks lower than had been previously thought; it certainly means, however, that *La Chute* ranks higher.

A gingerly approach to *La Chute* obscures the true greatness of Camus. This work can already be defined as a forgotten masterpiece. Camus is praised to the high heavens by some, while others deride his role as "directeur de conscience" of the middle class, but all this is done with only passing reference, or no reference at all, to *La Chute*. Most people ignore the fact that Albert Camus was the first one to react against his own cult. Here and there, some voices are raised in defense of a truth that no one, it seems, is really eager to hear. Philippe Sénart, for instance, maintained that Camus refused to be the infallible pope of his own new neohumanism:

Il ne voulait être que le *pape des fous* et il écrivait *La Chute* pour se tourner en dérision et il s'accusait en se moquant. Clamence, avocat déchu, qui avait "bien vécu de sa vertu," qui se trouvait, avec coquetterie, "un peu surhomme," était, dans le bouge où il se déguisait en juge pour mieux rire de lui, le Bouffon de l'humanité, d'aucuns disaient le Singe de Dieu, comme Satan. Clamence, l'Homme-qui-rit, c'était l'Anti-Camus.[4]

In one of the speeches pronounced when he received his Nobel Prize, Camus opened still a new line of investigation to the critics of his work:

> Le thème du poète maudit né dans une société marchande (Chatterton en est la plus belle illustration), s'est durci dans un préjugé qui finit par vouloir qu'on ne puisse être un grand artiste que contre la société de son temps, quelle qu'elle soit. Légitime à son origine quand il affirmait qu'un artiste véritable ne pouvait composer avec le monde de l'argent, le principe est devenu faux lorsqu'on en a tiré qu'un artiste ne pouvait s'affirmer qu'en étant contre toute chose en général.[5]

Throughout the *Discours de Suède*, Camus dissociated himself from his own past as much as the occasion permitted. Here, he relates the type of literature he himself had practiced for so long not to an awe-inspiring philosophical tradition, as in *L'Homme révolté*, but to French Romanticism. He chooses as the archetype of *révolte*, *Chatterton*, the one work of Alfred de Vigny with which contemporary readers are likely to find most fault. He suggests that the tragic conflicts set forth in his own early works are really a *degraded* form of Vigny's Romantic drama.

An earlier Camus would certainly have rejected this *rapprochement* out of hand in spite or rather because of its extreme relevance. *L'Etranger* is really much closer to *Chatterton* than to the *conte philosophique* because the *conte* has a concrete content and it fights for definite objectives, whereas *Chatterton*, like *L'Etranger*, is primarily an abstract protest of the discontented ego. A work that is against everything in general is really against nothing in particular and no one actually feels disturbed by it. Like Dostoevski's underground man, Meursault says: "I am alone and *they* are together." The work spells the final democratization of the Romantic myth, the universal symbol of the separated ego in a world where almost everyone feels like an "outsider."

Chatterton, like Meursault, was conceived as a lonely figure, as a man who refuses "to play the game." Both men live in a world of their own that contrasts with the unauthentic world of other men. Both of them suffer and die because society makes it impossible for them to live according to their own lonely, infinitely superior ways.

There is a difference, however. When Chatterton is offered the same type of third-rate job Meursault holds, he refuses haughtily. In his eyes, this menial way of life is incompatiable with his mission. We find it rather easy to interpret Chatterton's destiny in terms of Romantic pride. Camus's hero appears very humble by contrast; he does not view himself as a man with a mission; he has no visible pretensiòns and he is ready to do whatever is necessary to sustain his mediocre existence.

This modest appearance really hides a more extreme form of Romantic pride. Between Chatterton and other men there is still a measure of reciprocity, whereas none is left in the case of Meursault. Chatterton gives his "genius" and the community must give him food and shelter in return. If society does not fulfill its share of the contract, the poet cannot fulfill his role as a great poet; the crowd grows spiritually hungry and the poet grows physically hungry. This general starvation is less tragic, no doubt, than Greek or classical tragedy and it is so because Chatterton is less deeply involved with his fellowmen than earlier tragic heroes. Real tragedy demands genuine involvement. It is somewhat ironic, let us note in passing, that a doctrine with such ethereal pretensions as 1830 Romanticism could produce only alimentary tragedies of the Chatterton type. But this last meager resource is still truly present, whereas it is gone in the case of Camus. The poetic life cherished by Chatterton has become a part of the shameful game that the real individual must refuse to play in order to remain "authentic." L'Etranger should not end in a Chatterton-like tragedy; it should revolve around the closed circle of a perfectly self-sufficient personality. An endless succession of cafés au lait, Fernandel movies, and amorous interludes should provide a scale model of the Nietzschean eternal return.

Romantic pride separates Chatterton from his fellowmen; greater pride cuts Meursault off so completely that no tragic possibilities remain. In order to grasp this point, we may compare Meursault with another Romantic in disguise, Monsieur Teste, the solipsistic hero of Valéry's youth. Monsieur Teste is infinitely brilliant and original but he alone is aware of his own worth. He is satisfied, like Meursault, with a third-rate job; he does not mind looking quelconque and remaing unknown. He will never be a grand homme because he refuses to sacrifice anything to the spirit of the crowd. Meursault is really a Teste without a Ph.D., a Teste who prefers café au lait to higher mathematics, a super-Teste, in other words, who does not even bother to be intelligent.

The idea of turning Teste into a martyr of society would have sounded ludicrous to Valéry. The only thing a solipsist is entitled to ask of society is indifference, and indifference he will get if he behaves like a Teste or a Meursault. Valéry was perfectly aware that, as individualism becomes more extreme, the possibilities offered to a writer shrink; and he rejected as "impure" all types of dramatic literature.

L'Etranger begins like *Monsieur Teste* and it ends like *Chatterton.* Unlike Valéry, Camus does not perceive or he refuses to assume the consequences of his literary solipsism. He resorts to the device of the "innocent murder" in order to retrieve the structure of the *poète maudit* or, more generally, of the "exceptional man persecuted by society." The *crimen ex machina* saves the author from the limitations of his own attitude.

Contemporary readers sense that there is something contrived in *Chatterton,* and yet Vigny did not have to turn his exceptional man into a murderer in order to present him as a martyr of society. *L'Etranger* should appear even more contrived, but we do not understand the disturbing role that violence plays in it, probably because the novel is the latest successful formulation of the myth of the Romantic self.

Chatterton already prefers to be persecuted rather than ignored, but we cannot prove the point because it is plausible that society will prevent a poet from fulfilling his destiny as a poet. In the case of Meursault, this same preference for egotistical martyrdom can be proven, because it is not plausible that society will prevent a little bureaucrat from fulfilling his destiny as a little bureaucrat. Camus takes his hero out of society with one hand only to put him back with the other. He wants Meursault to be a solipsist, then turns him into the hero of a trial, that quintessence of diseased human relations in our modern society.

Why does Camus crave solitude and society at the same time; why is he both repelled and fascinated by *les autres?* The contradiction is really inherent in the Romantic personality. The Romantic does not want to be alone, but *to be seen alone.* In *Crime and Punishment,* Dostoevski shows that solitary dreams and the "trial" are the two inseparable facets, the dialectically-related "moments" of the Romantic consciousness. But this proud consciousness refuses to acknowledge openly the fascination it feels for the others. In the days of Vigny a discreet return to society was still possible because a few bridges were left between the individualist and his fellowmen. The "mission of the poet" was one, romantic love another. Camus has destroyed these last bridges because the urge to be alone is stronger in him than ever before. But the unacknowledged urge to return to other men is also stronger than ever. And this second urge can no longer be satisfied within the context created by the first.

The murder is really a secret effort to reestablish contact with humanity. It reveals an ambivalence that is present in all art with solipsistic tendencies but that has probably never been so visibly written into the structure of a work. This contradiction is also present in *Monsieur Teste* because it can never be eliminated completely. Monsieur Teste lives and dies alone, but not so much alone that we, the readers, are left in the dark about his superhuman and invisible qualities. The egotistical *Deus* is never so *absconditus* that it does not have its priests and mediators. The ambiguous narrator plays the part of the "innocent murder" in *L'Etranger*. He is an artificial bridge between the solipsist and ordinary mortals. He is close enough to Teste to understand him and close enough to us to write for us. Such a man, by definition, should not exist and the work should never have been written. Valéry was so aware of it that he remained silent for twenty years after writing *Monsieur Teste*.

Camus, too, should be silent and he is at least partly aware of it since, in *Sisyphe*, he discusses literature and concludes that it is a fitting pastime for the knight-errant of *l'absurde*—provided, of course, it is not oriented to *les autres*. This a posteriori justification must be read primarily as evidence that the problem was a significant and important one for Camus at the time. The pure doctrine of solipsism is not in *Sisyphe* but in *L'Etranger*. Meursault does not read or write; we cannot imagine him submitting a manuscript to a publisher or correcting galley proofs. All such activities have no place in an "authentic" existence.

Both the young Valéry and the young Camus cherished literature; both knew that it offered an avenue of escape from their equally mediocre stations in life. And yet both of them held views that made the practice of their art almost impossible. Romantic individualism becomes so exacerbated with these writers that it verges on a certain type of neurotic behavior.

We all know, outside of literature, that certain people are too proud to acknowledge a situation as painful. These people may even do their utmost to perpetuate or even aggravate this situation in order to prove to themselves that it is *freely chosen*. The creation of Meursault certainly reflects an attitude of this type. The life of this hero is objectively sad and sordid. The man is, indeed, a derelict; he has no intellectual life, no love, no friendship, no interest in anyone or faith in anything. His life is limited to physical sensations and to cheap pleasures of modern mass culture. The uninformed readers—American undergraduates, for instance—often perceive this essential wretchedness; they grasp the *objective* significance of the novel because the *subjective* intention of the creator escapes them. The "informed" reader, on the other hand, rejects the objective significance as naive because he readily perceives the subjective intention, and he feels very sophisticated—until he reads and understands *La Chute*. Clamence alone is aware that there are two layers of significance, subjective and objective, and he picks the latter as the essential one when he states that his "good criminals" were wretched people *at bottom*. The most lucid view justifies the most naive; the truth belongs to the reader who takes *nothing* or *everything* into account, and to no one in between.

The undergraduates quickly learn, of course, that it is not smart to pity Meursault, but they vaguely wonder, for a while, why his living hell should be interpreted as paradise. This hell is the one to which, rightly or wrongly, Camus felt condemned in the years of *L'Etranger*. There are psychological, social, and even metaphysical reasons, as well as literary ones, for *L'Etranger's* mood of repressed despair. These were troubled times; opportunity was scarce; the health of the young Camus was not good; he was not yet a famous writer and he had no assurance that he would ever become one. He *willed*, therefore, as many did who came before and after him, the solitude and mediocrity from which he did not see any escape. His was an act of intellectual pride and desperation reminiscent of Nietzschean *amor fati*. Valéry's *Monsieur Teste* stems from a comparable experience in a world somewhat less harsh. A young man who feels doomed to anonymity and mediocrity is compelled to repay with indifference the indifference of society. If he is very gifted, he may devise a new and radical variety of Romantic solipsism; he may create a Teste or a Meursault.

Even more relevant here than a purely psychiatric interpretation are the passages of *The Sickness unto Death* dedicated to what Kierkegaard calls "defiance," or "the despair of willing despairingly to be oneself."

This too is a form of despair: not to be willing to hope that an earthly distress, a temporal cross, might be removed. This is what the despair which wills desperately to be itself is not willing to hope. It has convinced itself that this thorn in the flesh gnaws so profoundly that he cannot abstract it—no matter whether this is actually so or his passion makes it true for him—and so he is willing to accept it as it were eternally. So he is offended by it, or rather from it he takes occasion to be offended at the whole of existence. . . . To hope in the possibility of help, not to speak of help by virtue of the absurd, that for God all things are possible—no, that he will not do. And as for seeking help from any other—no, that he will not do for all the world; rather than seek help he would prefer to be himself—with all the torture of hell, if so must be. . . . Now it is too late, he once would have given everything to be rid of this torment but was made to wait, now that's all past, now he would rather rage against everything, he, the one man in the whole of existence who is the most unjustly treated, to whom it is especially important to have his torment at hand, important that no one should take it from him —for thus he can convince himself that he is in the right.[6]

The absurd of which Kierkegaard is speaking, needless to say, is not Camus's *absurde*. It is rather the opposite of it, since it is the final rejection of nihilism, rejected by Camus himself and dismissed as facile optimism in *Sisyphe*. The young Camus thought he could dispose of Kierkegaard in a few sentences but Kierkegaard on Camus goes much deeper, paradoxically, than Camus on Kierkegaard: "such self-control, such firmness, such ataraxia, etc., border almost on the fabulous. . . . The self wants . . . to have the honor of this poetical, this masterly plan according to which it has understood itself. And yet, . . . just at the instant when it seems to be nearest to having the fabric finished it can arbitrarily resolve the whole thing into nothing."[7]

This highest form of despair, Kierkegaard informs us, is encountered solely in the works of a few great poets, and we perceive the bond between the Vigny of *Chatterton*, the Valéry of *Teste*, and the Camus of *L'Etranger* when the philosopher adds: "one might call it Stoicism— yet without thinking only of this philosophic sect." The genius of Kierkegaard cuts through the maze of minor differences that help a writer assert his own individuality, thus obscuring the fundamental significance of his literary posture. The whole spiritual structure is grasped through a single act of intuition. The essential features are revealed, common, as a rule, to two or more writers. The following passage enables us, for instance, to account for the similarities between Teste and Meursault:

One might represent the lower forms of despair by describing or by saying something about the outward traits of the despairer. But the more despair becomes spiritual, and the more is the self alert with demoniac shrewdness to keep despair shut up in close reserve, and all the more intent therefore to set the outward appearance at the level of indifference, to make it as unrevealing and indifferent as possible. . . . This hiddenness is precisely something spiritual and is one of the safety devices for assuring oneself of having as it were behind reality an enclosure, a world for itself locking all else out, a world where the despairing self is employed as tirelessly as Tantalus in willing to be itself.[8]

This last reference might as well be to Sisyphus rather than to Tantalus. Camus's *Sisyphe*, like *Teste*, is a "rationalization" of Kierkegaardian despair, whereas *L'Etranger* is the esthetic, or naive and, as such, most revealing expression of that same despair.

Here again, we must not let the hollow specter of the "biographical fallacy" interfere with our comprehension of an author's fundamental problems. We do not confuse the creator with his creation. The relationship is not a simple one. Meursault is the portrait, or even the caricature, of a man Camus never was but swore to be, at the end of his adolescence, because he feared he could never be anyone else. The scene with the employer is revelatory. Meursault, as we all know, is offered a trip to Paris and the possibility of a permanent job there. He is not interested. The incident has only one purpose, which is to demonstrate Meursault's total lack of ambition. And it does what it is supposed to do; it does it, in a sense, too well; it is just a little too pointed. Why should *any* little clerk with a penchant for sun bathing want to move to Paris, with its dreary winter climate? At the lower echelon, which is Meursault's, sunny Algeria offers the same possibilities for advancement as the French capital. As Meursault refuses, with studied indifference, to live in Saint-Germain-des-Prés, we can hear Camus himself protesting that he has no literary ambitions.

Camus left Algeria for Paris; he wrote and published quite a few books; he submitted, at least for a few years, to the various indignities that the fabrication of a *grand homme* demands. The conclusion is inescapable: Camus, unlike his hero, was not devoid of ambition, especially literary ambition. This truth is as obvious as it is innocuous, but it sounds almost blasphemous; we are still living in the atmosphere of puritanical egotism that fosters such works as *L'Etranger* and that prevents us from reading them critically.

The urge to escape solitude was stronger than the self-destructive dynamism of repressed pride. But this urge had to prevail in an underhanded fashion. Camus could not contradict himself too openly. The style of the novel reveals how he managed to deceive himself. Rhetorical ornaments are systematically avoided; the author uses none of the gestures that serve to emphasize a good point. We feel that he is not looking at us and that he hardly unclenches his teeth. He rejects even the affectation of vulgarity and profanity that the preceding generation had adopted in an earlier attempt to destroy rhetoric—with the sole result, of course, of creating a new one. The famous rejection of the preterite—or of the present—the two tenses of formal narration, for the *passé composé* that is a conversational tense, amounts to an abandonment of all approved techniques of story telling. The author refuses to be a *raconteur* who performs for an audience. His *écriture blanche* gives an effect of greyish monotony that is the next best thing to silence, and silence is the only conduct truly befitting a solipsist, the only one, however, that he cannot bring himself to adopt.

This style bears a striking resemblance to the style of Meursault's actions prior to the murder. We feel that someone, on some fine day, handed Camus a pen and a piece of paper and Camus did the natural and mechanical thing to do, in such circumstances, which is to start writing, just as Meursault did the natural and mechanical thing to do, when you receive a gun, which is to start shooting. The book, like the murder, appears to be the result of fortuitous circumstances. The overall impression is that *L'Etranger* was written in the same bored, absent-minded, and apathetic fashion as the Arab was murdered. We have a crime and we have no criminal; we have a book and we have no writer.

Camus and his hero have sworn to forsake all but the most superficial contacts with their fellow men. Overtly, at least, they both kept their oaths. Meursault refused to go to Paris; Camus criticized writers and thinkers naive enough to believe in communication. But the oath was not kept so firmly that Meursault refrained from killing the Arab or Camus from writing *L'Etranger*. A murder and a book are not superficial contacts but, in the case of the murder, the destructive nature of the contact as well as the casual way in which it was obtained make it possible to deny that there is any contact at all. Similarly, the antisocial nature of the book, as well as the furtive nature of its creation, make it possible to deny that the solipsist is really appealing to other men.

Camus betrays solipsism when he writes *L'Etranger* just as Meursault betrays it when he murders the Arab. The close analogy between the murder of the Arab and the style of the novel is not difficult to explain; every aspect of the work bears the imprint of a single creative act that stands in the same relation to its own consequence, the book, as Meursault's behavior to his murder. The "innocent murder" is really the image and the crux of the whole creative process. Clamence is aware of that fact when he insists that he, as a lawyer, had the same hidden motives as his clients. He, too, craved publicity but he did not have to pay as dearly as the actual criminals for the satisfaction of that impure desire. He should have shared in the punishment as he had shared in the crime, but he was acclaimed, instead, as a great moral leader:

> Le crime tient sans trêve le devant de la scène, mais le criminel n'y figure que fugitivement pour être aussitôt remplacé. Ces brefs triomphes enfin se paient trop cher. Défendre nos malheureux aspirants à la réputation revenait, au contraire, à être vraiment reconnu, dans le même temps et aux mêmes places, mais par des moyens plus économiques. Cela m'encourageait aussi à déployer de méritoires efforts pour qu'ils payassent le moins possible; ce qu'ils payaient, ils le payaient un peu à ma place.[9]

Camus does not want us to believe that his motives, as a writer, were those of a literary opportunist writing cheap best sellers. From the higher standpoint of *La Chute*, he realizes that his own involvement in the tragic conflicts represented in his work was rooted in his own ambitions and in that stubborn need for self-justification to which we all succumb. *L'Etranger* is a real work of art since it can be apprehended as a single structure; its stylistic features are reflected in its plot and vice versa. We must not speak of the novel's *unity*, however, but of its consistent duality and of its radical ambiguity. How could the novel be one when its creative process is truly "divided against itself"? Every page of the work reflects the contradiction and the division inherent in the murder; every denial of communication is really an effort to communicate; every gesture of indifference or hostility is an appeal in disguise. The critical perspective suggested by *La Chute* illuminates even those structural elements that the esthetic approach makes its essential concern but that it ultimately leaves out of account because it isolates them from the content of the work and its many-sided significance.

Can we really understand the murder of the Arab, the structure of the novel, its style, and the "inspiration" of the novelist as a single process? We can if we compare this process to certain types of immature behavior. Let us imagine a child who, having been denied something he wanted very much, turns away from his parents; no blandishments will make him come out of his retreat. Like Meursault, like the first Camus, this child manages to convince himself that his sole desire is to be left alone.

If the child is left alone, his solitude quickly becomes unbearable but pride prevents him from returning meekly to the family circle. What can he do, then, to reestablish contact with the outside world? He must commit an action that will force the attention of the adults but that will not be interpreted as abject surrender, a *punishable* action, of course. But an overt challenge would still be too transparent; the punishable action must be committed covertly and deviously. The child must affect toward the instruments of his future misdeed the same casual attitude as Meursault toward his crime or as Camus toward literature.

Look at Meursault: he starts mingling with underworld characters inadvertently and casually, just as he would associate with anyone else; the matter is of no real consequence since other people do not really exist for him. Meursault, gradually, becomes involved in the shady dealings of his associates but he is hardly aware of this involvement. Why should he care, since one action is as good as another? The child's behavior is exactly the same; he picks up, for instance, a box of matches; he plays with it for a while, absent-mindedly; he does not mean any harm, of course, but all of a sudden, a match is aflame, and the curtains too if they happen to be nearby. Is it an *accident* or is it *fate*? It is "bad faith" and the child feels, like Meursault, that he is not responsible. Objects, to him, are mere fragments of substance lost in a chaotic universe. The *absurde*, in the sense popularized by *Sisyphe*, has become incarnate in this child.

L'Etranger was written and is usually read from the warped perspective that has just been defined. The secretly provocative nature of the murder is never acknowledged and the reprisals of society are presented as unprovoked aggression. The relationship between the individual and society is thereby turned upside down; a lonely individual, Meursault, is presented as completely indifferent to the collectivity, whereas the collectivity is supposed to be intensely concerned with his daily routine. This picture is false, and we all know it. Indifference really belongs to the collectivity; intense concern should be the lot of the lonely and miserable hero. The real picture is found in the few truly great works of fiction of Cervantes, Balzac, Dickens, Dostoevski, and, we might add, the Camus of *La Chute*.

The truth denied in *L'Etranger* is really so overwhelming that it comes out almost openly at the end of the novel, in Meursault's passionate outburst of resentment. Many readers have rightly felt that this conclusion rings more true than the rest of the novel. The resentment was there all along but pride silenced it, at least until the death sentence, which gave Meursault a pretext to express his despair without losing face in his own estimation. The child, too, wants to be punished, in order to express his grief without confessing its real cause, even to himself. In the last sentence, Meursault practically acknowledges that the sole and only guillotine threatening him is the indifference of *les autres*. "Pour que tout soit consommé, pour que je me sente moins seul, il me restait à souhaiter qu'il y ait beaucoup de spectateurs le jour de mon exécution et qu'ils m'accueillent avec des cris de haine."

The structural flaw in *L'Etranger* becomes intelligible when the novel is assimilated to a type of behavior that has become very common, even among adults, in our contemporary world. Meursault's empty life, his sullen mood, his upside-down world, no less than his half-hearted and secretly provocative crime are typical of what we call "juvenile delinquency." This social aspect can easily be reconciled with the ultra-Romantic conception of the self that underlies the novel. Observers have pointed out the element of latter-day Romanticism in juvenile delinquency. In recent years, some novels and films dealing openly with this social phenomenon have borrowed features from *L'Etranger*, a work that, outwardly at least, has nothing to do with it. The hero of the film *A bout de souffle*, for instance, half voluntarily kills a policeman, thus becoming a "good criminal" after Meursault's fashion. The *theme* of juvenile delinquency is absent from *L'Etranger* because the novel is the literary equivalent of the action, its perfect *analogon*.

L'Etranger is certainly no accurate portrayal of the society in which it was created. Should we say, therefore, as the formalists do, that it is a "world of its own," that it is wholly independent from this society? The novel *reverses* the laws of our society but this reversal is not an absence of relationship. It is a more complex relationship that involves negative as well as positive factors and that cannot be expressed in the mechanical terms of the old realism or positivism. It is an indirect relationship that must be apprehended if we want to apprehend the esthetic structure itself. We have just seen that the only way to illuminate the esthetic structure of *L'Etranger* as an integrated structure is to resort to the social phenomenon called "juvenile delinquency." *L'Etranger* is not independent from the social reality it overturns, since this overturning is a social attitude among others and a very typical one. The autonomy of the structure may appear absolute to the writer at the time of his writing, and to the uncritical reader, but it is only relative. *L'Etranger* reflects the world view of the juvenile delinquent with unmatched perfection precisely because it is not aware of reflecting anything, except, of course, the innocence of its hero and the injustice of his judges.

Camus wrote *L'Etranger* against the "judges" or, in other words, against the middle class who are his sole potential readers. Instead of rejecting the book as the author had half hoped, half feared, these bourgeois readers showered it with praise. The "judges," obviously, did not recognize their portrait when they saw it. They, too, cursed the iniquitous judges and howled for clemency. They, too, identified with the innocent victim and they acclaimed Meursault as a Galahad of sun-worshiping "authenticity." The public turned out, in short, to be made not of judges, as the author had mistakenly believed, but of generous lawyers like the author himself.

Since all the admirers of the early Camus share, to some extent, in the guilt of the "generous lawyer," they too should be present in *La Chute*. And they are, in the person of Clamence's silent listener. The man has nothing to say because Clamence answers *his* questions and objections almost before they are formulated in *our* minds. At the end of the book, this man confesses his identity; he, too, is a generous lawyer.

Thus, Clamence is addressing each one of us personally, leaning toward *me* across a narrow café table and looking straight in *my* eyes. His monologue is dotted with exclamations, interjections, and apostrophes; every three lines we have an "allons," "tiens," "quoi!," "eh bien!," "ne trouvez-vous pas," "mon cher compatriote," etc. The style of *La*

Chute is the exact antithesis of the impersonal and antirhetorical *écriture blanche*. Gone is the false detachment of Meursault. We have shifted from the "restrained indignation" of the generous lawyer, as Clamence aptly defines it, to the open theatricality of a self-confessed and yet insurmountable bad faith. The studiously cheap and cacophonic symbolism of *La Chute* is a parody of the serious symbolic works of the past.

As he questions the authenticity of *L'Etranger* and similar works, Camus questions the question itself. *La Chute*, no less than *L'Etranger*, is directed against all potential readers because it is directed against the lawyers in a world where only lawyers are left. The technique of spiritual aggression has become more subtle but its aim has not changed.

Why does Clamence point out to us that his new posture is still one of bad faith? He undermines his own position in order to prevent others from undermining it. After deriding the generous lawyer, he mockingly describes himself as a penitent-judge. Slyly anticipating his readers, whom he knows to be adept at gleaning moral comfort from the most sinister parables, he gives a new twist to the now familiar serpent, hoping to keep one step ahead of everybody else in a game of self-justification that has turned into a game of self-accusation.

Let the judge repudiate judgment and he becomes a judge in disguise, a lawyer; let the lawyer repudiate the disguise and he becomes a penitent-judge; let the penitent-judge . . . We are spiraling down the circles of a particularly nasty hell, but this more and more precipitous *chute* is perhaps not so fatal as it seems. The penitent-judge does not believe in his role half as much as the generous lawyer did. The conclusion of *La Chute* is a final pirouette as well, perhaps, as the image of what may happen to a world entirely given over to the lawyers and the penitent-judges.

The universal need for self-justification haunts all modern trial literature. But there are different levels of awareness. The so-called "myth" of the trial can be approached from several mutually exclusive perspectives. In *L'Etranger*, the real question is that of the innocence and guilt of the protagonists. The criminal is innocent and the judges are guilty. In the more conventional ego-nourishing fiction, the criminal is usually guilty and the judges innocent. But this difference is really secondary. In both cases, "good" and "bad" are rigid concepts; the verdict of the judges is challenged but not their vision.

La Chute goes higher and deeper. Clamence is still busy proving that he is "good" and that other people are "bad," but his systems of classification keep breaking down. The real question is no longer "who is innocent, who is guilty?," but "why do we, all of us, have to keep judging and being judged?" It is a more interesting question, the very question of Dostoevski. In *La Chute*, Camus lifts trial literature back to the level of this great predecessor.

The first Camus did not realize how far-reaching, how pervasive the evil of judgment is. He felt that he was outside judgment because he condemned those who condemn. Using Gabriel Marcel's terminology, we may say that Meursault viewed evil as something outside himself, a *problem* that concerned the judges alone, whereas Clamence knows that he himself is involved. Evil is the *mystery* of a pride that, as it condemns others, unwittingly condemns itself. It is the pride of Oedipus, another hero of trial literature, always uttering the curses that result in his own undoing. Reciprocity between the I and the Thou asserts itself in the very efforts I make to deny it: "The sentence which you pass against your fellow men," says Clamence, "is always flung back into your face where it effects quite a bit of damage."

The outsider is really inside, but he is not aware of it. This lack of awareness determines the esthetic as well as the spiritual limitations of *L'Etranger*. A man who feels the urge to write a trial novel is not really "in love with the sun." He does not belong to the sunny Mediterranean but to the fogs of Amsterdam.

The world in which we live is one of perpetual judgment. It must be our Judeo-Christian heritage, still active within us. We are not healthy pagans. We are not Jews, either, since we have no Law. But we are not real Christians, since we keep judging. Who are we? A Christian cannot help feeling that the answer is close at hand: "thou art inexcusable, o man, whosoever thou art that judgest; for wherein thou judgest another, thou condemnest thyself; for thou that judgest dost the same things." Did Camus realize that all the themes of *La Chute* are in Paul's *Epistles*? If he had, would he have drawn from the analogy, and from the answers of Paul, the conclusions that a Christian would draw? Nobody can answer these questions.

Meursault was guilty of judgment but he never found out; Clamence alone found out. The two heroes may be viewed as a single one whose career describes a single itinerary somewhat analogous to the itinerary of the great Dostoevskian heroes. Like Raskolnikov, like Dmitri Karamazov, Meursault-Clamence first pictured himself as the victim of a judicial error, but he finally realized that the sentence was just, even if the judges were personally unjust, because the Self can provide only a grotesque parody of Justice.

The universal dimension of *La Chute* can be reached only through its most personal, almost intimate dimension. The two are really one; the structure of the work is one and its significance is one. Openly, at least, this significance is entirely negative. But the positive aspects are summed up in one sentence of the Nobel Prize acceptance speech. Camus opposes, in their order, his two fundamental attitudes, as a creator and as a man, leaving no doubt as to the personal significance of Clamence's confession:

L'art . . . oblige . . . l'artiste à ne pas s'isoler; il le soumet à la vérité la plus humble et la plus universelle. Et celui qui, souvent, a choisi son destin d'artiste parce qu'il se sentait différent, apprend bien vite qu'il ne nourrira son art, et sa différence, qu'en avouant sa ressemblance avec tous.[10]

NOTES

1. J. D. Salinger, *The Catcher in the Rye* (Boston: Little, Brown and Company), pp. 223–24.
2. Of *La Chute*, Jacques Madaule writes: "En un certain sens, c'est comme une réplique et une réponse à *L'Etranger*" ("Camus and Dostoievski," *La Table ronde* 146 [1960]: 132). See also Roger Quilliot, "Albert Camus's Algeria," in *Camus: A Collection of Critical Essays*, ed. Germaine Brée (Englewood Cliffs, N.J.: Prentice-Hall, Inc., 1962), pp. 38–47.
3. Louis Hudon, "*The Stranger* and the Critics," *Yale French Studies* 25 (Spring 1960): 61.
4. Philippe Sénart, "Camus et le juste milieu," *La Table ronde* 174–75 (July–August 1962): 113.
5. Albert Camus, *Discours de Suède*, in *Oeuvres complètes*, ed. André Sauret, 6 vols. (Paris: Imprimerie nationale, 1967), 3:452.
6. Søren Kierkegaard, *Fear and Trembling and The Sickness unto Death*, trans. Walter Lowrie (New York: Doubleday, 1954), pp. 204–5.
7. Ibid., p. 203.
8. Ibid., pp. 206–7.
9. Albert Camus, *La Chute* (Paris: Gallimard, 1956), pp. 33–34.
10. Camus, *Discours de Suède*, p. 442.

3

The Underground Critic

A writer's career, like that of a scientific researcher, generally develops over a period of many years. It often revolves, or seems to revolve, entirely around a small number of themes and problems taken up again and again by the author. He would not consider these thematic repetitions necessary if he had nothing new to say. Or at least it would be natural to think so. It might be assumed that these successive modifications are made under the pressure of completed works either no longer satisfying or never having satisfied the author. These new works, in relation to the older ones, have a negative and critical side that one can attempt to bring from the shadows in order to illuminate their principles.

This still abstract hypothesis conflicts with the widespread contemporary notion that readily recognizes that many writers revolve for a lifetime around the same themes; but this is invariably conceived as an obsession. Thus, if there is any progress other than the purely technical, it will be understood in terms of the obsession itself still reinforcing its effects. The critic compares successive literary works but does not purport to draw from this comparison the principle of his analyses. One does not ask the obsessed for the final word on his obsession.

In order to illustrate this perspective it is necessary to summon literary works that, to all evidence, end just as they began, and there is no lack of them. The outcome is the elaboration of the point of departure, its glaring and parodic confirmation. A merit of recent criticism is to have shown this by following some of these works step by step. Of course, the themes are never repeated in exactly the same manner, but their successive divergencies cannot be defined in terms of a rupture.

I accept this scheme for the greater majority of modern works without the slightest reticence because I myself have sketched out similar examples. For instance, the older Victor Hugo became, the more the obsessive character of his genius, which had been undeveloped in his

This essay appeared under the title "Présentation," in *Critique dans un souterrain* (Lausanne: L'Age d'Homme, 1976), pp. 7–34. It has been translated by Paisley N. Livingston and Tobin Siebers.

early works, revealed itself. The symbols of good and evil invert themselves along the way, but this is not a true revolution as it operates in the general direction of the obsession; it was "programmed" from the start. These structures only progress toward self-simplification, detaching their lines of force and becoming more and more readable, until finally they turn into their own caricatures in the universe they had created, a universe entirely reduced to an exasperated Manicheism of a symphony in black and white.

The case of Dostoevski strikes me differently. In his first works, a furious obsession is outlined. Everywhere the same scheme reappears, the same triangular relationship of desired woman and two rivals. We cannot simply say that these rivals struggle with each other for the woman. The principal hero conducts himself in an obscure and complex fashion. He flutters about the desired woman, but this only contributes to the rival's success and union with the loved one. The *dénouement* makes the protagonist desperate, of course, but not completely: he dreams of building himself a little place as third party in the couple's future existence. Regarding the rival, tokens of hostility alternate with gestures of servility, with the signs of a fascinating attraction.

The early Dostoevski interprets this kind of conduct within the framework of romantic idealism; he only sees "greatesness of the soul" and "noble generosity." The least attentive reader has suspicions fully confirmed by Dostoevski's own triangular relationship with his future wife and the rival Vergougnov, as revealed in the Siberian correspondence. To discard this correspondence under the pretext that it has no right to intervene in the consideration of literary works is a futile gesture. Certain letters and certain literary works are hardly distinguishable. To worry about a possible confusion of "reality" and "fiction" is to fall into fiction oneself, not to see that everything here springs from fiction. Everywhere, the same fascinations are presented in the guise of duty and morality.

But even in cases as clear as this one, certain champions of esthetic sovereignty once refused, and still refuse today, to admit their defeat. They are afraid to concede to extraliterary disciplines, notably psychoanalysis, the right to examine literary activity as a whole. Thus, they heroically close their eyes, clinging forever to the postulate of the "autonomous" work; they declare untouchable even those texts most visibly deformed by misunderstanding, most evidently governed by mechanisms escaping them.

These champions of the work of art have already succumbed to the prestige of what they call science. They are convinced that the mastery of obsessional mechanisms, if it exists, can only be their enemy, de-

voted to a *demystification* without nuances, avid to establish its totali-
tarian domination over the smoldering ruins of what they love. We
must admit that what is going on around us can hardly encourage them
to think otherwise.

The triangular relationships and the obsession with the rival will
never disappear from Dostoevski's works, but beginning with *Notes
from the Underground*, he abruptly renounces the idealist reading. He
himself brings out the obsessional character of the rivalries. "Greatness
of the soul" and "generosity" remain, but are presented in a satiric
light. The vague malaise caused by the early works, the vague questions they suggest but fail to pose directly, are succeeded by the
malaise and silence not of the work but of the characters, a malaise and
silence now possessing the thickness and consistency of a real human
being, the very object of the Dostoevskian research. Even if his art
prohibits him from directly explaining himself, Dostoevski clarifies this
malaise, he responds to our questions. The very perfect correspon-
dences between the two types of works are so numerous and precise
that no doubt remains possible. The obsessions dramatized on stage in
the second type are the very ones that directed the first without leaving
the wings.

No one, or almost no one, reads the works preceding *Notes from the
Underground*, but this is not an injustice to be regretted. The real
Dostoevski begins afterward; he begins with a rupture whose essential
character must be recognized even if the continuity of themes hides it.
Beginning with *Notes from the Underground*, the writer reexamined
the obsessional relationship that had victimized him for so long, and he
manages little by little to capture it in his works. He did not cease
creating characters resembling the writer he had been. This is no
longer a vain repetition of the early works, but an always more assured
progression where each successive book marks another stage, a dynamic enterprise where a more and more powerful novelistic instrument is forged.

In the works after the rupture, a *knowledge* is constituted and applied to an obsessional universe reflected but not revealed in the first
works. Before calling on extraliterary disciplines to enlighten the
"Dostoevski case," it seems to me the least a critic can do is to examine
this knowledge, to render it fully explicit so as to compare it with
nonliterary disciplines such as psychoanalysis. Curiously enough, this is
just what no one does. Those who champion all literary works indiscriminately would never dream of this method, since they do not admit
the existence of self-deceptive works. Those who do admit the existence of such works would never dream of it because they know of no
other kind. They mean to monopolize critical insight. The idea of

conceding even the tiniest parcel of it to literary works seems scandalous to them.

Blinded, perhaps, by their divisions, all of these critics demonstrate an excessive confidence in labels and conventions. For them, science is always science and literature can only be literature; the genres should never be mixed. If the boundary of scientific knowledge is not as fixed as imagined, then it would indeed be a matter of genre distinctions as debilitating as Boileau's would be if contemporary intellectual opinion obliged us to respect them.

A rigorous conception of desire, imbricated in the textual interlacings of the great works, comes to light in Dostoevski. A systemization of this conception is not without its dangers; however, it can be all the more attractive if we place the last works, here the direct sources, next to the first, thereby permitting us to inspect them. These are no longer rough sketches, but experimental subjects, a new kind of guinea pig used only by Dostoevski himself and still waiting to be used by us.

In Dostoevski, desire has no original or privileged object. This is a primary and fundamental break with Freud. Desire chooses its objects through the mediation of a model; it is the desire of and for the *other*, which is nonetheless identical to a furious longing to center everything around the self. Desire is essentially torn between the self and the other, who appears more and more masterful, more autonomous than the self. Here lies the paradox of a pride identical with this desire, its inevitable failure. The model designates the desirable while at the same time desiring it. Desire is always an imitation of another desire, desire for the same object, and, therefore, an inexhaustible source of conflicts and rivalries. The more the model transforms itself into an obstacle, the more desire tends to transform the obstacles into models.

The more desire learns about itself, the more self-defeating it becomes; it believes that by adoring the obstacle it moves more quickly toward its goal. From then on, desire is rekindled each time the conditions for a new failure seem to be present. In the psychiatrists' limited view, desire aims at this failure. Thus, psychiatrists invent for this misunderstood phenomenon a label, masochism, that definitively clouds its intelligibility. It is not failure that the so-called masochist seeks but the success of the rival that makes him fail.

We now grasp the importance, in *Notes from the Underground*, of episodes that at first glance seem to be simple burlesque. For example, the jostling in the street immediately turns the insolent stranger into one of the fascinating obstacles, simultaneously rival and model, that I have just defined. In this instance rivalry is indeed primary; there is no longer an object masking this truth; the rivalry is not the accidental convergence of two independent and spontaneous desires on the same object. Here everything is imitation, but a negative imitation that we fail to recognize and that the caricatural art of Dostoevski successfully manifests. Nietzsche vaguely suspected the importance of this book, but unfortunately for him and for us he never pursued it.

The sentiments the obstacle-model inspires, a mixture of hate and veneration, are those called "typically Dostoevskian." Nothing is more intelligible in the mimetic perspective than that alternating impulse to overthrow and "fuse with" the monstrous idol. Indeed, such is the mechanism of desire in the later Dostoevski. And the vision becomes more constraining if held in opposition to the early works. In fact, if this grid is imposed upon romantic and idealist interpretations, clearly, it successfully fills textual gaps, it rectifies the perpetual rifts between avowed intentions and their concrete manifestation. To explain the early works satisfactorily, to dissipate their malaise, it is necessary to see them not as the beginning of a deciphering but as symptomatic traces of a desire that only great works manage to unravel. One partial exception to this rule is *The Double*, a first advance toward Dostoevski's future genius that was quickly blocked by Belinski and his friends.

If desire is mimetic by nature, all consequent phenomena must necessarily tend toward reciprocity. Already at the level of the object, all rivalry has a reciprocal character no matter what its cause. Reciprocity will also intervene at the level of desire if each becomes an obstacle-model for the other. Desire spots this reciprocity. It observes, always accumulating more knowledge of the other and of itself, but this knowledge can never break the circle of its "alienation." Desire tries to escape the reciprocity it discovers. Under the effect of violent rivalry, every model must change itself sooner or later into an anti-model, differing instead of resembling. All want to break the reciprocity, but this reciprocity is only perpetuated in inverse form.

Two pedestrians see they are approaching one another. Each wishes to avoid the other and moves in the opposite direction of the one they envision the other is taking. A stand-off occurs. . . . Any example this simple necessarily springs from a domain where the investment of desire is next to nothing; it hardly suggests, as a consequence, the mechanism's craftiness, tenacity, and power of diffusion and contamination.

After Dante, almost no one but Dostoevski reveals how truly infernal desire can be, not in the absence of the object and the incapability of reaching it, but in the constant attachment to this double, a slavish imitation growing all the more invincible as escape is attempted. Even where all the positive data seem to preclude it, the relationship of rivalry moves irresistibly toward reciprocity and identity. Indeed, this causes the anguish of the Eternal Lover, model and rival of the Eternal Husband, where each alternately enters the other's game in spite of himself. Both of the doubles become entangled in the obligatory reciprocity of one and the very same game.

This disconcerting return of the identical exactly where each believes he is generating difference defines this relationship of the doubles, and it has nothing to do with the *imaginaire*. Doubles are the final result and truth of mimetic desire, a truth seeking acknowledgment but repressed by the principal characters because of their mutual antagonism. The doubles themselves interpret the emergence of the doubles as "hallucinatory."

Almost all of modern thought from Romantic literature to psychoanalysis sees the relationship of the doubles as only a fantasmatic and fantasmagoric phenomenon. Modern thought expels its own inherent truth in order to establish a difference that it never stops trying to grasp but that flees from it nonetheless. This is the mechanism of fashionability and modernism that Dostoevski never ceased to describe.

The hallucinatory reading is really a ruse of desire that must progress toward madness because it intends to pass itself off as mad in the only domain where, in reality, it sees clearly. By insisting that the double is only a "narcissistic reflection," that is, an unintelligible sign of a pathological state having no contact with the real, all modern thought remains tributary, the accomplice of the same alienations it pretends to combat.

In the early works of Dostoevski, the rivals are always doubles, but—and again *The Double* is an exception—the young writer always seeks to contradict this truth, even though it is already inscribed in the structure of the texts. He means to differentiate the rivals, to convince himself each time that his is "the good" and the other "the bad." On the other hand, in the great works the relationship of the doubles becomes more and more explicit.

In the works of Camus, *The Fall* acts as a rupture analogous to Dostoevski's. Like the early Dostoevski, the early Camus strives to differentiate a relationship permitting the mimetic rivalry to represent and invest itself in this representation. For example, in *The Stranger*, the "good criminal" brings out the "villainy" of the judges. All the passion of the work is concentrated in this message of difference.

It is not surprising that *The Fall* is marked by the appearance of doubles, by bizarre incidents contradicting much too impudently the flattering image that Clamence has carefully elaborated for himself not to be indignantly rejected. Clamence wants to be faithful to the dogma of difference, but his system collapses like a house of cards; everything is reorganized in function of the doubles, this time solidly and without possible contention. If the judges are guilty of killing and judging, the "good criminal" is also guilty of murder and judgment, since he has killed and done so only to provide the judges with a good occasion for condemning him, to put himself in the position of judging his own judges. The more Clamence strives to break the symmetry, the more he enforces it.

Like the great works of Dostoevski, *The Fall* makes possible a positive response to the question posed at the beginning of this essay. It produces within the works of a single author a rupture that confers on those following it a critical attitude toward the early works. *The Fall* makes an even more explicit response; it is nothing other than the critical reorganization of past themes in terms of the doubles. The critical force of the rupture is nothing but the doubles becoming explicit, the writer himself taking charge of them. This reading of certain works in terms of the doubles has only been articulated by other works; academic criticism has neither practiced nor conceived of it. All modern methodologies remain blind to the truth of the doubles.

In linguistic structuralism, the why and how of this blindness become manifest. Dual oppositions are marked out and rise to the foreground, but structuralism only conceives of them as signifying, that is, differentiating. The reflection of structuralism on the differential laws of language only confirms its own idea. Given that literary works are made of language, it is natural to imagine them as full of differential meaning and nothing else. This is true to the letter, but the letter here is not everything, or perhaps it is too much. In fact, it could be the vocation of great works to constrain language to say things that contradict its own laws, the sound and the fury of the relationship of the doubles, signifying nothing.

It is this *signifying nothing* that linguistic structuralism always allows to escape. It always creates one more signification in the manner of myths, which speak of the *doubles* as twins and sacred monsters, or in the manner of psychotherapy, which speaks of them as imaginary meaning, but nonetheless as meaning. Structuralism simply does not see—cannot see—the rupture in Dostoevski and Camus because this rupture does not correspond to any typically structural modification. These are still the same dual oppositions but from now on they are differentiated in appearance only. Structuralism does not see the effacement of difference in the senseless violence of the relationship of the doubles.

Far from revolutionizing criticism, linguistic structuralism systematically fulfills its traditional mission, which consists in saying and resaying meaning, paraphrasing and classifying significations. If structuralism can combine so well with Marxism and psychoanalysis, it is because they always reduce manifest significations to other hidden significations, to another differentiating system, for instance, the well-known Lacanian formula: "The unconscious is structured like a language."

It is not surprising that structuralism and modern criticism in general are so insensible to the formidable simplicity of the greatest literary effects, the comic and tragic. This does not mean that this criticism is actually a stranger to these effects; perhaps every day it moves a little closer, perhaps it is already mixed up in this business. These doubles, of course, perpetuate their own sometimes laughable, sometimes terrifying misunderstanding of the doubles.

The works I have just discussed and other analogous works all carry themes or symbolism of the rupture. I myself speak of these works in terms of a rupture made by the writer himself. Of course, at this point there will be well-intentioned people who will warn me that the "rupture" and "fall" are only literary themes. It is naive, they say, to relate literary themes to extraliterary references.

These people think I speak the way I do because I rely primarily on this theme or this symbolism of the rupture that figures strikingly in the crucial works. The reader of the preceding pages can verify that this is not the case. I begin with the relationship between "differentiated" works and the works coming to grips with the doubles. If desire is invested in a differentiated system, and it evidently is, then it is just as evident that the collapse of this system cannot fail to be noticed by the one most concerned. For what collapses is the flattering self-image that the author fought to create and perpetuate.

When Camus wrote *The Fall*, he did not have a fictional character in mind, but only his past work. *The Stranger* then seemed naive to him, not in a pleasant sense of innocence, but in an antipathetic and somewhat grotesque sense of an unrecognized *ressentiment*. This could not have been an agreeable experience. When Dostoevski wrote *The Eternal Husband*, he must have had his own fascination for real rivals like Vergougnov in mind, a fascination he had lived and could live again, but also that he had written about, glorified, and falsified for the world. This new awareness could not have been an agreeable experience either, at least initially.

Nevertheless, some would like me to remark that contemporary criticism can no longer permit itself to slide from text to author and from author to text as was once done. This is an excellent rule, but it aims, on the one hand, at the naive application of texts to the "author," and,

on the other hand, at the use of biographical data. I do indeed speak of
the author but, inconceivable as this may seem, I speak of him without
naively basing myself on the text and without depending upon material
other than the texts. The author springs from the rupture between two
types of texts, as the necessary experience of this rupture.

I am aware that works grounded in the rupture always carry a theme
or symbolism that suggests it. It is perhaps regrettable but undeniable.
Even so, I cannot believe that what we have here is a simple coincidence. Elementary logic obliges me to conclude that the author,
through the mediation of his characters, alludes to an experience that
he must be undergoing, since the comparative analysis of texts demonstrates its necessity. This comparative analysis is foremost and essential, not the themes or symbolism alluding to the rupture.

I refuse to consider this theme or this symbolism as gratuitous under
the pretext that critics will not see its textual correlative and therefore
believe that I am violating a rule applicable to thematic elements
alone. They fail to see the unchallengeable evidence for the reality of
the rupture. If I am told once more that this is impossible, that there
can be no unchallengeable evidence because all evidence is either
naively intratextual or naively extratextual, I will repeat once more that
this is not the case: there is a third possibility, mine, the intertextual
evidence.

In the case of Dostoevski, the writer's Christianity is inseparable
from his novelistic experience. Many readers might judge this affirmation as more inadmissible than the rest. They will conclude that there is
a distortion of the textual analysis pressured by a particularly harmful
a priori ideology, an a priori religious stance.

The novelistic experience destroys the myth of personal mastery that
feeds on servile dependency toward others doubled with flagrant injustice. Hate no longer hides from the writer his own fascinations. It
seems evident that this experience is extremely fertile for the esthetic
act. The writer at last has the possibility of creating truly memorable
characters by tracing the most odious and ridiculous traits of the other,
the rival, faithful mirror of his own intimate self; the previously impossible fusion of "observation" and "introspection" is achieved.

The character of Frédéric Moreau, among other examples, demonstrates that something of this kind occurs in all great novelistic
experiments. This character combines many of the author's own experiences and judgments with the irritating manner of Maxime du
Camp, formerly condemned in the correspondence and monopolized in
the early version of Sentimental Education as a negative and oppor-
tunistic double of the central hero who otherwise should have in-
carnated the author's own idealism.

Here we can also invoke the Proust of *Remembrance of Things Past* as he sifts through this memory, or perhaps his papers, in an attempt to make the ridiculous, archetypal snob Legrandin speak just as Proust wrote and spoke at the time of *Jean Santeuil*. At that time, Proust had not yet completely understood that hatred for the snob is only a facet of snobbery. This is why *Jean Santeuil* is a flat and self-serving work when compared to *Remembrance of Things Past*.

This novelistic experience is indeed an experience of the "fall," having a prodigious creative power. It is possible that the existential dimension of this experience may be limited, but it can never be wholly absent, and it can be read in many philosophical and religious keys.

These religious approaches strike me as particularly rich, and those of Judeo-Christianity are the richest of all, the most favorable for the development and explication of the experience. First of all, because Judeo-Christianity conceives of its own ascendency at the individual level, not as a shamanistic, ecstatic possession, but rather as a depossession. Secondly, because this depossession, even if it remains readable in the traditional language of *exorcism* (see, for instance, the expulsion of Gerasa dear to Dostoevski), is defined more essentially in the context of the relationship to an other who can only become a neighbor insofar as he ceases to be that sacred and profane idol that desiring *mimesis* seems to make of him.

Christianity is not a postulate exterior to the work, some sort of oath distorting the content of the work from the outside; it is the novelistic experience, the experience of rupture, that relates to Christianity and allows itself more and more to be interpreted by it.

Here again there is no recourse to biographical data separate from the works. Just as we can and must speak of the novelistic experience without leaving the texts, so we can and must speak of Dostoevski's Christianity because at the level that interests us these two things become identical. It is the texts that oblige us to conclude that their own story is inseparably linked to what they themselves understand through Christianity. To sever Dostoevski from his Christianity is to fall into prejudice because elements indispensable to his work's intelligibility are arbitrarily eliminated. This is rarely seen today; for most people the absence of prejudice implies a military obedience to the imperative commanding that religious belief and irrational "mysticism" are one and the same. On the contrary, this constitutes a good example of prejudice.

In *The Fall*, the religious reading is never adopted. And yet even here it constitutes a possibility present in the author's mind. This must be so, since the author judged it important enough to have his hero repeatedly and explicitly reject it. It must be concluded that there is something in the experience of "the fall" that calls or recalls certain religious experiences, at least to a particular type of mind. The fact that some respond negatively and others positively to this appeal does not matter very much.

The fact that Clamence's "fall" immediately turns into imposture, that it becomes transformed into a new enterprise for the recuperation of difference, is no objection either. Why should it not be so? Many of Dostoevski's heroes resemble Clamence. It would be ridiculous to think that the writer should represent only saints and heroes.

I have never said, I repeat, that in order to determine the reality, or especially the nature of the experience, we should rely exclusively or even essentially on the texts alluding to it. On the contrary, I affirm that only the relationship between texts can enlighten us; once this relationship is established we cannot fail to take account of the texts *speaking* of the rupture, whether they surround it with religious fervor or treat it with cynicism.

The collapse of difference is at stake in the illusory and frenzied antagonism between those becoming doubles; it is evident that no other experience is as susceptible to degree, manipulation, and falsification as the attempt to come to terms with the doubles. Judging the writer on ethical or religious grounds is not conceivable or even desirable. But such is not the problem that confronts the critic. He should try to, and, up to a point, he usually can, distinguish between texts founded on an illusory differentiation of the relationship set in motion and those founded on a recognition of the doubles. The superiority of the second over the first is not the secret of an intellectual clergy; it is nearly always ratified, even if unwittingly, by the "judgment of posterity."[1]

A few years ago, Julia Kristeva, inspired by the works of Bakhtin, notably on Dostoevski, proposed a distinction between *monologic* and *dialogic* works. It seems this distinction aims well but is not entirely on target, because as in Bakhtin the notion of the *carnavalesque* designates the form of what no longer has form and thereby remains the prisoner of formalism, like rites themselves. The notion of the *dialogic* inflicts all sorts of miseries on the linguistic structures, strives radically to weaken them, multiplies their substitutions and oscillations, but nonetheless in the final analysis remains the prisoner of linguistic structuralism. To escape the latter it would be necessary to understand that the total of this operation always equals zero. This would instantly free us from all methodological *préciosité* and grant us access at last to the doubles, that is, the essential.

In the case of these authors whose complete works are divided by a "rupture," I have discovered an analytic tool that first of all and in a privileged fashion is applied to the works occuring before the break. It cannot be said that critical specialists reject this tool, for they do not even see it. To explain this strange phenomenon, it is necessary to recognize that the doubles and the blindness toward them do not simply have a local implication limited to the works that take them into account. Little by little we are led to grant a broader range to the analytical principles outlined, to widen their application to critical and literary works that remain blind to the rupture not because they are fundamentally different or radically foreign to what this rupture reveals, but because, having never experienced it, they do not perceive their own doubles as such.

In short, the question arises: can we view those works without ruptures, those of a single block, as if they all took place before the break? Can Hugo be read according to the perspective of the later Dostoevski, in terms of a collapse of difference never occurring in his works, in terms of the doubles that never explicitly appear but that will be regarded as the truth of all antagonistic relations?

Before responding to this question, it is necessary to note that it leads the interpreter into less favorable terrain than the works previously considered. By abolishing difference, the interpreter contradicts an intention, deliberately discards a message that the author never himself put in question. He cannot count on the author to guide his approach retrospectively. He no longer breezes through a double series of texts. He no longer rediscovers this tight network of references that diminishes his role as his pleasure and certainty increase, and that confers on the enterprise a character I would willingly qualify as luxurious.

The response seems positive to me, nevertheless. The Manicheism of values has more esthetic glamour; there is more brilliance in the later Hugo than in the early Dostoevski or the Camus of *The Stranger*, but all contain the same dualism visibly rooted in the same type of conflict. It is still the same difference supported by identifications and exclusions that are revealed to be arbitrary at the level of the text itself. The interpreter must recognize in the heroes and traitors of *The Man Who Laughs* the doubles never acknowledged by the author, but doubles nevertheless.

Even though the author is no longer present in the works of "a single block," the doubles and mimetic desire will still affirm themselves, we might say, in his absence and in spite of him. Beyond a certain threshold, their truth is spectacularly asserted in the irruption of madness. When madness begins, we frequently see the doubles associated not with fictional relationships but belonging to those of the writer's existence. These relationships are arranged in a dual and ternary manner and we easily recognize in them a true epiphany of mimetic desire.

The double Nietzsche experiences in Genoa is probably no stranger to Zarathustra. But this double should, above all, be related to the triangle that emerges just before the definitive breakdown in order to disrupt every other Nietzschean theme: Dionysus-Nietzsche, Ariadne-Cosima, Richard Wagner, or *Nietzsche contra Wagner*. It is impossible here, even though it might be blasphemous, not to consider the extremely similar relationship presiding over yet another great literary madness, the relationship of Hölderlin and Schiller. Both men are separated and united by their common stake, a glory too divine to be shared, a formidable and empty genius appearing to oscillate from one to the other, granted and then stolen away again by the sometimes imperceptible vicissitudes of the atrocious alternation of benedictions and maledictions. The fact that *only one* goes mad in this case does not exclude the fact that this madness has its underlying principle in the realm of real relationships. Many other examples could be given. Charles Castella's book suggests to me that Maupassant's madness is of this kind.[2]

Everywhere we rediscover the doubles and the Dostoevskian triangle, a triangle that is, of course, the same as in *La Nouvelle Héloise*. Everywhere we repeatedly uncover the delirious exchange with the same monstrous idol, always beaten down, always climbing back again. Everywhere we rediscover the alternation of gods and sacrificial victims governed by the ups and downs of these violent exchanges; once again, Dionysus and the Crucified, *Ecce Homo*; the superman and the underground man, *Rousseau juge de Jean-Jacques*.

In works of this type, the continuity is that of mimetic desire itself, of its evolution, or better yet, of its historicity. This continuity moves from the more or less "Manichean" divisions already present in so-called normal perception (of doubles and triangulations haunting the most "average" existences) to the madness of a Hölderlin or a Nietzsche. The accelerating reciprocity of mimetic relationships engenders a sinister dynamism. The play of the obstacle-model determines a system of feedbacks, a vicious circle that is forever tightening. Beyond a certain threshold, the individual can no longer master or even hide this mechanism, it overwhelms him.

If this is the case, these are works where madness constitutes not only an insurpassable limit but an inevitable term, a true destiny, but naturally on the condition that its thrust be powerful enough and that nothing deter it. This madness reappears too often and in forms too analogous for me to tolerate the thesis of the accident, which has always repressed the interesting questions. Unfortunately, these questions will no longer interest anyone once the delirious escalation triumphs, at least rhetorically, over the last anxieties concerning madness. Today madness is openly claimed in the forms that were once the most clinical, officially enthroned as the supreme avatar of the Romantic ideal. Of course, this involves turning away from its real structure more than ever.

Given the obsessive character of certain works, there are in the last analysis only two ultimate possibilities, either they progress toward madness or they break from it in the manner of the Dostoevskian rupture. In all cases, with Rousseau, Hölderlin, or Nietzsche, as with Dostoevski, there exist the same doubles, the same mimetic configurations coming to light. At whatever level we view them, these convergences in so many great modern figures are striking; it is astonishing that they attract so little attention.

The reader must avoid confusing these two extreme types of works. In one case, the emergence of the mimetic scheme is achieved in and by delirium, in the midst of a catastrophe as definitive for the author as for the work. In the other, on the contrary, this emergence is achieved by a progress in perceptiveness. It constitutes for the work and sometimes for the author something like a second birth; it casts on mimetic desire and the doubles the best light available. In the first case the obsession masters the works, in the second the work masters the obsession.

If the negative side of a criticism derived from literary works may shock literary purists, the positive side—the fact that this negation proceeds from other works and consequently recognizes in them the highest critical moment, in short, provisionally considering them "irreducible"—will certainly displease the demystificators more ambitious than I can be here. Thus, this project may well pass as retrograde and obscurantist.

And yet it seems to me I have succumbed neither to a mystique of the literary work nor to a religious mystique. I believe there exists in certain works a knowledge of desirous relationships superior to any proposed. It is not at all a matter of challenging science, but of searching for it wherever it might be found and in no matter how unusual a place.

This affirmation may be surprising and must be justified, most notably in relation to psychoanalysis. The systemization attempted above approaches psychoanalytic theses at several points. A comparison imposes itself. It is necessary to include Freud's article on Dostoevski in the dossier. For Dostoevski is an author who wrote a novel about a

patricide and who we know hated his own father, a man of rare violence, many think, who was assassinated by his serfs. Freud should
have found in him the ideal literary subject. All this seems so evident
that the larger part of criticism automatically inclines itself in the direction of the oracle.

In Freud's article, we sense the weight of a certain malaise. After a
few appropriate remarks, a demonstration is begun, but stops short.
Freud forgets or flees from Dostoevski, taking refuge in a short story
by Stephan Zweig that more adequately suits his purpose.

Faced with a work like *The Brothers Karamazov*, psychoanalysis is
beside the point, and Freud is too perceptive not to sense it, even if he
fails to admit it. The mythic elements of *Oedipus Rex* are absent.
Freud leads us to understand that such a work must have symptomatic
value, like the epileptic fits, but at what level? For there to be neurosis,
the rivalry with the father and the desire to kill him must remain
unconscious. In all evidence this is not true here. It is necessary, therefore, that the Dostoevski case be much more or much less serious than
it appears. Freud explores the first possibility. He sketches a bold out-
line of a criminally insane Dostoevski. But this too is obviously unsatisfactory.

In whatever manner patricide fails to appear or, on the contrary,
manages to appear in a text, it should have a symptomatic character if
it is to bring water to the psychoanalytic mill. Without patricide there
is neurosis. With patricide it is even worse! It is quite evident that *The
Brothers Karamazov* is bound only with difficulty in this straight jacket.
After all, Dostoevski's father was really assassinated by serfs.

There is nothing more embarrassing, in the end, than the outright
surfacing of this "patricide" in such a striking work. If Freud begins his
article by granting that the work of art occupies a separate space, that
it cannot be analyzed, this is not merely an oratorical precaution. He
truly cannot situate it without making it his equal, and this he absolutely refuses to do. It is necessary to expel this double, to cast it into
some beyond with the sacred monsters, to keep making it a fetish with
the rest of the nineteenth century. Since Nietzsche and Freud, however, fetishes have been more abused than venerated. When brought
out they are always upside down. This is what is called the inversion of
metaphysics.

In his article Freud summarizes the Oedipal doctrine. The small
child sees his father as a rival and desires to kill him, but he manages to
repress this desire. On the one hand he fears "castration" and on the
other he maintains a certain "affection" for the father who was initially
a model. This "affection," it seems to me, constitutes a particularly
weak link in Freudian reasoning. Since the least bit of doubt cannot be

expressed on the subject of Oedipus without being immediately accused of "resistance," I will try an especially underhanded method here. Suppose I accept the principles of the Oedipus complex, that I sincerely adhere to the notion of the child's desire for patricide and incest. Now, no one can accuse me of a panicked flight from this terrifying and profound revelation. But the difficulties are far from resolved. More than ever, in fact. I find myself confronted by this "affection," which Freud attributed to the little Oedipus but which seems to come out of a novel by Paul Bourget. Nothing resembles this affection more than the conventional sentiments expressed among themselves in public by a well-educated and decent bourgeois family. It is only in the context of such a family life that I would expect to find this affection. The more I adopt Freud's reasoning, the closer I move to the heart of his subject, the more ardently I say *yes* to patricide and incest, the more I want to say no to this affection, to see it as a vestige of an outdated mode of thought.

Given his point of view, Freud realizes that he cannot give this affection a heavy psychic charge. To account for neuroses as severe as those in Dostoevski, he finds it necessary to reinforce this somewhat fragile sentiment. Thus, he summons what he calls the "bisexual" component, something held in reserve for just this sort of case. The feminine element of this bisexual component urges the child to make himself a love-object for his father, in the same manner as his mother. This reinforcement operates for castration, feared more than ever because to love the father it is necessary to renounce the male organ, as well as for this famous "affection," which here takes a homosexual coloring and is deprived of its conventional character.

If certain Freudians tacitly discard the Oedipus complex, others, more faithful, remain attached to it and it is necessary to question their reasons. How is Freud led to construct such a heteroclite and baroque edifice? Even with the best intentions, it is difficult to enter his game simply because in the final analysis there is no single game here, but rather several modes and levels of heterogeneous explanations and interpretations. All this overlaps and is juxtaposed in quite a disconcerting fashion.

This confrontation with Dostoevski is not unuseful because it leads straight to the essential, that is to say, the neurotic data whose origin Freud wishes to reconstitute. Freud's brief remarks on pathological phenomena found in Dostoevski's works are extremely pertinent. Freud sees that "ambivalence," the "typically Dostoevskian" sentiments of mixed hate and veneration, predominate. He concludes, not without reason, that the author himself was afflicted with this ambivalence. Freud equally notes the morbid "tenderness" toward the sexual rival.

He observes, finally, that Dostoevski often demonstrates a great insight into situations that can only be explained by "latent homosexuality." Freud provides no examples, but I have already mentioned several. Whether in the early works, in *Notes from the Underground*, or again in *The Eternal Husband*, the fascination with the rival of the same sex will always give an impression of "latent homosexuality," especially if the observer does not understand the mechanism of rivalry.

Freud often observed these things in his clients and they were to be explained by the double formation of the Oedipus complex, especially by its abnormal variant. If we closely examine this double formation, we understand that its peculiarities are never without a cause; they are always destined to return to the Oedipus complex, to implant in it the phenomenon that Freud did not discover through Dostoevski but that he found with satisfaction in his works. Given the nature of this work, therefore, and considering the very special limitations that Freud imposes on himself by pretending that everything springs from the "Oedipus complex," it is clear why he is led to act and think as he does.

This neurotic ambivalence must be incorporated into the Oedipus complex, but as Freud postulates a spontaneous and independent desire for the mother he fails to see the conflicts as truly mimetic, despite certain inclinations along these lines.[3] He does not realize that only the mechanism of mimetic rivalry, the obstacle-model sequence, can truly produce the type of ambivalence he needs. Therefore, he searches to engender separately the two sides of this ambivalence, the negative and the positive. The negative poses no problems because the desire to kill the father is always there to explain it. Whenever anyone is made into a father figure by transference, the old hate can be reawakened.

But it is also necessary to account for the positive side, for this element of attraction or even fascination that figures visibly in the most normal rivalries. This is more difficult. Here Freud's inability to recognize the mimetic mechanism, or perhaps his obstinate refusal of it in order to preserve an inherently incestuous desire, makes itself sharply felt. Having nothing else to propose, Freud must resort to the old trunk of familial sentimentality from which he pulls the "affection" I have been discussing. This affection is all the more astonishing since Freud does not need it to explain his concept of "repression"; it is directed at the castration anxiety. The only motivation behind this affection that hovers at the heart of Oedipal savagery is the inescapable necessity of generating the type of ambivalence that is observed in Dostoevski and that dominates, according to Freud, all psychic life. The result of this *bricolage* is a bit strange, but we see clearly to what each element corresponds.

This familial affection completes the positive side of "normal" ambivalence (which Freud defines somewhat solipsistically by the opposition between ego and superego). It is a little too weak to deal with a more marked ambivalence. Freud maintains, on the one hand, that the more marked ambivalence has a character of "latent homosexuality." Freud hopes to kill two birds with one stone with *bisexuality*; he makes "familial affection" both abnormal and reinforced by transforming it more or less into a passive homosexual desire for the father.

Until now, the Oedipus complex has always been accepted or rejected, like an article of faith; it was never truly criticized because it was believed that nothing could oppose it. Freud is far from guessing that the material for this criticism is found in Dostoevski, that the perspicacity that he recognizes there rests on a theoretical substratum that can be elucidated.

What immediately stands out in a comparison of Freudian and mimetic readings of neuroses is the unity and simplicity of the latter. This reading has a single principle, that of the dynamics of desire, developing by itself its own consequences in the story whose logic is never denied. This principle is mimetic desire itself, the immediate interplay of imitating and imitated desire. Mimesis generates rivalry, which in turn reinforces mimesis. Here is a mechanism that seems too elementary and too simplistic to produce all the effects we need; it must be put to the test.

Freud clearly saw that there are degrees of ambivalence. He did not fail to recognize that the same thing is at work in both normal and abnormal Oedipal formations. If, nevertheless, he is obliged to resort to a double machinery, at least in part, it is because "latent homosexuality" remains irreducible in his eyes; he is incapable of recognizing it as a simple movement in a continuous dynamic. Once more, he misses the mechanism of the model-obstacle.

In the mimetic reading, the double machinery is revealed to be perfectly useless; to explain the aggravated ambivalence of the Dostoevskian variety including "latent homosexuality," it suffices to postulate a more intense mimetic interaction, an intensity that can be ascribed to diverse causes.

In the "normal" stages of mimetic desire, the object is already designated by the model but this model stays in the shadows; the object remains the principal pole of affectivity and desiring activity. When the mimetic mechanism of the subject tends to turn from the designated object toward the rival designating the object, the object fades away.

Consider, for example, the case of a sexual life governed by mimetic desire. The model of the same sex, soon to be a rival, designates for the subject an object of the opposite sex. It is quite evident that the subject's interest cannot be displaced from the heterosexual object toward the rival of the same sex without giving the impression of a "homosexual tendency" at work. Freud will describe this homosexuality as *latent* because even if it loses some of its importance, the heterosexual object designated by the model is still there.

This mimetic formation of "neurotic" desire, it should be noted, allows an understanding of why everything interpreted as "latent homosexuality" appears at the same time pervaded with "masochism." These two labels denote a single phenomenon, namely, the rival's predominance over the object and the growing fascination he exercises. Masochism, we have seen, is nothing but the fascination exercised by the obstacle in his capacity of potential and then actual model.

The homosexual tendency is indeed present; it is not at all a matter of denying it. However, it is necessary to avoid evoking it as if it were some independent essence, seeing in it, as did Freud, a biological component—not because such a component cannot exist, but because here we have something much more interesting, an integration of homosexuality into the mimetic dynamic, that is to say, a possible origin in mimetic rivalry. What must be supposed is that beyond a certain threshold, the truly libidinal element of desire will in turn desert the object and become invested in the rival.

It is not a question, I repeat, of denying the possible existence of a biological homosexuality. It only need be shown that if Freud resorts to this possibility in the present case it does not follow from a positive intuition, but is simply, for want of something better, a failure to see its integration into the dynamic of rivalry. Because he is incapable of linking "latent homosexuality" to anything real in the present structure of the relationships of desire, Freud only sees it as dead weight that must be transported with everything else into the Oedipus complex before being submerged, in the end, in a biological opacity. If homosexuality is dead weight it is because it always appears to aim at a "father substitute" rather than at the present rivalry. The regression of psychoanalysis, its Oedipal fetishism, the primacy of difference, and the inability to spot the working of mimetic rivalry all demonstrate the same shortcoming.

This mimetic mechanism may be preferable, because it organizes all the elements dynamically with an economy of means so prodigious that it quickly ceases, if we truly grasp its workings, to be disconcerting. The idea of desire, even libidinal, that is displaced from the object toward the rival is an astonishingly fertile principle—one that illuminates a crowd of until now discontinuous phenomena. It is clear, for example, that the structure of Proustian desire emerging from *Remem-*

brance of Things Past is always a structure of rivalry and mimetic exclusion, whether a matter of eroticism or snobbery, that in the last analysis turn out to be identical. We can show that Proust's analyses all tend to reveal this identity; they tend not toward Freud but toward the mimetic definition of desire.

Another reason why the mimetic reading is preferable is its dynamic and no longer regressive character. This reading admits without difficulty that the first mimetic episodes—notably those where an adult in a position of authority, perhaps the father, plays the role of first model and obstacle—may exercise a permanent influence and introduce a pattern that will determine not only the intensity but also the modalities of the ulterior mimetic mechanism. This reading, however, does not succumb to familial fetishism, it does not search exclusively in a distant past or in the depths of some unconscious for the cause of neurosis. The successive episodes always have their own dynamism as well as a cumulative effect, particularly regarding the knowledge they acquire themselves, knowledge subordinate to the desire that makes each stage a new escalation and that determines an ever-possible evolution toward insanity.

In my opinion, psychoanalysis has never succeeded in demonstrating why neurotic episodes, whose essence lies in an always more distant past and which should fade like the successive reproductions of an original, have on the contrary the tendency to become more intense. The unconscious can always be brought in, but this assumed intervention has an arbitrary character, is a *deus ex machina*. The obstacle-model mechanism not only accounts for the perpetual aggravation of these phenomena, but it also restores the very style of this aggravation. As the structures become more and more manifest, bringing out and emphasizing the naked lines of force, we finally reach the glaring evidence of the Nietzschean triangle, completely based on its doubles that oscillate psychotically between autoadoration and adoration of the other. These are, of course, what psychiatry will call megalomania and delusions of inferiority.

Mimetic desire and mimetic rivalry, unlike the Oedipus complex, possess an exclusively destructuring value. No principle of structuration is to be found here. It is not a matter of an origin analogous to that of the Oedipus complex. The mimetic mechanism of desire can be set in motion anywhere, at any moment, and with the appearance of literally anyone.

In *The Brothers Karamazov*, the relationship of the sons to the father is perhaps a mimetic relationship anterior to all others, perhaps more destructive, but fundamentally identical to them. Thus, the resemblance

to the Oedipus complex is superficial. While in Freud father would not
be father and son would not be son without unconscious rivalry, in
Dostoevski the rivalry is perfectly conscious, even if some of its consequences are not. The father is less the father as he more readily
becomes the rival of his own children. The primordial crime is not patricide, as in Freud, but infanticide. Despite his title of father and his role
as progenitor, father Karamazov is nothing but a bad brother, a sort of
double. We are in a universe where there are no more fathers in the
sense meant by Freud.

The Oedipus complex is one particular case of mimetic rivalry, made
sacred and mythic by a false radicalism whose real goal is to hide the
father's disappearance. Psychoanalysis can only treat mimetic doubling
as an escape mechanism. But confronted by the mimetic reading, psychoanalysis is the escape mechanism, even in the case of a Dostoevski,
crushed as he was by his own father. The patricide and incest perpetually exhibited are only a diversion, a mock secret masking the truly
inadmissible secret. To evoke the father and mother is never to admit
the role of the other in desire, for example, the role of the other writer if
the subject is a writer. This amounts to our never asking: who is the
Schiller of the Hölderlin I may be, who is my Belinski, or my Turgenev
if I am Dostoevski. The rival to be revealed is almost never the father,
a rival of the past, the idol buried in the unconscious, but the present
and future rival reduced by psychoanalysis to a bit part in a drama
really performed on "another scene" (*l'autre scène*). Nothing suits
desire more than the minimization of the only idol fascinating it.

It suffices to uncover the dynamic of mimetic desire in order to see
simply and logically integrated into it not only "bisexuality" and
"latent" and "manifest" homosexuality but most of the phenomena that
psychiatrists attempt to describe, such as identification, masochism and
sadism, megalomania, delusions of inferiority, the phenomena of doubles, etc. In comparison, the contradictory conceptions of diverse
psychotherapies, notably psychoanalysis, seem less like completed
constructions than fragmentary, heterogeneous and rigid sketches. In
light of this dynamic the nonintegrable traits of these psychotherapies
denounce themselves as traces of the fascination for the obstacle-
model.

It seems to me the true scientific spirit would be responsive to the
efficiency of the mimetic theory, to its unifying power, to the extraordinary coherence that it grants. Perhaps it is too strong to call this a
theory. Actually, it is a structural dynamic, or rather a destructuring
dynamic. Unlike psychoanalysis, this dynamic does not demand a position regarding the nature of the real; if it has an implicitly critical

character toward numerous theories it has a positive stance in and of itself.

It is not probable, however, that this reading will be taken seriously. Paradoxically, it will touch only those people who remain responsive to certain intuitions of the Freudian type and the desire for scientific systemization accompanying them. Now these people, for obvious reasons, are all the more faithful to Freud now that they find all around them a certain abandonment to incoherence, a withdrawal from the scientific spirit which Freud has always demanded.

On the other hand, we collide with the tradition associating all serious research with a method of didactic exposition, that is, the abandonment of all fiction and drama. The direction of the interpretation is given a priori. Everything must begin with a work of explicit scientific vocation and must return to it. The idea that Dostoevski could have something to teach Freud, that he could be more capable of interpreting Freud than Freud would be of interpreting himself is still considered unthinkable by many. This tradition does not deny that a writer may have striking intuitions, but begins, nevertheless, with the principle that these will always be fragmentary, that they can never form a coherent whole. The analogies and divergences between Freud's and Dostoevski's visions of desire are such that they allow Dostoevski some ground without compromising the empire of psychoanalysis. Dostoevski is accorded timely "presentiments" of a truth that essentially will rest in Freud's hands. Freud will always act as the supreme arbitrator and absolute reference.

This refusal to question established truths seems contrary to the scientific spirit. If Freud has nothing decisive to say about Dostoevski, it is necessary to ask if Dostoevski does not have something more decisive to say about Freud. We must conceive of the inversion of the relation between psychoanalysis and Dostoevski. I would like to conclude by showing with one more point how this step is possible and that it can be fertile.

In regard to literature, I have said, Freud demonstrates "ambivalence." He sees in it only a tissue of misconceptions, and yet he venerates it, puts it on a pedestal, sees it as the most beautiful ornament of humanistic culture, and so on. What would the greatest writers, what would Dostoevski think of such an attitude?

The writer sees himself defined by Freud as a character who enjoys an extraordinary narcissism. We must let our writer examine the figures of pure narcissism proposed by Freud in *On Narcissism: An Introduction*, the suckling infant and the wild beast. When well fed these creatures seem so serenely autonomous, so indifferent to others that they evoke in Freud a sort of nostalgia like that in all those, he observes, who have renounced part of their narcissism through maturity and responsibility.

I believe that if Dostoevski could have read this text he would have remarked on the metaphors of Freud's desire. It is possible to ask if the entire theory of narcissism is not a projection of this desire. In Freud narcissism only exists in others, and in others never treated as equals, always a little more or less human, always made a little sacred or bestial in the sense of the metaphors in *On Narcissism: An Introduction*—the woman, the child, the writer.

What desire never sees with equanimity, what prodigiously agitates it, is the apparent absence in the other of the lack it finds in itself, the absence that seems like the desire of self, a divine autosufficiency. It is always this, in Freud and modern thought in general, that unleashes the passion for demystification. The desire for a superb autonomy has been renounced, the naive stages of desire have been left behind, and the demystificators desperately want everyone else to corroborate them by doing the same. Nothing is more irritating for those who know than those who do not know or pretend not to know. The universal demystification is aimed at them. Only this demystification can assure that there is nothing to be desired anywhere, that no one is to be envied. It is along this bias that the demystificating urge and with it many forms of modern thought, including psychoanalysis, are connected to desire.

It is necessary to note that Freud discovered and named "narcissism" following a noncritical reading of the myth of Narcissus, a pure and simple rewriting of the apparent meanings of this myth. These could well hide, once again, the violent and violently denied reciprocity of the doubles, the unrecognized mechanism of mimetic desire. This very mechanism appears to be well signified and consequently masked by the theme of the mirror.

No one ever desires himself except through the mediation of someone else. This is called coquetry, and the reader must avoid accepting the traditional reading of it as narcissism. The notion of narcissism cannot explain coquetry because it never restores the paradoxical and essential role of the other. The narcissistic reading remains at a level of "common sense" that is almost always that of desire. This is probably why this reading and narcissism in general have entered so well into our language and mores in the very same sense that Freud gave them, that is, in a perfectly mythical sense.

The metaphors of narcissism dehumanize their objects. They begin, notably in Freud's examples, by turning these objects into infants, animals, and finally monsters. At a more extreme stage, all life is withdrawn, tending toward a sort of petrification. This metaphorical trajectory reflects a constant exasperation of desire faced with an always more unreachable and desirable obstacle-model. It is this desire, therefore, that moves toward death. We would say that Freud saw this, but probably in postulating an independent "death wish" he once again missed the formidable unity of the whole dynamic of desire, which, in the end, is more convincing than the mere addition of discontinuous concepts we have in Freud.

We must, however, recognize that the value of *On Narcissism* is not slight. It was the first time that someone theoretically approached certain relations of desire, which had until then been dealt with only by writers. Freud unfortunately went astray and, as always in this realm, it was under the effect of desire. The equivalent of the notion of narcissism can be found in a writer such as Marivaux, but the greatest writers, especially Dostoevski and Shakespeare, dissipate its mirage. Behind it are found the hidden investments of desire, the same ones that produce mythology.

To make the weakness of *On Narcissism* obvious, the text must be compared to all those that did not inspire Freud because he never truly read them, the great discoverers of mimetic desire, Cervantes, Shakespeare, and Dostoevski. The agreement of these writers on certain fundamental relationships, most notably the doubles, should strike the modern observer who is still crushed beneath a Babel of contradictory theories. The objection might be made that Shakespeare invented a profusion of metaphors analogous to those I have criticized in Freud. This is true. *A Midsummer Night's Dream* is a reworking of Ovid's *Metamorphoses*. Looking closely, nevertheless, we find that Shakespeare proposed with these metaphors and metamorphoses a criticism of them so radical that no one, not even Freud, has understood it.

Freud treats literature as a sort of voodoo charm, and the notion of narcissism serves him well. For him, the works of Dostoevski and literature as a whole are a homogeneous mass, a solid block of "repression" and "sublimation." Freud will never admit that the work of a writer is the fruit of an intellectual enterprise like his own, with its inevitable errors, its unsuccessful experiments, and its risks of definitive failure, but also its chances of success, all through a process of trial and error. He never grants the writer's ability to exercise a real thought, to engage in an intellectual adventure in the fullest sense.

If the scientific pretensions that have dominated twentieth-century thoughts are revealed in the final analysis to be deceiving, we must admit it without falling into the defeatism that negates all science or believes that science is only possible once "man" has been eliminated. We must rediscover what the waning dogmatisms have disdained, notably, the greatest literary works. It is not a matter of passing from one idolatry to another or of canonizing indistinctly all literary tribes, it is a matter of giving the floor, in a climate devoid of scientistic terrorism and esthetic futility, to those writers who are capable of going much farther than has ever been gone toward the understanding of the relations of desire.

NOTES

1. Some will say that *The Fall* is not a masterpiece. First of all, we must be aware of the role of trend in this judgment, the role of the secret mistrust of themes that go too far—the role, in short, of the unshakeable modern refusal to accept the doubles. It must be admitted, however, that *The Fall* does not enjoy, in comparison to *The Stranger*, the same incontestable superiority that *The Eternal Husband* has over Dostoevski's early works. This is perhaps especially true for reasons of form and even genre, which, while not touching the being of the novel, dim its brilliance. Camus criticizes his previous works too directly not to depend a little too narrowly on them. *The Fall* does not succeed perfectly as fiction. It remains, however, too fictive to be read and tasted at its true level of literary and intellectual confession, a genre merely touched upon by the Sartre of *The Words* and still waiting to be invented. In a world where truly novelistic works are perhaps no longer possible, *The Fall* failed to find its voice. Its eminently critical character renders it particularly valuable to us given our concerns here, but weakens it as an independent work.

2. Charles Castella, *Structures romanesques et vision sociale chez G. de Maupassant* (Lausanne: Editions de L'Age d'Homme, 1972).

3. See René Girard, *Violence and the Sacred*, trans. Patrick Gregory (Baltimore: The Johns Hopkins University Press, 1977), ch. 7.

4

Strategies of Madness—
Nietzsche, Wagner, and Dostoevski

Any effort to make Nietzsche's insanity intelligible will have to focus on those triangular relationships that are at the core of Freud's psycho-analytical theory. This does not mean that we have to be Freudian. We may try to read Nietzsche in the light of the mimetic conception of desire I outlined in *Deceit, Desire, and the Novel* (Baltimore: The Johns Hopkins University Press, 1976) as well as in *Des Choses cachées depuis la fondation du monde* (Paris: Grasset, 1978).

Nietzsche's obsession with Wagner was obviously more than a youthful infatuation, an early error of judgment, easily rectified when the thinker reached "maturity." One cannot dismiss the Wagner prob-lem with the traditional arguments on the incommensurability between the "life" and the "works." Wagner is very much a part of the "works." Nietzsche kept writing *for*, then *against* Wagner during his entire career, sometimes directly, praising him and attacking him by name, at other times indirectly. As the final breakdown approaches, even though Wagner is now dead, he is still a haunting figure, perhaps more than ever.

Far from providing an approach that would take Wagner seriously, the reading of the traditional Oedipus complex or Jacques Lacan's theory of symbolic "forclusion" and schizophrenia, illustrated in Jean Laplanche's *Hölderlin et la question du père*, make it possible, once more, to avoid the real issue.

The history of Nietzsche's relationship to Wagner corresponds per-fectly to the successive stages of the mimetic process. First, Wagner is the explicitly acknowledged model, the openly worshiped divinity. Later he becomes an obstacle and a rival without ceasing to be a model. The psychoanalyst would say that the relationship has become "ambivalent." To seek the cause of this "ambivalence" in some dead

This essay appeared under the title "Superman in the Underground: Strategies of Madness—Nietzsche, Wagner, and Dostoevsky," in *MLN* 91 (December 1976): 1161–85.

father is to blind oneself to the reality of the conflict. While Wagner is fast becoming the cultural hero of the German people, he prevents his disciple from reaching the goal that he sets for him. This is the same double bind that we find in the cases of Schiller and Hölderlin, and of Rimbaud and Verlaine. Freud and the other theoreticians of psychoanalysis refuse to understand its terrible simplicity; they always direct our attention away from the truth, toward some ludicrous fable. But in order to be reminded that this double bind exists we only have to look at their own relations with their disciples, at the psychological ruins they leave in their wake. At the time of the Bayreuth triumphs, a horrified Nietzsche must suddenly confront, infinitely multiplied, his own idolatry for Richard Wagner.

Bayreuth is presented by Nietzsche as Wagner's monstrous effort to organize his own cult. Nietzsche may not be completely wrong, but *Ecce Homo* is exactly the same thing. It is Nietzsche's effort to organize his own cult. It is Nietzsche's reply to Bayreuth, an act of retaliation, and like all such acts it is the same thing as the act against which it retaliates. The only difference, of course, is that Wagner has real worshipers, whereas Nietzsche has no one but himself. He must play the two roles of the worshiper and the worshiped, something that no one can successfully accomplish for very long. The complete silence around him forces Nietzsche into more and more histrionics, the type of behavior that must be acknowledged as characteristically schizophrenic even though the continuity with earlier and more moderate expressions of self-praise is unbroken. The difference between the healthy man and the sick one, at this stage, may be their more or less successful relationship to the crowd.

Everything here is obvious, but the obvious is never clearly formulated. The piety of Nietzsche's disciples—the sanctimonious and blind piety that surrounds only dead models, of course, in our Nietzschean world—prevents the truth from being heard or even uttered.

In order to undermine the Wagner cult, Nietzsche has resorted to many ruses, as when he suggested Bizet as a substitute musical god. Even a child would not be fooled, but we all are or pretend to be. Western intellectuals can practice on Nietzsche the useful art of deviating even from the most schizophrenic party lines.

Victory and defeat are two positions in the same structure of rivalry and they are constantly exchanged between Wagner and Nietzsche. The fact that the two partners do not share equally in victory and defeat or that there may be other partners, unknown to us, does not prevent this manic-depressive structure from being first of all a concrete relationship of doubles, a mimetic reciprocity that keeps fulfilling itself in the very efforts Nietzsche makes to undo it. Any effort to separate *Ecce Homo* from the Wagnerian cult is a misrepresentation of an important moment in the growing schizophrenia of German and European culture.

In *Ecce Homo*, Nietzsche claims that everything he wrote about Wagner in the past, all the praise he lavished upon that false idol must not be disregarded and forgotten; rather, it must be restored to its rightful owner, who is Nietzsche himself. Every time the name of Wagner appears, the name of Nietzsche must be substituted. The maddening thing, of course, is that Nietzsche's own written words, in *The Birth of Tragedy*, for instance, testify against him and in favor of Richard Wagner. Modern dictatorships can rewrite history. Writers cannot rewrite their own books. If we read chronologically, we can see the moment when the "ambivalent" but still "rational" response to the model as obstacle and the obstacle as model gives way to the nightmarish "identity crisis" and "megalomania" that characterize the last stages. The patient returns not to his early childhood but to his early relationship with the mediator, when the model, having not yet turned into an obstacle, was openly worshiped. Through what now appears to him as a diabolical trap, the victim realizes that he himself consented and connived in the unjust triumph of the mediator. He is dispossessed of his own self and he tries more and more desperately to fill the vacuum not only with the elusive Richard Wagner but with whatever historical or mythological models happen to strike his fancy.

If we follow too hastily the psychoanalyst's lead and describe Wagner as a substitute father, the rivalry is emptied of its real intellectual and artistic content and the problem becomes unintelligible. This does not mean that there are no sexual elements in the rivalry. If we examine these elements, we will find that the Oedipus complex is totally unable to account for them even though the facts of the case, at first glance, look favorable to Freud.

In Nietzsche's last notes, the name of Richard Wagner appears once more in a configuration that even the observer most impatient with "triangular criticism" must resign himself, for once, to name a triangle. The other two names are those of Wagner's wife, Cosima, and of Nietzsche himself. There is a mythological version of this triangle in which Richard Wagner appears as Theseus, Cosima is Ariadne, and Nietzsche himself is Dionysus. In those final days, however, Nietzsche can sign indifferently "Dionysus" or "the Crucified," in sharp contrast to an earlier formula, Dionysus *versus* the Crucified, which figures at the very end of *Ecce Homo* and which expresses, of course, the philosopher's fierce opposition to Christianity.

The mythological triangle alludes to the episode in which Dionysus receives Ariadne from Theseus. According to Nietzsche's sister, the first reference to this mythical story came from Hans von Bülow. When his wife abandoned him for Richard Wagner, Cosima's first husband never lost his urbanity and wit. He would explain that, for a woman torn between a man and a god, it is excusable to choose the god.

We have a first triangle, therefore, with real-life characters playing mythical roles mostly different from the ones in the final triangle. Richard Wagner plays the role of Dionysus. Nietzsche is not even there. Cosima alone remains in the same place. The matter is not inconsequential. Even though Hans von Bülow's *bon mot* was made more in the spirit of Offenbach than of *The Birth of Tragedy*, it corresponds exactly to Nietzsche's view of the situation at the time. Nietzsche, too, has his own mythology in which the role of Dionysus is also assigned to Wagner. This first triangle, from which he, himself, is excluded, must still be very much on his mind when, at the edge of insanity, he writes the new version. He now occupies the place formerly reserved for Richard Wagner; but Richard Wagner is still there and Nietzsche expects to receive Cosima from his hands, just as Richard Wagner had received Cosima from Theseus–Hans von Bülow. The possession of Cosima and the identification to Dionysus are both explicitly at stake in the replacement of the first set of characters by the second. The possession of divinity and the possession of the woman go together.

The temptation to classify Cosima in the role of a parental substitute must be resisted. Reflex Freudianism provides only an illusion of light. The operation of the triangle becomes unintelligible.

Every time Nietzsche became involved with a woman, it seems that a common friend acted as a go-between, and this common friend was also interested in the woman or, if he was not, Nietzsche thought he was. In 1876, for instance, Nietzsche asked a friend, Hugo von Senger, to propose marriage, in his name, to a woman whom Hugo later married. The episode with Lou Salomé is somewhat similar. When Nietzsche met her, she was associated with Paul Rée. Very hastily, once more, Nietzsche asked Paul Rée to convey to Lou a marriage proposal, which she rejected.

Freud is interested in these triangles. His awareness of the rival's role is limited to what he calls "ambivalence," the love-hate relationship. He does not realize that there is a functional way to account for this "ambivalence": the metamorphosis of the mimetic model into an obstacle. For an explanation he relies on the "Oedipus complex." As long as the fascination for the rival remains moderate, the "normal" version of the complex appears adequate. The woman is a mother substitute; the rival is a father substitute. The subject is supposed to "relive" the original sentiments of the Oedipus complex: desire for the mother, hatred for the father as a rival, "normal tenderness" for the father as a father.

In triangles such as Nietzsche's, the fascination for the rival is extreme and the "normal" Oedipus model cannot account for it. That is why Freud had to invent his "abnormal" Oedipus genesis. Since he did not apprehend the mimetic principle at all, he could not realize that, with this principle, it is possible to account for everything as a single dynamic process in which the other becomes more and more fascinating as a model even as he turns more and more into an obstacle and a rival fascination for the obstacle. This triangular process also accounts for the homosexual effect, since this obstacle is a rival of the same sex.

This homosexual aspect of the fascination for the rival is really the only element of the picture that Freud clearly perceives, but this aspect is bound to be misunderstood by anyone who does not understand the primacy of imitation over rivalry. The fascination must be described as a "latent" homosexuality for the simple reason that a woman is also present in the picture and she remains the only direct object, so to speak, of mediated desire.

The second Oedipus is nothing more, really, than the addition of a homosexual element to the first Oedipus. In addition to the "normal" desire of the little child for his mother, which must be retained since there is a woman in the triangle who will be the usual mother substitute, Freud is forced to postulate a desire, in the little child "to be loved by his father as a woman."

Thus, we have two kinds of Oedipus genesis, a "normal" and an "abnormal" one. There is no doubt Freud would have resorted to the second in the case of Nietzsche. There exists another great writer who dealt with women and men, both in his life and in his work, in a triangular manner extremely reminiscent of Nietzsche. The writer is Dostoevski, and Freud's essay on him invokes the "abnormal Oedipus" to account for phenomena strikingly similar to the ones mentioned above.[1]

The rival plays exactly the same role in Dostoevski as in Nietzsche. Here again, hastily conceived proposals of marriage are made through the mediation of friends whom Dostoevski had reason to believe were themselves interested in the women. When the mediator finally makes his own move, Dostoevski—or his heroes, many of whom resemble him in the extreme—are always ready to yield to the rival. In the first works, or in the early correspondence, this sort of behavior is always presented as "magnanimous" and hope is expressed that, thanks to this "magnanimity," it will be possible to welcome the woman back from the rival or to share her with him in a very modest way, perhaps as a helpful old friend.

Does the *abnormal* Oedipus account for this type of situation? The Freudians will answer that it does, and in a sense they cannot be wrong because the abnormal Oedipus was devised specifically for this type of triangle. Except for writers, Freud was the first one to observe this type of configuration and to attempt a scientific interpretation of it. Thus he could not fail to do so better than anyone before; but it is easy to show that, in spite of his very great merits, he did not come up with the right interpretation nor did he even observe the triangular operation properly. These two failures are really inseparable from each other because the reality of the mimetic process is simply too closely knit to permit a distinction between the theory and the description of the facts.

In all these triangles, the goal is less to wrench the loved one from the mediator than to receive her from him and to share her with him. The presence of the rival is indispensable. If this rival tries to disengage himself, the subject will do his best to drag him back into the picture. Why? Is there a direct homosexual drive, as Freud believes? There is nothing of the sort. The subject is unable to desire on his own; he has no confidence whatever in a choice that would be solely his own. The rival is needed because his desire alone can confer on the girl whatever value she has in the eyes of the subject. If the rival disappears, this value will also disappear.

Even though the rival may be a rival first and a model later, in the actual sequence of events producing a triangle, this reverse order is still derived from the order suggested above. The rival must be interpreted first as a model. As soon as we recognize this primacy of mimesis, everything falls into place and becomes intelligible.

It is not enough for the subject of these triangles to have the mediator designate a love object to him; the mediator must continue to desire that object so that her value will remain constant. That is why the subject always wants the other man to play an active role as a go-between, as a *mediator*, literally, between himself and the object.

The subject does not want to win the girl decisively; if he did, he would lose the mediator and he would lose all interest in the girl. The mediator must not win too decisively either; if he did, the subject would go on desiring intensely but the risk of being permanently excluded would be too great. No resolution of the deadlock is really satisfactory. The only tolerable situation is for the rivalry to go on. The triangle must endure.

For the subject, the essential thing is the continued bond between the girl and the rival, a bond that seems to achieve the perfect autonomy and self-sufficiency the subject is dreaming of. The only narcissism is the narcissism of another, here of two others, of a happy couple, of a couple's happiness, which becomes the object of desire rather than either the man or the woman.

If we understand this *raison d'être* of the triangle, we shall perceive that Freud failed in his attempt to account for this phenomenon. Freud imagines two separate desires, one for the woman, which must come from the mother, the other for the rival, which must come from the father. Hence the weird fairy tale of the little child selecting his father, however briefly, as a homosexual lover.

Freud does not understand that the mediator's desire is the essential factor in the desirability of the woman. The subject needs the desire of his rival to sustain and to legitimize his own desire. In Oedipal terms, this would mean that the son wants the father's desire to sustain and legitimate his desire for the mother. If there is one thing the Oedipus complex will not allow, it is certainly that. It would mean that the mother is not desired "for herself," that she has no independent value of her own, that she is desired primarily as an object for the father. In addition, it would mean that the father is not the incarnation of the law against incest. The two pillars of the Oedipus edifice crash to the ground.

The main difference between the mediation principle and psychoanalysis is that, in Freud, the desire for the mother is intrinsic. Freud thought that an intrinsic, though later repressed, desire was necessary to account for the incest taboo. All relationships remain fundamentally independent of each other. In the love-hate relationship with the father, the love and the hate are juxtaposed rather than truly united. Only the mimetic process can make the three characters within the triangle truly dependent on each other; only that same process can show that the same drive makes the mediator venerable as a model and hateful as an obstacle.

The truth is that the Oedipal triangle is not functional. One does not really know why it should go on generating substitute triangles. We understand very well, on the contrary, why the mimetic triangle must be perpetually repeated, why it is a search for successful rivals. If the model keeps interfering with the subject's desire, ultimately it is this interference itself that will be actively sought, as a designation of the most desirable object, and the triangle will be there. We understand very well why advanced cases of the mimetic disease will go on patterning their desires on the desires of more successful friends. Only one genesis is needed, since the exasperation of the vicious circle that constitutes the relationship with the mediator accounts perfectly for the varying degrees of fascination vis-à-vis the rival and for the gradual shift away from the heterosexual object to the rival and model of the same sex. Before he is an object, the homosexual partner is a rival.

The mimetic alternative makes it possible not only to arrive at a satisfactory solution, but to see exactly where Freud went wrong and why he had to come up with the type of hypotheses he finally adopted. These are certainly false but they are not gratuitous.

The mimetic alternative does not exclude the possibility for the original parental triangle to be, at some time or other, a triangle of mimetic rivalry. But this possibility is not inherent in the family life of the child. Rather, it is the opposite that is true. The more the father is a father in the sense of the law, the more unlikely it is that he will be a mimetic rival. He may be an ideal model, he may be a hated tyrant, but the mimetic rival is something else again. Far from being compatible and from combining easily, the role of the father as an incarnation of the law and the role of the mimetic rival are normally separate and divergent.

If Freud was misled, if he tried to reconcile the irreconcilable, it is in part because of historical reasons. Working at a time when the additional father still retained some of his former power, while mimetic rivalry was on the increase, Freud and others found it not unnatural to think that these phenomena were closely related and to attempt a single explanation of both. Dostoevski also lived in that ambiguous time when these two types of phenomena were constantly juxtaposed. But, in his later work at least, he distinguished them better, perhaps, than anyone else. As a result, he was a better interpreter than Freud both of the law and of mimetic rivalry. In *The Brothers Karamazov*, Freud saw little more than evidence of "Oedipal problems." The convenient thing about Oedipal interpretation is that there is no better evidence for it than the absence of a murdered father, except, of course, the presence of a murdered father.

Another important work that Freud apparently did not even read is *The Eternal Husband*, the most powerful interpretation of the type of triangular relationships I have been discussing. Here the obsessive rival is clearly revealed as a model of desire, and this short novel has been my constant guide in the preceding pages.

What about the *ideas* of Nietzsche? Even if mediated desire has a bearing on the writings about Wagner, one might still argue that his philosophy remains unaffected. It can be shown, I believe, that such is not the case. In the opinion of many scholars, the "will to power" is one of the most important ideas of Nietzsche. An objective examination clearly reveals that the will to power provides an intellectual justification for the most self-defeating behavior demanded by the acute stages of the mediation process.

At first, Nietzsche used the will to power for purposes of psychological "demystification" only. The expression appears in connection with behavior secretly motivated by an extreme regard for the opinion of others. Of actions commonly attributed to "altruism" and other good sentiments, Nietzsche wrote that they were rooted in "a will to power." Walter Kaufmann rightly observed that the will to power, at that stage, had an unfavorable connotation; Nietzsche "did not exhort people to develop a will to power, nor did he speak of it as anything glorious."[2]

The late Nietzsche often presents the will to power as the force that moves the entire universe. Heidegger thinks that Nietzsche turns the will to power into the basis of a metaphysical system. To espouse one's will to power and to develop it as fully as possible becomes the only virtue.

This does not mean that the deplorable consequences earlier attributed to the will to power are forgotten or ascribed to some other force. There is only one force, the will to power, but it branches off into two contrasting varieties. The first could be called the "authentic" will to power and the other is often called *ressentiment*, a word that Nietzsche used a few times and that became popular because of a book by that title, not by Nietzsche but by Max Scheler, who freely extrapolated on the Nietzschean theme.

Why is *ressentiment* so different from the authentic will to power? On this subject opinions vary. Many commentators, in one way or another, posit a difference of *essence*. Nietzsche's vision is turned into one of the countless inverted ethical Manicheisms that the contemporary world produces in such abundance. Nietzsche's fierce originality is destroyed.

The truth is that Nietzsche himself clearly rejected that solution. It is really incompatible with the monistic character of his metaphysics. The distinctiveness of the will to power is that it is a form of energy and cannot be differentiated except in terms of quantity. How can a difference purely quantitative to start with eventually become qualitative? The answer lies in the competitive and conflictual nature of the will to power. Those individuals who have more will overcome those who have less. The strong must dominate the weak and the weak will bitterly resent their inferiority. They will do all they can to escape its consequences, even deny its reality. But they know that in any new loyal encounter they would be once more defeated and they are thus condemned to devious means.

These weak and defeated people are the victims of *ressentiment*. Since they are extremely numerous, they can unite to invent religions and philosophies that sound very "altruistic" but whose sole real purpose is to reverse the natural hierarchy of the will to power. These are the religions and philosophies that declare that the meek and the humble will have their day. *Ressentiment* hides behind an outraged sense of justice. The Judeo-Christian tradition is the prime example. Its "slave morality" becomes institutionalized in the egalitarian institutions of modern democracies.

We must ask ourselves what Nietzsche means when he enigmatically alludes to the crushing weight of the will to power. We have just noted that the only way to avoid *ressentiment* is to overcome other wills. This is stated over and over. Nietzsche always prescribes *victory* as the true medicine for the human spirit.

Medical kit for the soul. What is the strongest healing application? Victory.[3]

What will happen if we start judging Nietzsche according to his own criteria? Where are his *victories?* Was not his life an almost continuous defeat? Is not defeat *the worst bacillus for the soul?*

The purely quantitative definition of the will to power and the criteria of selection to the Nietzschean pantheon assuredly place a formidable burden upon the man who espouses the mystique in full awareness of its implications. If he does not prove capable of overcoming all opponents, he cannot have any illusions about himself. The usual subterfuges of *ressentiment* will not be available to him. He cannot find any comfort in some "morality of the slaves."

There is a real problem, therefore, of Nietzsche's evaluation of himself in the context of the will to power mystique. It is a problem no one ever considers; the answer appears to go without saying. To us, Nietzsche is a genius. He says so himself, and with decreasing inhibitions as he moved closer to insanity. How could we suspect that he might not possess the inner strength to uphold an opinion of himself that he asserted so vigorously and that happens, besides, to coincide with our own?

To write as he did, Nietzsche had to assume not only that there are undefeated champions of the will to power, but also that he must be one. His whole work is a hymn to that higher will. Had he not shared abundantly in the ultimate principle of the universe, how could he have discovered it? How could he stigmatize *ressentiment* and the slave morality as fiercely as he did?

What I want to suggest, of course, is that these appearances are misleading. There were moments when Nietzsche felt unable to meet the demands of his own mystique. The facts of the case become obvious when we realize that Nietzsche's relationship to the will to power cannot be separated from his relationship to Wagner (and other possible mediators, although Wagner is certainly the most important).

Dionysus and the higher will are one and the same thing. If Nietzsche did not feel secure in his identification with the first, he certainly did not feel secure in his possession of the second. The fear that the mediator might still be the "true" Dionysus is the same thing as being deprived of the higher will, the same experience as being overwhelmed, vis-à-vis Richard Wagner, by an irrepressible *ressentiment*.

It will be objected that my brutally quantitative and competitive definition of the will to power is not widely accepted at the present time. This is certainly true. In the hands of the French Nietzscheans, notably, the will to power has become a dainty little idealistic gadget that does not resemble at all what I have been talking about. The question is: why do these people find it necessary to deviate from the abruptness of the Nietzschean concept? The answer, I think, is obvious. The Nietzscheans never spell out the self-defeating consequences of the real will to power, yet they must be vaguely aware of them since they are so successful in neutralizing them. What they really would like, of course, is to preserve the vitriolic force of Nietzsche's "demystification" without running any risk of having it boomerang against themselves. They want to make it safe as a tactical weapon, one that will not explode in their hands as it actually did in his.

We are surrounding Nietzsche with all those pieties he himself so fiercely rejected. The myth of the noncompetitive will to power stems from the existence of two kinds of competitiveness in Nietzsche: one belongs to *ressentiment*, and all the objectionable traits usually associated with competitiveness in general are reserved to that kind. *Ressentiment* is feverishly competitive, always on the lookout for petty victories gained at the expense of mediocre adversaries. The other kind belongs to the authentic will to power, and it is generous and noble. But it is no less ardent. It is the unashamedly competitive and conflictual nature of Greek culture that testifies to the superiority of the Greek will. Walter Kaufmann is right, once more, when he defines the Greek will to power as the will of the Greeks "to outdo, excel, and overpower each other."[4]

As for Nietzsche himself, what he says about his own competitive and aggressive urge must be carefully examined: its implications are far-reaching.

I attack only causes that are victorious. . . . I attack only causes against which I cannot expect to find allies. . . . I attack only causes against which I shall stand alone.[5]

This chivalrous behavior is in keeping with the demands of the mystique, no doubt. But it can also be described as a feverish enterprise of self-destruction, especially in a man who attaches as much importance to victory as Nietzsche does. What the mystique adds up to, really, is a Herculean and systematic effort to bring about its own metamorphosis into *ressentiment*.

Is it not still possible, though, that an exceedingly strong will, looking as hard as it can for still stronger opponents, will not find any and will remain gloriously undefeated? What Nietzsche seems to envision is a series of fair battles with other knights of the will to power: the best will emerges victorious. This is not very different from the dreams of Don Quixote. Our two knights-errant never seem to realize, however, that the "world" is largely indifferent to the type of challenge they represent.

When the lion keeper opens the door of the cage and Don Quixote faces the monsters, the monsters simply refuse to fight back; they yawn and go back to sleep. Don Quixote is still sensible enough not to force the keeper to prod the beasts into a rage. He finally bows to the latter's terrified entreaties and he beats a dignified retreat after declaring glorious victory. I cannot help feeling that Nietzsche would have felt secretly offended by the nonchalance of the lions.

Nietzsche did not like Cervantes, whom he accused of harsh *Ironiesirung* against what he called the "higher ideals."[6] He should have listened instead. There is more in *Don Quixote* to help a man like Nietzsche to retain his sanity than in all of psychiatry and psychoanalysis combined. To Nietzsche as to Don Quixote, the greatest peril is the indifference of the world that his classical mixture of ego-and-other centeredness is bound to misinterpret. He constantly overestimates his own potential for scandal; he always exaggerates both the acceptability of his works and their lack of acceptability.

It is *de rigueur*, of course, to deplore the great indifference of the world toward its geniuses. This great reservoir of unconcern may play a role in our social existence equivalent to the quantitatively predominant nitrogen in our atmosphere. It may be indispensable to the mental health of mankind as a whole. To a Nietzsche, however, this element of sanity turns to poison. The knight of the will to power counts as having lost a multitude of battles that simply never took place.

In the Nietzschean indictment of Bismarckian Germany, of its complacency, bad taste, and general mediocrity, there is a note of shrillness that betrays a deeper wound than Nietzsche and the Nietzscheans allow. Nietzsche's relationship to the university is not as one-sided as it is often pictured. The detached superiority, the superb indifference are certainly present but not at all times. There are other times when this one-sided relationship, like all other one-sided relationships in Nietzsche's life, unexpectedly turns around in the most agonizing manner. It is still one-sided, but to Nietzsche's detriment rather than to his benefit. The problem with Nietzsche is that he never allowed these reversals full expression in his works. The mystique of the will to power did not permit it. This heroic silence may be a factor in his final breakdown.

It is not necessary to analyze one by one the fallacies of the will-to-power mystique. A comparison between this mystique and the mimetic process will provide a more radical critique.

Many features of *ressentiment*, as Nietzsche describes them, resemble the consequences of the mimetic process. *Ressentiment* is really a thwarted and traumatized desire. The very word evokes the image of an immovable obstacle against which the initial "sentiment" did in fact collide and to which it keeps obsessively coming back, only to be frustrated again and again.

There is a great discrepancy, however, between the Nietzschean conception and the mimetic process. In Nietzsche, there are desires, very few perhaps, but some, that escape entirely the traumatic consequences of rivalry. Logic seems to be on Nietzsche's side. If conflict is of the essence, a differentiated outcome seems in order. The stronger wills should win and the weaker should lose. A few wills should escape unscathed because they must be always victorious. On the face of it, Nitzsche's view looks like tough and uncompromising realism.

If desires are truly mimetic, they are bound to clash with other desires, as Nietzsche believes; not because they freely choose to do so, as he apparently assumes, but because they are copied from each other. The final outcome is disastrous because it results not from the relative strength of the desires that happen to clash together, but from a mimetic propensity that cannot be let loose without turning into a search for, and if need be a creation of, the insurmountable obstacle. All our observations suggest that indifference itself can be turned into the most invincible obstacle. There is always enough indifference in the world to destroy the most powerful will to power.

As in the case of the Freudian *libido*, the energetic perspective is not the tough realism that it appears to be. It is not the "scientific" destruction of all myths. It is an excuse to disregard what some would call, today, the "communicative" nature of our desire. All desires say to each other "imitate me" and "do not imitate me" almost simultaneously, which is the same thing as saying that mutually frustrated desires generate and reinforce each other.

If we examine the will-to-power mystique from the perspective of mediated desire we shall find a very significant misrepresentation that can be prompted only by desire itself; there is not one feature in it that does not promote the illusions and the "interests" of desire, that does not threaten, in other words, to be disastrously self-defeating for the victim of that mystique.

Ressentiment is a very perspicacious analysis of effects that truly belong to the entire Nietzschean *Weltanschauung*, but these effects are not presented as universal; they are reserved only to the weaker will to power. Nietzsche teaches us that we can escape these effects, that ours can be a privileged and exceptional desire if only we follow the rules of noble and chivalrous competition that he enunciated. These rules mean nothing if they do not mean that the knight of the will to power must move heaven and earth to find the man who will teach him the lesson he certainly deserves. The mystique justifies the search for the insurmountable obstacle characterizing the more advanced stages of mediation. It presents, in a glorified style, what is already a "pathological" compulsion. It has nothing to do with genuine courage and real adversity. It is a quest for self-engineered adversity. This is precisely what Cervantes means when he says that Don Quixote is mad.

The Nietzschean mystique is both a mask for the mimetic disease and a sophisticated justification for the type of behavior it demands. We observed earlier that desire learns more and more from its own defeats, but that it puts this knowledge in the service of more desire, making even more catastrophic defeats inevitable.

The will-to-power mystique might be called the *ideology* of mimetic desire, if it is true that ideologies are actively engaged in furthering ends that are best furthered by not acknowledging their true natures. Compared to earlier romantic mystiques, in the egotistical and solipsistic vein, the will to power certainly reflects a worsening of the disease. It is the ideology of the world in which we live, no less competitive in the intellectual world than it is in business or politics.

The will-to-power mystique is really a religion of success, truly astonishing and "heroic," coming as it does from such an unsuccessful man. This is precisely why it is so deadly. It turns Nietzsche's own worldly failures into a metaphysical curse that cannot be appealed, a kind of mundane last judgment from which there is no rescue. Nietzsche is his own implacable judge.

I have said earlier that the reversal of all the one-sided relationships in Nietzsche's life usually finds no expression. Nietzsche reveals chiefly the *manic* side of his obviously manic-depressive condition. There are striking exceptions, though, such as the following text, which is written not in Nietzsche's own name but in the name of an anonymous "madman."

This text really does not say or do anything we have not seen before;

the same terrifying process can be read in it, but more directly this time, since its subject is the road to insanity.

Make me insane, I beg you, o divine power. Insane, so that I may finally believe in myself. Give me delirium and convulsions, moments of lucidity and the darkness that comes suddenly. Make me shudder with terror and give me ardors that no mortal man ever experiences; surround me with thunderbolts and phantoms! Make me howl, moan and crawl like a beast, in exchange for faith in myself! Self doubt devours me. I have killed the law and I feel for the law the horror of the living for a corpse. Unless I am above the law, I am the most reprobate among the reprobate. A new spirit possess me; where does it come from if it does not come from you? Prove to me that I belong to you (o divine power). Insanity alone can provide the proof.[7]

The true reason for the manic-depressive oscillation is mentioned and it is *lack of belief in oneself*. But the truth is not complete, since a cause is suggested for that lack of belief—and it is not the real one. Why does the madman feel like the most reprobate among the reprobate? Because he has killed the law, we are told. The statement is important and I will come back to it. For the time being it is enough to note that it is manifestly insufficient as an explanation. How can a dead law cause a lack of self-confidence in the heroic murderer? No dead law, or any other object for that matter, will do. Self-doubt must result from a *comparison* not with something but with *someone*. This someone is not named.

Everything tells us that the manic-depressive oscillation must take place between a mediator and the subject. Still, to withhold that truth and to say as much as Nietzsche does, in the passage above, is an amazing *tour de force*. The revelation is almost complete and yet the one missing character makes it completely misleading.

The mediator is the real center around which everything revolves in proportion to the madman's desire to have everything revolve around himself. As a result, the text must be generated by desire itself. The absence of the mediator is the surest clue to his continued omnipotence, the infallible sign that the fires of mediation will go on burning higher and higher. If we understand this, we also understand what the madman means by *certainty*, and why he counts on *insanity* to provide it. Insanity is what the madman already possesses and yet he wants more of it. Insanity is *doubt*, since it is the manic-depressive alternation, and yet a still more extreme insanity would mean the resolution of that doubt.

Outwardly, thus, the text still subscribes to the old romantic notion of insanity as a sign of election, a proof of kinship with "the divine powers." In the absence of the mediator, everything must be "literary" in the most limited sense of the word. The madman is surrounded by thunderbolts and phantoms. He is performing vertiginous acrobatics for reasons that remain vague and mysterious. This is still the *interior landscape* of the Romantics.

Behind these lyrical frills, however, another explanation is lurking and it cannot fail to crystallize as we realize that the madman's wishes correspond to the evolution of Nietzsche's illness. More insanity can and does obviously mean more and more oscillations, manic-depressive ups and downs so sudden, so extreme and violent that finally the whole pendular mechanism must break down. Only then will the oscillation of Dionysus between the subject and his mediator be interrupted forever; only then will the *lack of belief in oneself* be eliminated. Only in that sense, I believe, does more insanity mean the end of the doubt that is a lesser degree of insanity. It is striking that the only certainty and stability the madman can envisage is the destruction of his own mind, the triumph of madness, misrepresented as his own triumph.

The embrace of insanity as "divine" and the refusal, or inability, to name the mediator are one and the same thing. It is not in vain, therefore, that the madman calls on the power of insanity. We can be certain that his prayers will be answered. He himself is seeing to it. As we observed before, the terrible irony of mimetic desire is that it always gets exactly what it demands.

This demand for insanity may well date back to *The Birth of Tragedy*. To embrace Dionysus "in the raw" as Nietzsche does is to court the divine *mania*, and the god does respond with the *manic*-depressive alternation. The nonritualized Dionysus of Nietzsche is the god of furious revenge from whom any sane man would keep away. The manic-depressive alternation is tied to a very modern and hidden form of revenge, as Nietzsche himself well understands and demonstrates when he speaks of *other people*.

If a pious Greek had read *The Birth of Tragedy*, he might have prophesied a dreadful outcome. Why should an ancient Greek know more than our most brilliant minds? The ancient Greek was not Nietzschean and, dimly, at least, he could see a truth from which an entire world, our Nietzschean world, is turning away. Most of us turn away from that truth in such a prudent and clever fashion that the consequences, outwardly at least, are hardly visible. Not so with Nietzsche. In him alone this rejected truth fights back and fulfills itself in the most terrible and grandiose manner.

The greatness of Nietzsche is not that he was right in any sense but that he paid so dearly for being wrong. He never got away with anything, which is the closest thing to being right.

It may be objected that my commentary is unfaithful to the spirit of Nietzsche's text. Insanity in it appears as something positive, a conquest of sorts. This is true of the passage quoted above, but other texts can be found in which the same phenomena are described and presented as something awful, as a disease. The only difference is that *ressentiment* is attributed to Christianity. Here is an example from *The Will to Power:*

What is it we combat in Christianity? That it wants to break the strong, that it wants to discourage their courage, exploit their bad hours and their occasional weariness, convert their proud assurance into unease and distress of conscience, that it knows how to poison and sicken the noble instincts *until their strength, their will to power turns backward, against itself—until the strong perish through orgies of self-contempt and self-abuse:* that gruesome way of perishing of which Pascal provides the most famous example.[8]

Is it unfair, is it too cruel to point out that it was not Pascal who went mad but Nietzsche?

In order to bring the points I am trying to make into sharper focus, I will turn back briefly to Dostoevski, potentially helpful in this situation because, in the second phase of his career, he managed to portray more accurately and completely than anyone else, including Freud, the kind of psychic life that his own first phase, no less than the writings of Nietzsche, imperfectly and symptomatically reflect.

Dostoevski must be viewed, not merely as a writer of "fiction," not merely as a victim of mediated desire, which he certainly was, and for a very long time, but as the greatest modern revealer of that desire, in all those works of his that are superior, even though the source of their power is not generally acknowledged.

In connection with mediated desire, some short works, notably *Notes from the Underground*, acknowledged by Nietzsche himself as a masterpiece, are more immediately relevant, even though the element of the grotesque, which brings the contours of the process into sharper relief, may increase the reluctance of some to acknowledge the validity of the *rapprochement.*

The underground "hero" is a small Petersburg bureaucrat. His egotistical ambitions stand midway between 1830 Romanticism and a crude but unmistakable version of the Nietzschean will to power. During his hours of solitude, he dreams that his most farfetched aspirations come to pass. Thanks to his brilliant imagination he rises to a plane of tremendous exaltation.

When he reaches a certain level of enthusiasm, the underground man must simply rush out to "conquer the world," only to encounter there the most extreme disappointment, and worse. Any slight unpleasantness that his puny physique and general insignificance may provoke is fantastically magnified. Mere indifference is felt as an insult. Even anonymous offenders become fascinating figures around whom the "self-conscious mouse" will endlessly gravitate.

The main point is not the superiority of solitude over "gregariousness," as romantic and existentialist anthologists repeat *ad nauseam*, but the regular alternation between an imaginary omnipotence of the *self* in solitude and the real omnipotence of the other in society. The *other* is anyone, literally, who happens to cross the hero's path or stand in his way or simply look at him with real or imagined irony. A cycle of petty revenge is immediately triggered. The other is the quintessential mimetic obstacle.

Notes from the Underground operates at the same level of awareness as *The Eternal Husband*, earlier mentioned in connection with the sexual triangles of both Dostoevski and Nietzsche. The two stories exemplify the same prodigious change. Long the mere puppet of a process to which his first writings belong, really, since their distortions, the general *sensiblerie* they exude and, above all, the refusal to acknowledge the true role of the mediator are nothing but the reflection and the instrument of mediated desire, Dostoevski finally masters that mimetic desire itself. The latter works are nourished by a retrospective understanding of a compulsive behavior from which all signs suggest the author is also moving away in his life, however slowly.

The intuitions of a Dostoevski are no more ineffable and capricious than the intuitions of a Cervantes or a Shakespeare. I think they can be systematized along the lines of the mediation process. The task is essential, I believe, to counter the harm done by the absurd postulate of a total separation between psychological knowledge and literature. Freud did a lot to spread a myth responsible for the sterility of much contemporary criticism. It is important in truly great writers to make the systems of human relationships as readily available as the concepts of Freud and others, so that a psychoanalytical pseudodiagnosis will not be automatically and triumphantly plastered all over the mediation process, making it invisible.

The elaboration of models and of a conceptual system that will finally do justice to the rigorous perception of a Dostoevski is no less necessary to psychiatry than to literary studies. In my view, it is the only direction that can revitalize both and turn these disciplines into the allies that they should be. Only a pseudoscience runs counter to the greatest works of our literary heritage. A real science will justify their vision and confirm their superiority.

The last remark may be viewed by some as a clear indication that the type of analysis recommended here is traditional and "conservative." In reality, the mediation principle is less acceptable than either psychoanalysis or Marxist analysis because it is more radical. It goes to the heart of individual motivation in the cultural field, studiously avoided or camouflaged by these methodologies.

We can see this quite well in the case of Nietzsche. It is misleading to define such themes as "Dionysus" or the "will to power" exclusively as we find them in their final state of metaphysical quintessence and frenzied abstraction. This final state is the result of a process that must be viewed in its entirety and that begins in a very different key.

At the beginning, imitation and rivalry are already present but they still have a recognizable object, an object that is still concrete to us, average intellectuals, in the sense that it appears worth fighting for. If we had to define this object, we would say that it is intellectual and artistic omnipotence. It is that supremacy or hegemony in the cultural world that Nietzsche and Wagner are both striving for. Most intellectuals will say, of course, that they are only striving for excellence. As far as they are concerned, at least, the competitiveness is something to which others are addicted, not themselves. They all understand, however, the tremendous bitterness that may develop as a result of even the most outwardly insignificant opposition. The intellectual world is one in which the covert judgment of peers, in the absence of objective criteria, must play a decisive role. This state of affairs cannot fail to breed a large amount of delusion. In such a world the built-in potential for so-called "paranoid" distortions is always considerable.

This modern intellectual world really begins before the French revolution, toward the middle of the eighteenth century, at the time when the prestige of intellectuals makes their judgment more important to other intellectuals than the opinion of aristocratic benefactors. With the advent of that world, a certain type of mental disturbance acquires a great importance on the intellectual stage. The most influential works are affected by it. The first great examples that come to mind are Rousseau in the French-speaking world and Hölderlin in Germany. Nietzsche is another example.

Neither the sociologist nor the psychoanalyst of literature really goes to the heart of the question. The first is always concerned with the problem of the bourgeois versus the aristocrat. This is certainly relevant, since the transformation I am talking about is a consequence of a broad social evolution; but it is more indirectly than directly relevant. The pressures from the world at large are real but they are filtered and often distorted by the microenvironment of the intellectual world, which should be the most immediate object of study, not as mere statistical data but as a network of complex and unstable relationships at least partly governed by mediated desire. In this microenvironment, the most important relationships are not between social superiors and inferiors but between peers, even though these are rarely experienced as relationships of "equality."

The more or less hidden violence of these relationships cannot be without consequence on intellectual creation. Yet this influence is never formally acknowledged and studied. The idea of *sublimation* on which much psychoanalysis still bases its theory of cultural creation is a prime example of the mystified way in which intellectuals can conceive their own world.

In the present historical situation, the crumbling of the last traditional hierarchies makes the presence of the metaphysical rival more and more obsessive, and something like psychoanalysis may be indispensable as a last ditch maneuver against the revelation of the mimetic process. Psychoanalysis makes it possible to acknowledge the obvious, but in such a manner as to empty it of its content and displace our attention toward the specious scandals of a "parricidal" and "incestuous" desire.

What psychoanalysis says about a writer like Nietzsche is always what desire wants to hear. It says that Wagner, the real Wagner, is not that important to Nietzsche after all, and this is what desire is most eager to hear. This, therefore, is desire itself. The mediator, we are told, is not what truly obsesses us. The triangle is only a replay. The only drama that counts is a very old one, and it is circumscribed by two narrow circles, with the subject alone at the center of both. One is the circle of the immediate family, whose major actors are by now dead or reduced to senility. The other is the even narrower circle of a supposedly "narcissistic" ego.

Objectively, the psychoanalysis and the sociology of literature function as screens between us, intellectuals, and the truth we are most unwilling to face: *The insanity of a Nietzsche and of many others is rooted in an experience with which none of us can be really unfamiliar.*

The clatter of broken taboos, all around us, is supposed to be deafening and we should not be misled. The show is fake. It has been going on for too long with only minor changes in the plot and in the cast of characters. The real taboos are elsewhere and they are rigidly enforced. Our fiercest demystifiers quickly regress to the most antiquated conventions when it comes to the really delicate problems. How piously they adhere to the myth of the "good" Nietzsche versus the "bad" Wagner.

If Freud is a last line of defense against mediation, he also comes closer to the truth than anyone before—as close as you can come and still manage to keep the truth out. This transitional status of the Freudian doctrine, its role as an immediate precursor and as a last resistance against a full apprehension of the mimetic process can be specified, I believe, if we situate Freud's treatment of the "law" in the context of the passage of *Dawn* quoted above. In that passage, let us recall, the law is "murdered" by the madman himself and its "corpse" is held responsible for everything. This accusation is false, of course, but it is not without reasons. The law is truly responsible in the sense that it is not there anymore to prevent what is going to happen in its absence, i.e., the mimetic process.

The law differentiates and separates the potential doubles; it channels mimetic desire toward goals that are truly transcendental in the sense that they are exterior to the community. These goals are common to all and nondivisive. As long as the law is alive, it prevents "differences" and "identities" from being dissolved and returned to the warring confusion of the doubles. According to the Greeks, the murderers of the law are responsible for that warring confusion. They saw what they mistook for a "god," lying apparently within their reach, just beyond the law that they did not hesitate to transgress. It is that "god" who now appears to oscillate between the doubles, and he still eludes their grasp as they reach for each other's throats.

This Nietzsche will not say, and, in order not to say it, he suggests that the law, even though it is dead, may be the cause of the disaster. This scapegoating of the dead law is not the solution for Nietzsche alone. In one form or another, it is the solution of a whole era now coming to a close. It is the solution handed to us by Freud. The Oedipus complex is supposed to be the means through which the law is transmitted to the child. This law is already a dead law. It is already transgressed, in spirit at least, even before it is born, since the parricidal desire comes first. Because of that law, Freud was left with his sempiternal father and never discovered the mimetic rival, with its formidable potential, as a truly functional principle of psychiatric systematization. He never realized that with this one principle, he could discard his two varieties of Oedipus, his unconscious, his narcissism, etc., and reach a more efficient, more intelligible, and better integrated organization of *more* data.

Freud could not have missed the mechanism of mimetic rivalry if he had not been so intent on incriminating the law for troubles that have nothing to do with it. The reasons are the same as in Nietzsche's case. The indictment of the law is a fruit of desire itself, which refuses to face its own truth. And it is also a last protection against the full revelation of that truth, a revelation that spells the end of all peace and sanity if it does not spell the end of desire itself.

Today, Marx, Nietzsche, Freud, all the giant killers of the law, formerly antagonistic, are mustered together in an effort to bolster the intellectual system of the dead law. The unity of an era is becoming visible in its death throes. The corpse of the law is the last sacrificial object, the last *difference* that still *defers* a little the face-to-face encounter of the doubles. The harder we beat that dead law, however, the sooner we shall realize how trivial an activity that is. It is not really the dead law that the doubles want to beat; it is each other.

History itself is now separating the elements mythically joined by Nietzsche, Freud, and others. In that situation, Dostoevski, sooner or later, will be better understood because he is the only one who already understands. He understands that the law is not responsible for the mimetic crisis. He also understands that the modern world is a mimetic crisis unlike any other. At his worst, he only looks back with nostalgia at the comfort of the law, while it still lived. At his best, he knows that there is no return.

There is no return because those who naively boast they have killed the law are not responsible for its death either. The problem is more complex and mysterious. The real killer of the law is the law itself, or whatever passes for it in our universe; the murderer is that same *Christianity* that is being murdered.

The two texts of Nietzsche quoted above, the one from *Dawn* and the other from *The Will to Power* are interesting in connection with that belief of Dostoevski. They describe the same phenomenon, basically, and yet they describe it in a very different light, ascribing it to different causes. One madman is gloriously mad because he has killed the law; the other, Pascal, is distressingly mad because he has not killed it. It is strange that, dead or alive, the law would work the same effects in the superman and the slave. Which of the two versions are we to believe? Nietzsche never reconciled them, really, but they can be reconciled in Dostoevski's idea that this strange law of ours is the real killer of the law.

It is not a matter of indifference, of course, that the megalomania of Nietzsche is presented under the title *Ecce Homo* and that he signs both as Dionysus and the Crucified. Each time Nietzsche feels like a god for a little while, he must pay for it dearly and becomes the Crucified. The would-be god is really a victim. Here, finally, and only here, the self-defeating process at work everywhere in Nietzsche becomes manifest. The confusion between the god and the victim is the climax of the manic-depressive oscillation. In the shift from Dionysus *against* the Crucified to Dionysus *or* the Crucified, in the collapse of that supreme difference, we have the collapse of Nietzschean thought.

To the historian, of course, or the philosopher, this confusion is nothing but insanity, sheer nonsense in other words, distressing or glorified nonsense but still nonsense. In reality, the god is always a victim, in pagan theology no less than in Christianity. Why would Nietzsche reach this identity of the two as the circle of his insanity closes in upon him? An identity that destroys so many false differences cannot fail to be more than nonsense, much more. As the era of Nietzsche's "will to power" draws to an end, this identity of the god and the victim points to possibilities that still lie beyond our grasp, possibilities unheard of, truly vertiginous.

NOTES

1. Sigmund Freud, "Dostoevsky and Parricide," in *Dostoevsky: A Collection of Critical Essays*, ed. Pierre Wellek (Englewood Cliffs, N.J.: Prentice-Hall, Inc., 1962), pp. 98–111.

2. Walter Kaufmann, *Nietzsche: Philosopher, Psychologist, Antichrist* (Cleveland: Meridian Books, 1962), p. 159.

3. Friedrich Nietzsche, *Morgenröthe*, 5. 571, in *Gesammelte Werke*, 23 vols. (Munich: Musarion, 1920–28), 10:352. Quoted in Walter Kaufmann, *Nietzsche*, p. 167.

4. Kaufmann, *Nietzsche*, p. 166.

5. Friedrich Nietzsche, *Ecce Homo*, 1. 7, in *Gesammelte Werke*, 21:186. Quoted in Kaufmann, *Nietzsche*, p. 114.

6. Nietzsche, *Gesammelte Werke*, 9:445. Quoted in Kaufmann, *Nietzsche*, p. 372.

7. Nietzsche, *Morgenröthe*, 1:14. *Gesammelte Werke*, 10:22–23. My translation.

8. Friedrich Nietzsche, *The Will to Power*, ed. Walter Kaufmann, trans. Walter Kaufmann and R. J. Hollingdale (New York: Vintage Books, 1960), p. 146.

5

Delirium as System

Deleuze and Guattari place the Oedipus complex on the side of repression as if it were its displaced representative: "Oedipal desires . . . are the lure, the disfigured image by which repression entraps desire."[1] The family becomes a simple "agent delegated to repression" (delegated by society, of course, which sees in the repression a means of enforcing its oppression). It becomes a stage for the Oedipus complex, following the rules that are taught by psychoanalysis but that in the final analysis spring from all the social mediations imprisoning desire.

Thus, the Oedipus complex is reduced to the level of "resistance." And what it resists is "true" desire, a multivalent and polyvocal force foreign to the demands of representation and imprisonment in structures. This desire is defined in terms of a flux cutting other fluxes, thereby delimitating "partial objects"—which in the first place are improperly named because they are not taken from "whole persons" but rather precede them. "True" desire is unconscious. What we perceive as such at the level of "whole persons" is the result of complex operations, frayages, and codings that change its regime and increasingly set desire against itself, inscribing it first on the body of the earth and primitive societies, then on the body of the despot, and finally on capital in modern society. This last inscription gives rise to a widespread decoding that society perpetually seeks to thwart with "archaic recodings," such as the Oedipus complex. In order to "domesticate" a less and less coded desire, psychoanalysts unflaggingly return it to the "eternal triangle" and put all our dreams and desires through the "Oedipal meat grinder."

If true desire is unconscious and still crushed by repressive codings, even in capitalism, how do the two authors know it exists? It is especially the delirious forms of schizophrenia that inform them, since these forms explode suppression in order to free true desire. In this delirium, all effective attitudes, all structural positions, all conceivable and in-

This essay appeared under the title "Système du délire," in *Critique* 28 (November 1972): 957–96. It has been translated by Paisley N. Livingston and Tobin Siebers.

conceivable identifications appear juxtaposed, without exclusion or totalization of any kind, in perfect openness and readiness to accept constantly new forms. Delirium can thus serve as a weapon against analytic formalism. The authors certainly do not intend to exclude the Oedipus complex, at least at a certain moment in the critique, but they want to include and absorb it on the same grounds as everything and anything, dispelling its full import through an excessive inclusion, so to speak. The schizophrenic is complaisant; ready when it suits him to rave an Oedipus complex just as he would rave anything else, but without remaining there, without becoming forever fixed on the parental appellations that psychoanalysis demands: "In delirium, (I feel that) I become God, I become woman, I was Joan of Arc, and I am Heliogable, and the Great Mogul, a Chinese, an Indian, a Templar, I was my father and I was my son. And all criminals. . . ."[2]

An Oedipus complex drowned in polyvalent delirium—what a marvelous invention! To challenge this logic by calling it demented is useless, since it already labels itself as such. It is certainly impossible to place Heliogable and Assurbanipal on the same plane with papa and mama. Deleuze and Guattari do not deny that the nondelirious are incapable of doing so; for them it seems that papa is always there, nearby, while Assurbanipal is not. Thanks to delirium, once more, Deleuze and Guattari make this fact work to the advantage of Assurbanipal, at the expense of common sense and psychoanalysis, both probably very astonished and worried to find themselves for once on the same side of the fence.

Desire, we have seen, has nothing to do with persons. On the side of the unconscious, there are only parts in "desiring machines." This is the level we can call infraindividual, here called "molecular." At the other extreme, there is the collective level, the "world-historical," also defined as "molar." There is nothing, or almost nothing, between the two. Deleuze and Guattari put considerable talent and staggering rhetoric at the service of a cause that they deem deserving: the destruction of everything in between and the avoidance of any concrete problematic of desire.

Some will say that it is not a matter of avoidance, but of a rigorous fidelity to the principle of the work, to its delirious claim. And this is certainly correct. The schizophrenic reaches at once, without all this sophisticated sophistry, the same result as L'Anti-Oedipe, the loss of that space at the heart of which we communicate, and which we, the others, the nondelirious, believe we have in common with our neighbors. A passage is made without transition from one "extreme" to the other, from nothingness to God, from the infinitely small to the infinitely large.

In my opinion, we must regret not the attack on psychoanalysis but the positions justifying it and making impossible any real confrontation with the essential Freud, any profound criticism of the fundamental psychoanalytic myth, the Oedipus complex. The real battle can only occur on the terrain abandoned without a shot by Deleuze and Guattari, who prefer their double problematic, "molar" and "molecular." We understand without difficulty the reason for this retreat and for this preference, at least on one level. Freud himself chose this terrain and occupies it with strength. To dispute his possession evidently involves great risks, and may even demonstrate temerity. Deleuze and Guattari do not want to be caught in a machine that they consider highly dangerous. The Oedipus complex functions like quicksand; its capacities for absorption are extraordinary. At first we believe that Deleuze and Guattari lack respect for Freud's genius, but we are quickly corrected.

L'Anti-Oedipe renounces, therefore, all frontal attack in favor of guerilla tactics, modeled necessarily on the schizophrenic come-and-go. Deleuze and Guattari try to outflank Oedipus, to run faster than he does and leave him behind. There are a thousand ways of proceeding. We have already seen the "drowning" in the acid bath of schizophrenia, there is also the "scorched earth" policy. These critics create a void before Oedipus, depriving him of all resources, and try to starve him to death. If the eternal complex resists all this bad treatment, they can still try to break it into little pieces:

The father and mother only exist in pieces . . . explode into fragments which skirt the agents of the collectivity. The father, the mother, and the subject are at grips and in direct contact with the elements of the historical and political situation . . . which at every instant shatter all triangulation.[3]

Deleuze and Guattari are always on the offensive, their attacks are often pointed, their mockeries amusing, but the projectiles launched are heteroclite, striking haphazardly. *L'Anti-Oedipe* displays, for example, a most complete disdain for myth and tragedy, offers no encompassing reading, but does not hesitate to turn toward them each time they seem to be possible allies.

I agree with Deleuze and Guattari when they refuse to see in early childhood the locus of a pathology of society, the cause of "civilization and its discontent." But first of all, since it is this discontent that is in question, why not leave childhood to its toys? We are all so thoroughly conditioned by psychoanalysis that we still retain its formal framework even when we have stopped believing in it.

The digressions on flux lead nowhere. The song of "true" desire can only be a lyric overture. Once the final chord has been struck, it is necessary to return to the problem obsessing us, to the "repressions," "suppressions," and conflicts. Either we accentuate the primary repression, which in *L'Anti-Oedipe* precedes all "molar" formations, and once again cast doubt on this marvel of innocence, ignorance, and spontaneity defining until then the unconscious and all its "molecular production," or we accentuate the molar formations and again find ourselves in the midst of whole persons and their misunderstandings. In both cases we return, sooner or later, to the problematic that we wished to short-circuit.

Long live the Deleuzian unconscious! But this unconscious is all the same to us if the "good" desire of infants has the bad habit of being transformed among adults into a frenzy of repression and oppression, and if we are destined to "oedipalize" and castrate each other until the end of time. It is this transformation that is worth considering. Its mystery is what should be penetrated. Deleuze and Guattari understand this perfectly well. The logic of their subject returns them little by little to the maleficent regions they wanted to avoid. They get caught in the machine; they are slowly sinking into the quicksand.

In the beginning of the book, it would seem that the Oedipus complex is only a false problem: there is no Gordian knot. But this knot is, on the contrary, a reality. Deleuze and Guattari cannot return to the scene of the Oedipus complex, which they promised never to visit without rediscovering this same knot intact and always in place, where it has never relinquished control.

Thus, we witness an underhanded reaffirmation of the Oedipus complex. The concessions multiply as the real problems become more evident. The reader remembers the triumphant negations of the beginning, he expects them to be fully confirmed and demonstrated. Let us judge his disappointment: *"We do not deny that there is an Oedipal sexuality, an Oedipal heterosexuality, an Oedipal homosexuality, an Oedipal castration complex—whole objects, global images, and specific egos."*[4] Therefore, what remains to be denied? The essential, affirm Deleuze and Guattari, is that these are not "productions of the unconscious."

The Oedipus complex has nothing to do with the order of a "desiring production" always crushed by repressive and suppressive forces. On the contrary, it is everywhere in the project of domesticating the unconscious. Since this enterprise has completely succeeded, it suffices to say that the Oedipus complex is everywhere, and that's that. It does not matter if desiring production is theoretically independent of the social formations integrating it, since it is always dependent *in fact*. We are happy to learn that there is another and better unconscious behind the pseudounconscious of Freud and that it remains uncorruptible, but

this myth resembles the superior god of certain religions, so superior
and distant that we need not consider him. It cannot do anything for
us.

Deleuze and Guattari ferociously hunt down any kind of piety, but
their unconscious production sharply resembles a new form of piety
that is particularly ethereal despite appearances. Finally, do they not
limit themselves to placing beneath the shaken but intact Freudian
edifice, at either its bottom or top, a new layer of the unconscious,
whose repercussions on our little affairs would be just about as concrete as the discovery of a new layer of gas in Venus's atmosphere?

At times Deleuze and Guattari move even farther toward Oedipal
reconversion. After vigorously supporting the anti-Freudians in the
ethnological debate on the universality of the Oedipus complex, they
seem more or less to reverse their own position by an inexorable evolution. The universal Oedipus complex could indeed haunt all societies,
"but exactly like capitalism haunts them, that is, like the nightmare or
anguished foreboding of what would be the decoding of fluxes."5 Since
the decoding of fluxes triggered by capitalism is one and the same with
the absolute truth of history—given some oratorical precautions made
necessary by intellectual circumstances—we certainly cannot permit
ourselves to treat these "nightmares" and "forebodings" lightly.

We might ask if Deleuze and Guattari are not like the man who,
when forced to witness his wife's rape, congratulates himself because
he has transgressed once or twice the chalk circle that the rapist traced
around him and ordered him not to cross. It is even possible to ask
whether L'Anti-Oedipe retains this meager consolation to the end.
There are solemn vows to protect "desiring production" from all
Oedipal contamination, but there are also other passages that appear to
plunge the Oedipus complex once more into a sort of unconscious, or at
least to remove it from the conscious: "The Oedipal usages of synthesis
or of oedipalization—triangulation, castration—reflect forces a little
more powerful, *a little more subterranean than psychoanalysis, family,
and ideology, even when combined.*"6

Such formulas make us wonder, but it is easy to see what makes
them necessary. No one prevents us from asserting that the Oedipus
complex is only a chimera predicated by psychoanalysis. If we advance
the question a little further, we see the resurgence of the phenomenon
of "triangulation" that is habitually read in terms of the Oedipus complex. No one knows how to read, or can even imagine reading, "triangulation" in any other terms. Psychoanalysis always takes the blame,
but nevertheless we cannot say that it created all these triangles. Ever
since the age of the troubadours, for example, these triangles have been
at the center of Western literature. The quicksand has finally swallowed

its victim: *"psychoanalysis did not invent these operations, it only lends them the resources and procedures of its genius."*[7]

But there is still delirium, some will say, still the good news of delirium that Deleuze and Guattari undertake to proclaim. If delirium is truly the new Arcadia, the real Utopia, what do we care about the Oedipal machinery and all this old Greek theater, which, as the two authors emphasize, "is not even avant-garde?" It is a fact that neither Freud nor his successors succeeded in circumscribing or accounting for delirium. From this failure we may deduce that delirium is inexhaustible and infinite. Since delirium eludes psychoanalysis, we can probably elude it too and ride it toward unexplored horizons. Once more it is appropriate to recognize the prestige of psychoanalysis and the predominance it maintains even when we believe it repudiated. Where Freud fails, no one can succeed.

Who knows if failure is definitive regarding delirium? Who knows if it has not been already surmounted in part by certain literary works that psychoanalysis and other scientific pretensions of our time have literally prohibited us from deciphering? All our cultural disciplines are too uncertain of their own status in relation to science to treat literary works as equals, to hear them out.

The great works to be considered range from Greek theater to Dostoevski and Proust, passing through Cervantes and Shakespeare. I am convinced that it is possible to extract from these works a unified theory of desire, and therefore a systemization of delirium, through an essentially logical process the reality of which is verified by the sequence of great works.[8]

First of all, it is necessary to set forth the principle of mimetic desire, of a desiring mimesis prior to all representation and all selection of object. In order to support this principle, we could refer to direct observation and the works just mentioned as well as some others. But we can also be content to consider it simply as a postulate capable of engendering not a linear theory of desire but a logical development that is at the same time a historic process with a remarkably explanatory power in the most diverse and sometimes unexpected domains.

What desire "imitates," what it borrows from a "model," is desire itself, prior to gestures, attitudes, manners, and everything to which mimesis is usually reduced when it is understood only as representation. This mode of imitation operates with a quasiosmotic immediacy necessarily betrayed and lost in all the dualities of the modern problematics of desire, including the conscious and unconscious. This desire for the other's desire has nothing to do with the Hegelian desire for "recognition." Its existence is confirmed by cultural evidence of ex-

traordinary richness that becomes more rare, more fragmentary as we
approach the present and as the dogma of originality triumphs simultaneously with the complete banishment of mimesis. The great writers
mentioned above produced a quasitheory of mimetic desire that is
absent in Plato and the ancient world, and that is absent also in the
modern age. These authors are almost always the ones—and here the
coincidence is significant—whom modern esthetic theory reduces to
the perspective of realistic imitation, discarding once more the mimesis
of desire, nonrepresentational mimesis. I could, first of all, show that
"esthetic" and "realistic" and subsequently "formalist" and "structuralist" treatments constitute the source of the misunderstanding, the
instrument of the real repression.

These same writers are in truth "out of fashion," at least concerning
their essential preoccupations. The only one who plays a role in *L'Anti-
Oedipe* is Marcel Proust. Deleuze believes it possible to attract Proust
into the orbit of his "molecular" desire by relying particularly on a
single scene, where a kiss is given to Albertine. His approach seems to
justify an objection: "Finally, in exaggerated proximity, everything dis-
solves like a mirage, Albertine's face shatters into partial, molecular
objects, while those of the narrator's face reconnect to the organless
body, closed eyes, prim nose, full mouth."[9]

It would not be necessary to reconsider this description if it had not
been presented, at least implicitly, as an apotheosis of desire. Really, it
is quite the contrary. It is the collapse of desire that Proust wishes to
describe, the extinction, death, and bankruptcy of desire. At a time
when he was not so completely carried away with partial objects,
Deleuze evoked this same scene and reproduced in a note a subsequent
sentence that formally contradicts the reading in *L'Anti-Oedipe*: "I
understood by these detestable signs that at last I was kissing the cheek
of Albertine."[10]

To affirm the mimetic nature of desire is to deny it any privileged
object, whether a unique or well-determined object such as the mother
in the Oedipus complex or else a class of objects as narrow or vast as
might be supposed. It is equally necessary to renounce all psychic or
biological entrenchments, including, of course, the pansexualism of
psychoanalysis. We must renounce all entrenchments of desire in need.
This does not imply a minimalization of sexuality or needs; quite the
contrary, these are nearly always involved in the matter and can play
the role, among others, of masking or obscuring mimesis. Mimetic
desire is at times so inextricably mixed with other things that probably
no kind of analysis can isolate it; it is nonetheless necessary to pose the
other extreme of need and appetites, a pole of desire itself, which,
while both evident and mysterious, is not libido but mimesis.

Desiring mimesis precedes the appearance of its object and survives, as we shall see, the disappearance of every object. In the end, this desiring mimesis engenders its objects, but nevertheless it always appears to the outside observer as a triangular configuration the angles of which are occupied respectively by the two rivals and their common object. The object always comes to the foreground and mimesis is hidden behind it, even in the eyes of the desiring subjects. The convergence of desire defines the object. It is truly impossible to fix the origin of and responsibility for the rivalry, whose inexhaustible source is mimesis. Mimesis cannot spread without becoming reciprocal; at every instant the rivals assume the roles of model and disciple. Mimetic desire always plays off a desire that is already mimetic. Desires attract, ape, and bind one another, creating antagonistic relationships that both parties seek to define in terms of difference. But in reality, the relationship is nondifferentiated. In fact, at every instant, mimesis engenders new reciprocities by a constant redoubling of the same ruses, the same strategies, and the same mirror effects.

The definition proposed here permits an escape from all differentiated desire, from all the divisions that poison every problematic of desire from the Platonic theory of mimesis to the double conception of Nietzsche.

The conflict of desires results automatically from their mimetic character. This mechanism necessarily determines the characteristics of what Nietzsche calls *ressentiment*. The re- of *ressentiment* is the resurgence of desire colliding with the obstacle of the model-desire. Necessarily opposed by the model, the disciple-desire returns toward its source to poison it. *Ressentiment* is only truly intelligible if we begin with mimetic desire.

Unlike Freud, who remains entangled in his fathers and mothers, Nietzsche is the first to detach desire from all objects. Both despite and because of this extraordinary progress, which permits him to uncover a problematic of mimetic conflict and its psychic consequences, Nietzsche does not cease marking man's desires with sometimes positive and sometimes negative signs. The Nietzschean division has even known extraordinary success. For the majority of contemporary antimoralities, it serves as a model, sometimes in combination with psychoanalysis, as in *L'Anti-Oedipe*.

Next to *ressentiment*, Nietzsche posits an original and spontaneous desire, a desire *causa sui* called the will to power. If desire has no object unique to itself, on what can the will to power be exerted? Unless it is reduced to exercises of mystical gymnastics, it will necessarily pursue objects valorized by others. The power is revealed in the rivalry with the other, this time in competition undertaken voluntarily.

Either the will to power amounts to nothing or it chooses objects in function of the rival desire in order to steal them. In other words, the will to power and *ressentiment* have one and the same definition. Both are reduced to desiring mimesis. A notion such as the will to power can only surface at that moment when desire, no longer able to hide its mimetic nature, openly claims it in order to perpetuate its illusion of mastery. In the end, desire rushes headlong into the disasters awaiting it.

Do not some desires assert themselves more strongly than others? Probably, but the difference is always secondary, temporary, relative to the results. As long as desire is triumphant in rivalry, it can believe that it owes the other nothing, that it is truly original and spontaneous. On the other hand, desire cannot face defeat without recognizing its own *ressentiment*, now all the more humiliating since it originally believed it could transcend as will to power. There can only be a will to power in victory.

And this victory is nothing but a myth. The more ardent the desire, the more it is destined for defeat. The question has nothing to do with desire's intensity, its objective aptitude for triumphing over rival desires. The "strongest" desire is the one that quickly finds its master in denied rivalry. The will to power is a Wagnerian giant, a collosus with feet of clay that collapses pitifully before an adversary who has withdrawn. Proust calls this "l'être de fuite." There are tactical retreats, of course, that desire has no difficulty recognizing and that reassure it, but there is also the sincere, absolute indifference of others who are not invulnerable but simply fascinated by something else. Whenever the will to power is not recognized as the center of the world, it will place the one who does not recognize it at that same center and render him a secret cult. It never fails, in short, to turn into *ressentiment*. Here is the theme par excellence of modern drama: Neron crushed by Junie, the cold Baudelairian beauty, the impotence of genius obsessed by stupidity—Flaubert, Nietzsche. The movement toward madness in Nietzsche is identical with a perpetual metamorphosis of the will to power into *ressentiment*, and this metamorphosis is identical to the schizophrenic oscillation of "extremes," the terrible alternation of exaltation and depression. The will to power is mimesis exasperated by the obstacle of model-desire; it recognizes its only essence only to present itself as a matter of deliberate choice.

In his book on Nietzsche, Deleuze translates will to power and *ressentiment* as active and reactive forces.[11] These two nearly symmetrical expressions suggest the correct critical direction to the reader. If we probed the remaining dissymmetry we would find that it disintegrates before our eyes, that all difference evaporates and that symmetry must absolutely prevail. Deleuze goes to great lengths, on the contrary, to prove that this is not the case. Nietzsche's madness is nothing but an always more delirious wish to sustain a mythical difference that succumbs more and more to hostile reciprocity.

In *L'Anti-Oedipe*, the will to power becomes unconscious desire, "desiring production." All real desire, all activity of a relational and social character—including, I presume, the writing of *L'Anti-Oedipe*—arise from reactive forces and *ressentiment*. Deleuze's enterprise can be defined as a new effort to differentiate the will to power from *ressentiment* in order to quarantine the active forces from contamination by the reactive forces, while burying the former deeply beneath the latter, abandoning to *ressentiment* all activities that Nietzsche was still too concrete, not modern enough, to cast away. The procedure is very efficient, but it is the efficiency of a miser who buries his treasure so well that he cannot find it again. The omnipotence of desiring production is absolutely indistinguishable, in practice, from a radical castration. We are told that desire is prodigiously revolutionary, but we search in vain for examples of the will to power in this book. I only see the small child playing all alone with his toys.

It is necessary to return to this mimetic desire whose pathological evolution is exemplified by the case of Nietzsche. In general terms we can describe this evolution as follows: desire learns to recognize the ever repetitious metamorphosis of the model into an obstacle. Instead of drawing the obvious conclusion, instead of recognizing the mechanical and inevitable character of the rivalry, desire chooses another solution, which permits it to survive the knowledge of its perpetual failure. It decides to see this obstacle, which reappears regularly, as that behind which the true object of desire must exist. It chooses the obstructed path, the forbidden way, as if it led necessarily to the destination sought. Thus, there seems to arise behind every obstacle this beautiful totality, this closed garden, this well-defended treasure described so frequently by the metaphors of desire. The fascination for the hardest obstacle is the fruit of the only reasoning desire can make in order to perpetuate itself when it has become aware of its own consequences. Through a disastrous but logical shortcut, desire now moves directly and by choice toward the type of overpowering obstacle that was only, at first, the indirect and unexpected result of its own mimetic and therefore competitive nature. Far from constituting an individual aberration, "masochism" and "sadism" are inscribed in the logical course of desiring mimesis; these perversions are the only future it can have unless desire abandons the impasse in which it has been engaged from the beginning.

Mimesis generates violence and violence accelerates mimesis. An offspring of mimesis, violence exerts a mimetic fascination without equal. All violence is modeled on earlier violence and in turn serves as a model. Between mimesis and violence there exist relationships that still remain hidden. With reciprocal violence we enter a critical phase that opens upon delirium and madness, of course, but also upon destruction and death.

Perhaps the best guide to this critical phase of mimetic desire is Dostoevski. In *The Double*, he clearly divides into two groups a range of delirious phenomena that appears to defy classification. The second group is only the negative side of the first, master then slave, divinity then nothingness. There are two moments—one of exaltation, another of depression—and they never stop alternating. Delirium is never solitary, and its relationship to the other resembles a balance that cannot permanently achieve equilibrium or disequilibrium. When one of the partners is above, the other is below, and vice versa. Why?

Desire is linked to mimetic violence, that is, to an exchange of reprisals that can indeed be invisible, *underground*, as Dostoevski would say, or even imaginary in its modalities, but that nonetheless is real in its basic principle. He who has struck the last blow rises above the other. He conserves the mythic prize as long as he can believe his triumph is definitive, as long as his adversary does not steal it back; in short, as long as he is not the object of a new reprisal. Dostoevskian doubles live in a universe already resembling our own, peopled by bureaucrats and intellectuals, a universe intensely and arbitrarily competitive, almost totally devoid of clear-cut elements, of objective signs of triumph or failure such as physical violence or the rules of competitive sports.

The perception of doubles and twins figures among the typical phenomena of delirium. Freud, psychiatry in general, and nearly all writers, including those of *L'Anti-Oedipe*, only see doubles as one delirious figure among many. Dostoevski sees them in an entirely different way. Implicity at least, he structures and explains delirium as a function of the doubles. It is delirium itself that insists on making the doubles a fantasmagoria without importance. The two partners experience exaltation, that divine possession, then depression, or more precisely depossession, much too passionately for them to grasp a conception of the whole, to recognize that they occupy in turn the same position in the same system of relationships. The illusion of nonreciprocity reaches its limit, but it is really a matter of revolving nonreciprocity, which in the last analysis returns to reciprocity. As the movement accelerates, the moments tend to become juxtaposed and reciprocity shows through. The experience of the double has a persistently hallucinatory character, and yet it incarnates the fundamental truth of the relationship and reciprocity is affirmed at the heart of delirious fantasmagoria.

We rediscover the oscillation of schizophrenia in the relationship between Nerval and his double, where sexual superiority is sacralized. It is also found in Hölderlin, and here, in the final analysis, perhaps because the sexual relationships are not *deficient*, the matter at stake has an exclusively literary and intellectual nature, especially with his double, Schiller. This fact should be of no small interest to those writing on Hölderlin, especially since they themselves are intellectuals and writers. However, the unusual thing, although perhaps not so very unusual, is that this fact is wisked away by literary fetishes and neo-Freudian interpretations of the Oedipus complex.

We find this same oscillation of megalomania and the inferiority complex in the relationship between President Schreber and his double, Flechsig, the asylum director to whom all previous doubles are visibly transferred. The theory of "nerve-contact" between God and men furnishes a "theoretical" justification for the circulation between the doubles of the sacred object, God himself. Good when with Schreber, he becomes evil and vindictive when he lets himself be controlled by Flechsig. Freud recognizes the rival in Flechsig, but as always he makes nothing of the double. No one is interested in the doubles.

Far from uncovering mimetic violence, the matrix of the doubles, *L'Anti-Oedipe* even denies the suffering it causes. The thesis of the book supposes a peaceful coexistence between the extremes of delirium. To affirm this possibility, it is necessary to adopt cleverly ambiguous formulas such as differences of intensity, which alone would separate the diverse elements of delirium and provide the two authors with exactly the difference that they need to avoid falling into indifference or violent exclusion. When it is a matter of the Oedipus complex, we have seen, Deleuze and Guattari voluntarily turn to extremes. When it is a matter of delirium, on the contrary, they suddenly desire to entrench themselves in that middle ground that no longer exists. They would thereby convince themselves that delirium is habitable or at least consumable and marketable, that it constitutes not only a free but a permanent diversion that may be advantageously substituted for all other reality.

The truth is that these alternating moments reciprocally exclude one another and produce the anguish characteristic of delirium. The process cannot be defined as only "subjective" or "objective," nor as an autoexclusion or as a real exclusion with a source in another domain of reality. Simplifying, we can say that the "exquisite sensibility" and the extreme ambition of the great schizophrenics of modern thought oblige them to assume the diverse forms of exclusions or ostracisms whose raw materials are always provided by the competitive and anonymous nature of modern society itself.

Mimesis is always a project of self-differentiation that seeks to realize itself, especially in the negative stage of violence and the obstacle. The more desire aspires to difference, the more it generates identity. Mimetic desire is always more self-defeating. As it progresses, its consequences become more aggravated, and this aggravation in the end is identical to delirium and madness. This is why we find exactly the same things in delirium as in the anterior stages of mimetic desire, only here the form is exaggerated, caricatural. At least in appearance, there is more difference and more identity because the doubles never stop imitating each other, and this time the imitation is quite visible because those observers probably the least inclined to follow us will speak here of schizophrenic *histrionics*. Delirium is nothing but the obligatory outcome of a desire that imbeds itself in the impasse of the obstacle-model. The impasse in question is the most general form of the double bind that Gregory Bateson sees as the source of psychosis. All desires ultimately trap each other in the contradictory double injunction, "imitate me, do not imitate me." When effects of the universal double bind become too extreme to stay hidden, we speak of psychosis. And naturally the observation of these extreme effects, for the first time, reveals the double bind as a relation of desire.

Far from acknowledging the reciprocity besetting it, desire always flees into more imitation in the insane quest for difference, which, in turn, leads to more and more reciprocity. We cannot escape from reciprocity into delirium without having it reappear in the ironic form of the doubles.

Unlike Deleuze and Guattari, I think delirium *means* something. Meaning to be in delirium, nonetheless, is opposed to the meaning in delirium. Delirium means the identity of the doubles, the nullification of all differences, it speaks the lie that is itself, and if we continue to ignore it, it will speak louder and louder. The expressiveness of delirium is identical to the caricatural element we have just identified. Mimetic desire is neither inexhaustible nor inexplicable; in fact, it becomes easier to explain as it exasperates itself. It systematizes itself and emphasizes its own contradiction. The more we turn from this revelation, the clearer and simpler the lines of force become.

If *L'Anti-Oedipe* is truly on the side of delirium, we must expect to find the unrecognized and obsessive relationship of the doubles. And in fact many doubles appear in this book, the most spectacular and evident being the primary antagonist, Freud himself.

Freud is everywhere in a legitimate and official capacity in those aspects of his work that are explicitly called upon because they can be used against the Oedipus complex or have been judged at least detachable from it. Deleuze and Guattari summon a good Freud, who in their eyes is better than the evil Freud of the Oedipus complex. They want to divide the great man against himself. But the expulsion of Freud by Freud never takes place. The work remains impregnated with Freud, especially where he is violently repudiated. The Freud chased out the front door slips in the window; so much so that at the end of this Freudian psychomachy he is entirely or almost entirely reinstated, a Freud in particles, perhaps even molecular, a Freud mixed and emulsified, but nonetheless Freud.

The insidious return of the Freudian double is essential and must be understood at the level of the mechanisms of thought more than at the level of themes. Deleuze and Guattari show profound insight when they reproach the psychoanalytical Oedipus complex for its ambiguity: "we easily rediscover it everywhere precisely because it is ambiguous; in this sense it is correct to say that it is totally useless."[12] But the most acute observations are those that boomerang most quickly against the observer. *L'Anti-Oedipe* itself swarms with undecidable concepts; for example, the notion of capitalism, with its decodings and recodings, about which the most contradictory statements can be made. Here we can take almost word for word some of the formulas used against the Oedipus complex and turn them against the notions that Deleuze and Guattari attempt to set forth in its place, beginning, of course, with desire. It is impossible to inscribe everything in desire without having everything flee in the end outside of desire. Accompanying the benevolent side of desire is also a malevolent side that is terribly significant because society as a whole arises from it. We constantly have the impression that our authors sustain a single and yet double project. They would suppress all differences that serve as escape mechanisms for their adversaries, psychoanalytical and others, but they also want to establish a new difference, a "true desire" previously undiscovered and belonging only to them and their friends. Here is a double bind imprisoning the book in a long and vigorous debate with itself:

From the beginning of this study, we have maintained that social and desiring production are one and the same, but also that they differ in regime, so much so that a social form of production exercises an essential suppression of desiring production, and also that the desiring production (a "true" desire) contains the potential disruption of the social form. But what is a "true" desire, since suppression, also, is desired? How to distinguish them? We demand the right to proceed with a very slow and cautious analysis. For, make no mistake, even in their opposing functions, *these are the same syntheses.*[13]

In short, it is always necessary to decide the undecidable, first in one sense and then in another, thanks to a series of ups and downs that, of course, bring us back to the schizophrenic method. Yet we must ask how this kind of demonstration can be inscribed in the claim for delirium. If delirium is speaking, or if one speaks in the name of delirium, why try to fix difference on one side rather than the other, why not let infinite movement carry us away? If delirium were really what they wished it to be, why not enjoy it without worrying about anchoring it in another logical critique of all nondelirious systems?

In the greater part of the work, the two authors strive to fix wandering differences. In spite of themselves, they never renounce the valorizations and exclusions that nonetheless remain incomplete and call forth the doubles from every page. Essentially then, the work corresponds not to the admitted content of the claim for delirium, but to the unadmitted content; the delirium overwhelming this work is not and could not be what is claimed. Its relationship to delirium is no less authentic as a result. It possesses the only authenticity compatible with the nature of a delirium that always mistakes itself and thereby engenders effects increasingly opposed to what it seeks. To achieve true and effective delirium, it is necessary not to abandon oneself to the giddy spinning and flight of difference, as *L'Anti-Oedipe* pretends to do, but to do what it actually does—persistently immobilize the entire system in those circumstances where the enterprise becomes hopeless. This, we have shown, provokes the giddy spinning and flight of difference. The desire to stabilize difference always renders it more unstable, like the clumsy fellow in his canoe who overcompensates for its rocking and capsizes himself.

The time comes when the force of symmetry becomes so strong, the presence of the doubles so obsessive, that there is no question of escaping them. What I have said so far is only valid for a part of *L'Anti-Oedipe*, the greater part. There are other passages, assuredly difficult to circumscribe exactly, where the authors, giving up the struggle for absolute difference, lend themselves to the play of encroaching identity and become complacent with it. Among the theses they defend there are those that it would be difficult not to read as mimetic variations of theses they have previously criticized, particularly those of structural psychoanalysis.

One example of this is the great *transcendental anus* that the authors solemnly employ to caricature the structuralist phallus. We already know that with delirium there is no need to exclude anything. To dispatch the spoilsports it suffices to advance into delirium, to submerge resistances in more delirium. To suppress the symbolic phallus—that is, at the *molar* level—is out of the question. Since *Bouvard and*

Pécuchet, this object has served us well, and it maintains an outdated charm that it would be foolish to discard. It is more amusing to reduce the thing to insignificance by elevating above it a new symbolic object. What is involved? The anus, of course, which they intend to turn into a superpotent machine. Thus, we have *schizoanalysis*, the new and improved product, truly designed for our contemporary life styles and capable of outselling all its competitors in the lively marketplace of psychoanalysis:

If in our societies the phallus has taken the position of a detached object distributing the lack to persons of both sex and organizing the Oedipal triangle, it is the anus which so detaches it, and overwhelms and sublimates the penis in a sort of *Aufhebung* constituting the phallus.[14]

Deleuze and Guattari must have had a good laugh while cooking up the sublime penis and the anal *Aufhebung*. Facing the fervent acceptance given to this new ritual unveiling, the old believers—who deserve it, we admit—are too dismayed or too occupied with their own conversion to notice that the practical jokers are verifying behind their backs the same old structural theory of psychosis. They think it possible to slip into schizophrenics without any trouble at all, they prance about a little and bang—As if the bottom fell out, in the end the symbolic becomes manifested as a hole!

After serious and enthusiastic pages, there are others in *L'Anti-Oedipe* that discourage all desire for discussion. We never know where true thought ends and the eristic farce begins. This ambiguity serves the designs of the two authors, we can even believe it is arranged to catch the reader in some sort of double bind. The thesis defended here, which maintains that the book constantly returns to the ideas it denounces and never manages to rid itself of either Freud or Lacan, destined as it is to drag these doubles along behind it—this too patiently elaborated thesis—will instantly be shown useless and superfluous. I can always be told that I have wasted my time and effort, that the authors know far better than I all that I pretend to show them. And this is not entirely false. We could cite as evidence the matter of the great anus and others of the same sort. Whatever he does, the critic is cornered. If he lets himself be preoccupied with the aspects of the work that appear most substantial, he will be accused of pontificating over a text that does not even take itself seriously. What good is it to dissect what is only a torch thrown into the decrepit structures of capitalist intellectualism? Yet if the critic lets himself laugh, on the contrary, if he says everywhere, "That's a good one," he will be reproached for misunderstanding the only enterprise that still has some validity in the convulsive decadence of our time.

Either case would not be entirely wrong. To take the book seriously or lightly are only two different ways of not seeing the critical stage we have reached and the manner in which *L'Anti-Oedipe* wishes to insert itself in this crisis. We are told that instead of bracing ourselves against this movement, we must embrace it. We must carry the artifice of contemporary thought even farther, exaggerate once more what is already a caricature. Under such conditions every procedure is legitimate. At times we rely on one thing to subvert another, and later, it is the other way around. To think logically against the logic of others is quite fair for Deleuze and Guattari, but we must not turn this weapon of logic back on them; we cannot ask them to be consistently logical because schizophrenia is speaking through their mouths and they own the copyright on true delirium. Oh! Isn't this schizoanalysis a beautiful invention! This will silence all opponents more quickly than all the "resistances" a psychoanalyst is so quick to invoke whenever he is contradicted.

To aggravate all perversions while relying on the arbitrariness of our cultural forms, to depend exclusively neither on delirium, play, nor political engagement, but to partake of all these attitudes and still more, so that this is impossible to enclose in any critical definition, we have here the infinite difference of a successful schizophrenia, one identical with the stance and strategy of *L'Anti-Oedipe*.

Here everything, up to a point, results from tactical calculations. Nevertheless, it is necessary to note the mimetic repetition of the doubles inscribed on the clinical chart of schizophrenic delirium. Deleuze and Guattari only mention briefly what they themselves call schizophrenic *histrionics*, and then only to minimize its role, a role that could, in the last analysis, be much more important for this chart and *L'Anti-Oedipe* than they would have us suppose. In other words, it could be that, at the level of the struggle between difference and identity, *L'Anti-Oedipe* conforms more to the reality of delirium than its claim for delirium would wish to admit.

In the greater part of their book, Deleuze and Guattari attempt to establish fixed reference points, to distinguish top from bottom and right from left. They seriously strive to separate the good unconscious from bad social desire, good revolutionary schizophrenia from bad reactionary paranoia, etc. I could endlessly discuss, at the level of the proposed methods and subsequent analyses, the success or failure of this project, the aptitude of "disjunctive syntheses" or even "differences of regime" to play the role they are intended to play. I believe, in fact, that it hardly makes sense to place on the social as such the responsibility for all human unhappiness. The attempt is nonetheless interesting, for it does not entirely succumb, even regarding psychoanalysis, to the ease of blaming all our troubles on the traditional sociological or ideological scapegoats. But due to this very fact it gives way to a real paralysis. Where it is necessary to have differences, it is also necessary to do away with them. Therefore, I must begin with this paralysis and the resulting confusion to explain the turnabout we have recognized, the sudden conversion of the champions of difference into buffoons of identity. Deleuze and Guattari want to believe that they have transformed themselves into madmen of philosophy and tricksters of psychoanalysis by their own free will, but it is necessary to look a little closer. The time comes when even the most extreme mobility, even the most sensational dialectic can no longer save difference from the undifferentiation penetrating it. It is at this moment when the doubles pursue them and when difference, locally, seems lost, that the two authors throw themselves into the cause of mimetic undifferentiation, into an enterprise opposed to what they had once pursued with equal ardor. But this undifferentiation is only a parody. Far from turning openly toward the doubles in order to ask what they mean, they prevent themselves from taking them seriously; the recourse to contentious parody makes everything ridiculous. In the end, it is a matter of making themselves and others believe that this game is not really that of the doubles, that it is not the doubles who direct the game but the two authors who have decided to play at doubles. The difference only seems important in the light of a certain project that consists of maintaining difference at any price, and it is all the more absurd because it reaches the same inevitable result, the destruction of all concrete difference, but only in the context of delirious histrionics that render that destruction inefficacious, uselessly transforming into the worst what should be the best.

As curious as we may find these stratagems, they are less interesting than the fundamental question of Oedipus and the complex, which is left in suspense. From beginning to end, Deleuze and Guattari use the word "Oedipus" and the neologisms they derive from it (oedipalize, oedipeanize) as perfect synonyms for *triangle* and its derivations. Both "triangulate" and "oedipeanize" designate one and the same operation. Correct me if I am mistaken.

In other words, as they have been schooled, the two authors docilely return to the Oedipus complex any relations of a triangular configuration, all mimetic rivalries, all the conflicts of doubles that they happen to observe. For example, they mention a declaration Stravinsky is reputed to have made just before his death, according to which all his life he wanted to prove his capabilities to his father.[15] Here Deleuze and Guattari see a confirmation of a universal brainwashing that runs rampant in contemporary society. Psychoanalysis does not need to invent the Oedipus complex, they say, subjects come to their analysts already completely oedipeanized. Here I must pose a question not to psychoanalysis, since it is not worth the trouble, but to Deleuze and Guattari, who pretend to be liberated from it. Is there anyone that Stravinsky could wish to prove something to without immediately being labeled a victim of the Oedipal injunction? With whom does he have the right to become a rival without falling under the power of psychoanalysis—his brother, his girlfriend, his housekeeper, other musicians? With no one, since each time the rivalry will be presented in the form of a triangle and will automatically return to the eternal Oedipus complex, abandoned without a struggle to the Freudo-structuralist machine.

If this abandonment is legitimate, if the Oedipus complex has a privileged point of view concerning all conflictual activities, the matter is settled. All that remains are the squabbles of the old guard, trifles and provocations. Desiring production is the Utopia of a universe without conflict, a vast cloud of ink destined to conceal an unconditional surrender. The Oedipal theory comes out of *L'Anti-Oedipe* intact, and toward the end it even collects a nice bonus: *L'Anti-Oedipe* itself thoroughly oedipeanized, since it is entirely structured in a triangular rivalry with psychoanalytic theoreticians, who furnish more than enough living and dead fathers to satisfy the most fastidious analyst. If Stravinsky's declaration is oedipeanized, it is no more so than the hundreds of pages of *L'Anti-Oedipe*. It is hardly more than the tiny mote in our neighbor's eye that prevents us from noticing the beam in our own, the enormous Oedipal beam that constitutes the work entitled *L'Anti-Oedipe*.

I am not establishing myself as a defender of psychoanalysis; quite the contrary. I maintain that Deleuze and Guattari have defended psychoanalysis despite themselves and have confirmed it by returning to a defeatist method. There is certainly a psychoanalytic brainwashing, but their definition of it only perpetuates and aggravates the misunderstanding. Fifty years of psychoanalytic culture have successfully transformed the reference to the Oedipus complex into a reflex that is activated whenever we are faced with any triangular or paratriangular configurations. It is not the content of conflicts, but the label that belongs to psychoanalysis. We must not let ourselves be impressed by the label to the point of believing that only a new solipsistic myth can rid us of Freud.

Certainly in many cases the reference to the Oedipus complex is made without reflection and does not correspond to any real consideration. Yet it is never without consequences and carries a host of prejudices that are impossible or nearly impossible to challenge. The Oedipus complex has become a quasiindestructible and fundamental premise, a real law of psychic gravity. *L'Anti-Oedipe* is an example.

The mimetic definition of desire allows us to explain rivalry without the Oedipus complex, it brings forth an unlimited number of doubles without referring to myth or the nuclear family. We find ourselves in the presence of a very general conception whose relation to mythical, tragic, and psychoanalytical Oedipus must be clarified. It is evident that the Oedipal crisis, as Freud envisions it, carries undeniable mimetic elements that are variable and never precisely stated. On the other hand, the mimetic relation is opposed to the Oedipal structure by its destructuring quality. Assuredly, mimetic desire is always inscribed in the existing structures that it tends to subvert. This does not mean at all that it can be defined as "imaginary."

We must examine the poorly defined relationship between the Oedipal, mythic, or psychoanalytic triangle and all the triangles and pseudotriangles of mimetic rivalry. The only hope for a true anti-Oedipalism lies in an effective critique of that univocal relation postulated by psychoanalysis between the Oedipus complex and all other triangles.

In all evidence this critique begins with myth. It is a new effort to explain myth. We recognize without difficulty, in many myths and particularly those concerning Oedipus, the traces of acute crises where the cultural fabric literally comes undone. As a result of modern formalism, Deleuze and Guattari believe that the signs of nondifferentiation and the presence of the doubles in myth do not correspond to any kind of reality. This attitude is part of the same general outlook as the refusal to systematize delirium in function of the doubles. It always reaches the same impasses. But here again, we must reconsider the problem beginning with real doubles. Innumerable indications, always indirect, of course, but marvelously convergent, suggest that the crises revealed behind cultural phenomena spring from mimetic desire and tend to reach a paroxysm in which physical violence and delirious manifestations are combined. These mythical indications range from the mythic plague, disguises, and festive hierarchical inversions to ritual mutilations, so called "totemic" ceremonies, as well as masks and cults of possession. There is no reason not to welcome the convergent evidence and to admit, at least as a hypothesis, that the violent loss of the cultural is the necessary condition of its restoration, that the metamorphosis of a community into a blind and demented mob constitutes the necessary precondition of all mythical and ritual creation.

Once there is nothing left but the doubles in confrontation, the slightest accident, the tiniest sign can cause all reciprocal hatred to be fixed on one of them. What mimesis has fragmented and infinitely divided can be in one motion unified again through a collective transference made possible by a general nondifferentiation, all of which can be understood as a real operation.

The homogeneity of the crisis, which is one with the interminability of violence and the false infinity of spiraling difference, ends when the scapegoat victim sorts out everything and everyone, once more, fixing difference and restoring a common direction for all. With this fact I can explain why so many myths of origin are presented in the form of conflicts between brother and mythical twins where only one perishes or is driven away, or even in the form of a creative collision between two symmetrical entities, mountains for example, from which order, meaning, and fecundity immediately spring. Ethnological structuralism deciphers the difference stabilized by the scapegoat victim and guaranteed by the religious; it cannot explore the underlying symmetry, the conflictual identity of the doubles that precedes all (re-)differentiation.

The scapegoat victim provides an outlet for violence by unifying the entire community against him. He appears, therefore, to carry with him into the grave a violence that he has polarized. An actual state of nonviolence is substituted for the reciprocal violence that was poisoning the community. Because the violence and nonviolence originate from the same process, a process never truly understood, human communities refer them to a single entity—the former scapegoat—that seems to become transcendent and beneficent after an immanent and maleficent visitation. The metamorphoses of the sacred are thus attributed to the mediation of a deified ancestor, a mythic hero, or a divinity; the mechanism of the scapegoat victim can always be recognized behind all religious operations.

Once we have uncovered this process that mimesis and the scapegoat victim constitute, we immediately see that only our ignorance could attribute primitive prohibition to pure superstition or fantasms. Their object is real: desiring mimesis and all the violence accompanying it. Assuredly, this fact can hardly be denied in the case of prohibitions against mimetic representation and all modes of doubling representation, such as those against the enunciation of proper names. The prohibitions aganst twins or even in some societies, the simple physical resemblances between blood-related people work the same way. Similarly, at least in principle, the incest prohibition affects all women inside all groups of cohabitation, whatever the degree of kinship; the danger of mimetic rivalry between those living together is thus eliminated. Plato's vaguely expressed fear of mimesis is still the primitive fear, the fear of uncontrollable mimetic rivalry in which cultural differences dissolve. This also accounts for the hostility of many traditional societies toward images, mimes, actors, and theatrical representation in general.

Many functionalist intuitions are correct, even if they do not justify themselves. The effectiveness and the relative insight of prohibitions are one with their origin. Prohibition is only the violence of the crisis suddenly interrupted by the scapegoat mechanism and transformed into proscription by a community terrified by the idea of falling once more into violence.

Ritual also springs from the scapegoat victim. It seeks to preclude any recurrence of the crisis by repeating the founding and unifying mechanism in the most exact form possible. The principal action will almost always consist, therefore, of a form of ritual immolation that imitates some real murder, certainly not that of the "father," but of the scapegoat victim.

Rite, therefore, is itself mimesis, which aims, this time, no longer at the other's desire, with the dissolving and destructive consequences familiar to us, but rather at unifying violence. Unanimous, ritual mimesis, combined with prohibitions and the totality of the religious, constitutes a real preventative of wandering and conflictual mimesis. Against bad mimesis, therefore, culture knows no other remedy but good mimesis. This is why mimesis is undecidable, notably in Plato, as Jacques Derrida demonstrates.[16] Everything touching the sacred is truly undecidable. The scapegoat mechanism furnishes the principle of all decision, even in ritual and pararitual repetitions as weak and desacralized as they might become. *Decidere*, in Latin, means to decide in our sense only because it first means to cut with a knife, to kill the sacrificial victim.

The final resolution is too closely integrated with the crisis for the rites clearly to distinguish the two. As a rule, this is why rites carry elements having an objective character of transgression, but constituting religious imitation of the process that has engendered the prohibition. This imitation is necessarily identical to the transgression of prohibition, especially when understood in terms of the latter. Thus we have reciprocal violence, crises of possession, that is, paroxysmal imitation, multiple forms of violent undifferentiation, ritual cannibalism, and, of course, incest. These phenomena always have a maleficent character; they only become beneficent with the rite, in close association with some form of sacrifice, that is, with the ritual element the most directly commemorative of the scapegoat victim.

If mimetic desire is a universal reality, if it moves toward infinite violence, that is, toward insanity and death, we must certainly envision the problem of culture in the context of the most extreme peril, of the violent delirium demanded by Deleuze and Guattari. *L'Anti-Oedipe* situates itself, therefore, at a point whose crucial character must be recognized, but it does so to accomplish the opposite of what it should. It repudiates *in extremis* the identity of the doubles by founding itself on delirium when it is really necessary to acknowledge the violent loss of language and differentiation. The real question is not how to achieve universal delirium, but why is there something besides infinite violence and delirium, why, in other words, is there something rather than nothing? The question is the same as that of the difference that appears to oscillate between the doubles but that actually has a stable reality relative only to the effective operation of a determined cultural order. In reciprocal violence and delirium, difference returns to its original nothingness. Only an exchange of reprisals remains, and it is most evident that no collective will in the sense of Rousseau's can found stable differential systems common to a whole society. Where such a thing as collective will exists, it is tributary to a preexistant system. Here is an unanswered question to which the hypothesis of the scapegoat victim can bring a solution too adequate to the data and too perfectly imbricated with mythic and ritual evidence for the disciplines concerned to avoid the examination it demands.[17]

If we recognize in the mimetic crisis and its resolution something more original than meaning, we will realize that the definition of the scapegoat victim as parricide and as incestuous has only a retrospective character: it can only be effectuated beginning with the law founded by the death of the victim. Parricide and incest signify and distort the crisis itself and the fact that this crisis is entirely pinned on a single victim.

We must ask why the accusation of parricide and incest, the obsession with Oedipal crimes, including infanticide, reappear in all great social crises, a fact witnessed by Greek tragedy and psychoanalysis among other things. In all collective violence of the lynching and pogrom variety, motivated by this kind of accusation, the same drama is repeated. The only difference in the modern world is that we no longer read the collective transfer in the mythic key of genuinely guilty heroes. In today's world, we have become able to observe collective violence and to read it as such; it is no longer productive, therefore, of ritual actions and mythological significance.

If the crisis is the propagation of mimetic rivalry, we easily conceive that, as it spreads, it eventually contaminates even relationships with parents. This transformation of father and son into mimetic rivals, into doubles, is repeatedly shown to us by tragedy. Therefore, the third side of the triangle can be occupied by the mother. At the horizon of all crises of the type defined above, parricide and incest must surface, not as fantasms, but as the extreme potential consequences of an extension of mimetic rivalry to the familial triangle. It is not necessary to ask if the passage to this extreme is effectively realized in order to understand that it can never be defined as merely imaginary or fantasmatic.

Thus, psychoanalysis cannot escape by claiming that the origin for violence proposed here does not cause it difficulty or contradict its theory, because the accusations against the scapegoat victim still can be unconscious desires and fantasms, etc. Parricide and incest do not have their origin in the family life of the child. That idea belongs to adults and to the community in crisis, as Deleuze and Guattari correctly remark. It bears no relation to early childhood and signifies the destruction of all familial law by mimetic rivalry.

Oedipus the King demonstrates the genesis of the accusation. This accusation is born of the protagonists' quarrel over the crisis, a quarrel that, in fact, *is* the crisis. Each adversary attempts to defeat his mimetic rival by attributing to him the responsibility for all public misfortune. This play of accusations is reciprocal. That this exchange successively beings forth regicide, parricide, and incest as it becomes increasingly embittered suggests an awareness, on Sophocles' part of the genesis I have just proposed. In the process of being transferred from the collectivity to the individual, the crisis is transfigured and reduced to the proportions of a transgression any individual can commit. This process is nothing but the pursuit of the scapegoat victim, which cannot end until the whole community is finally united against—and therefore around—a single victim.

Once unanimity is achieved, the epidemic of widespread violence between neighbors no longer exists; instead, only innocent citizens remain who face a single, guilty party. This scapegoat victim takes upon himself all the maleficent aspects and leaves to the Thebans only their blameless, passive contagion with the plague. When the oracle orders them to discover who is uniquely responsible for the crisis, it is actually telling them what they will do in order to resolve that crisis— not because such a responsible individual really exists, but because only the mimetically achieved unanimity against some mythical culprit can bring healing. The oracle unleashes the paroxysm of the crisis; dissent must peak before resolution can follow.

Mimetic desire has furnished us with a source of conflict that is rooted neither in the family nor in the Oedipal myth, since it makes possible a complete explanation of this myth that psychoanalysis can never achieve. Instead of relating mimetic triangles to the Oedipus complex, we must read that complex in light of mimetic desire. Mimetic rivalry does not find its origin and cause in the Oedipus complex; on the contrary, we must seek in mimetic rivalry the cause of all versions of the Oedipus story, whether mythic, tragic, or psychoanalytic.

If psychoanalysis clothes the works of desire and violence in a mythological parricide and incest, and this is what the myth already did, it must do so for the same reasons. It is not difficult to see that classical psychoanalysis functions like a rite, or to follow the formula of Lacan, the rite of the Oedipus complex.

In the traditional conception of the cure it is sufficient to bring the shameful desires to light in order to dissipate their virulence and permit men to assume them in a constructive mode. Of its enemies, then, the cure makes allies. The Oedipus complex is the disguised representation of the scapegoat or sacrificial victim that each of us must internalize and then externalize. It plays the double role of poison and cure.

Of course, this passage from the collective to the individual does not lack precedents. Classical shamanism displaces from the collective to the individual the general theme of expulsion constituting the fundamental interpretation of the scapegoat mechanism at the ritual level. Here what is expelled is a material object that supposedly has invaded the sick person's body. In the same way, psychoanalysis transposes the successively maleficent and beneficent *pharmakos* into a psychic expulsion, following more literally and precisely than it would care to believe the same mythic disguising of the scapegoat victim at work in ancient rites. If terms like *abreaction* and *catharsis* are now avoided, at least by the French neo-Freudians, in describing the benefits of the cure, it is not because they say poorly what they are supposed to say, but because they say it all too well. The parallels between ritual and modern cultural forms cause an undefinable discomfort.

Psychoanalysis is always the undecidable that is decided, first in one direction, then in the other. We rediscover this mystery not only in the conception of the cure, but also in a chronological view of Freud's work, and even in the history of psychoanalysis, which, although first seen by the pioneers as the scourge of God, was later metamorphosed into a pillar of social order. Freud himself, on his arrival in New York, believed that he brought "the plague" to the Americans, but in the last years of his life he spoke mostly of sublimation. What first seemed the most destructive element, parricide and incest, very quickly became the foundation of the psychoanalytical order, the building block for *homo psychoanalyticus*. The undecidable, once more, has pivoted upon itself. We must be careful not to reject these metamorphoses as a betrayal by the epigones, as a pretended "recuperation," or any other second-rate scapegoat.

To define psychoanalysis as a rite is not to minimize it, especially at the level of knowledge; for a rite to be effective it must be constituted in the proximity of the scapegoat victim. Certainly the generative mechanism is misunderstood, but less than in the weakened and derivative forms. We must see in the Freudian theory the byproduct of a powerful, double advance in the direction of the scapegoat victim; comprised on the one hand of the Oedipal problematic and on the other of *Totem and Taboo*. The closeness of the theory to the real mechanism confers on it a properly mythic power in a great number of domains ranging from medicine to esthetics and even to science, since it constitutes a source of inspiration for future research.

If Freud never reaches the scapegoat victim, we nonetheless would say that he always remains centered exactly on it. In other words, his advances, hesitations, and setbacks move along parallel paths that lead to the scapegoat mechanism and therefore remain almost equivalent. This explains the properly mythic equilibrium of the great Freudian notions, or, once again, their undecidable character. The critical and violent element is always exactly compensated for by an ordering and stabilizing element. The "complex" grants access to regular family and social life, as with the great rites of passage, only because it is primarily a real passage through maleficent violence, a submergence into disorder. Freud could not conceive of an Oedipus complex without crisis, without this foundation that is first of all the loss of foundation. It seems contrary to the true spirit of Freud to accentuate the problems of transindividual structures that *Totem and Taboo* would resolve through "phylogenetic heredity."

Freud never directly confronts the problem posed by the contradictory aspects, the structuring and destructuring, contained in the Oedipus complex. He lets the undecidable decide itself without him, and the mythic power of his theory is identical to this withdrawal. Liberating itself little by little from rite, the mind always wants to decide by itself, but as long as the scapegoat victim remains a mystery, it is best not to substitute the wrong principle of decision for the undecidable. The mind falls first into the stable disequilibrium of a false rationality, then into the unstable disequilibrium that leads to delirium.

In structural psychoanalysis (Lacan), the equilibrium is broken for the sake of the structure. What is lost is the reality of the crisis and this loss is partly compensated for by the discovery of a notion absent in Freud, a symbolic order independent of the objects in which it is actualized: a purely formal residue of transcendence that determines the final elements of all representation, orders the structural positions, and distributes the roles inside this structure.

In the present perspective, this notion of a symbolic order must seem like a partial intuition of the perpetuated effects of the scapegoat victim, even in a system seemingly deprived of all mythical-ritual foundation and even though all reference to a transcendental principle has disappeared. Thus, it is necessary to reject the reading proposed by *L'Anti-Oedipe*, which makes of the symbolic order a simple regression toward "archaic despotism."

Nonetheless, diverse factors tend to limit the usefulness of Lacan's contribution. The first factor results from entrenchment in psychoanalysis excluding direct sociological and cultural observation. Structural psychoanalysis is often nothing more than a structuralist misreading of psychoanalysis. The second results from structuralism itself, which can only be founded at the expense of the crisis, at the price of a fundamental decision that severs all the undecidables from their maleficent side. Certainly, it is excellent to reject the mythic localizations of the crisis stressed by Freud, especially those of early childhood. Nonetheless, the negation of all crisis, the loss of all intuition concerning it, falsifies the whole theory. Even at the level of symbolic order, which itself should not be made the object of a separate treatment, it should not be seen as independent of the oppositions of the doubles rejected and effectively neuralized in the ghetto of the imaginary.

Because they always recover and disguise the two faces of violence, the great symbols of the sacred symbolize at once all desymbolization and all symbolization. They only become the signifier because they have first signified the end of all signification. This is why they are always undecidable. We misrecognize them if we associate them exclusively with mechanisms, or rather with postulates of structuration too arbitrary to be productive at the level of cultural texts. For example, in sacred monarchies, incest can only signify stabilized difference, the established law and sovereignty, because it first of all signifies the loss of difference and real violence. Apprehended in itself and outside of all ritual context, incest is exclusively maleficent and destructuring. If there is ritual incest in certain societies, it is because there is first of all the scapegoat victim whose collective murder, the punishment for a supposed incest, has freed the community from the violence strangling it. It is necessary that the substitute victims of the ritual live and die as the original victim seems in retrospect to have lived and died, by virtue of the principle—same causes, same effects. The attempt is made to perpetuate and revitalize the effects of a primary and spontaneously unifying sacrifice.

Ritual incest has the same origin as the royal throne, which is really the same as the sacrificial stone. The proof is found in the formulas of African rituals that sometimes make the king a true scapegoat, not because of "sins," in the vague modern sense, but because of an ever-fermenting violence that might explode if it did not find a ritual outlet, here the king himself. In Ruanda, for example, in a ceremony where the king and his mother are attached to each other as if condemned to death, the following words are pronounced: "I impose on you the wound of the javelin, the sword, the cross-bow, the rifle, the club, the hook. If some man, if some woman has died of the wound of an arrow, a lance . . . I lay these blows on you."[18]

Ritual incest arises not from barbarous despotism, as Deleuze and Guattari believe, nor from some structural imprint constitutive of the human mind. The symbolic order is not an imprescriptible and inalienable given, analogous to the Kantian categories. L'Anti-Oedipe is right in rising up against this conception, but it lacks the resources for an effective critique.

In the structuralist perspective, the effacement of the symbolic is defined as some sort of deficiency, a "forclusion," somewhat analogous to organic deficiencies. All real identifications are "imaginary." Nothing that takes place between men can influence the destiny of the symbolic order. L'Anti-Oedipe notes well this absence of history, but cannot suggest a valid alternative. I suggest that the symbolic order is born of the scapegoat mechanism, that is, of a collective violence that is always at the mercy of reciprocal violence.

Far from reaching fundamental structures, Lacan's psychoanalysis proposes the hypostasis of a transitory historical moment. It takes the image of a particular moment, already deformed by its own eyepiece, for an inalienable given of the human mind. If we observe this system in the light of the preceding remarks, we must conclude that it belongs to the final stage of a cultural cycle, close to absolute disintegration. The symbolic order still distributes roles among real persons and continues to act as an organizing agent at the level of concrete relations, but it does so solely because it operates as a lack. We are supposed to believe that the phallus is the absolute sign of this structural law— phallic power always sought by desire, but always eluding it. The sacred is not even mentioned.

Transcendence *is*, in short, only because it serves as a deceiving object of rivalry. The symbolic order is passed off as being invulnerable to all the conflicts involving it, as being absolutely out of range. In reality, what we now observe is the result of this rivalry, a state of extreme ruin, a competitive action really destructive, but the structuralist does not foresee that destruction. He is far from expecting what will follow. The constant exasperation of the rivalry over the symbolic, notable in contemporary polemics, must lead to an even more complete ruin, an effacement of the symbolic as an objective power, not an absolute objectivity, of course, but one relative to the culture under consideration and to the differences that the symbolic stabilizes.

If we can now speak of a cultural advent of delirium, rather than of pathological aberration only or simple intellectual fantasy, then this effacement must indeed be taking place. It is not an accidental "forclusion" or an abstract negation. This is the news Deleuze and Guattari report when they negate the symbolic. Concerning this negation, I would have to repeat what I said earlier about their negation of Freud. In the swarming triangles and doubles, it often boomerangs against these authors. The negation is thus partially ineffective and remains ahistoric, like the previous affirmation, but it marks, nonetheless, a new stage in this same history. *L'Anti-Oedipe* is a sign of an aggravated cultural crisis. The elements, which before tended to reorganize themselves as a function of a misrecognized but real vanishing point, tend increasingly toward fragmentation and dispersion. Until now the absence of divinity was still a substitute for presence, which is now in the process of being effaced. At this time we might say that even the death of God has begun to die.

And here the spectacle of *The Bacchae* reappears among us, but in parodic form, the return of transcendence to an immanence that threatens to merge with pure violent reciprocity. As in La Fontaine's fable, the symbolic tree trunk sent to the frogs by Jupiter as their king and despised by them because it passively tolerated the worst indignities from it subjects is succeeded by some sort of schizophrenic crane, a great devourer of the little frogs that demanded a king or refused all kings, which is the same thing.

The process of reciprocal appropriation of the symbolic, the polemics concerning the city in crisis, is identical to the destruction of its object. This can be ascertained with a marvelous precision in the transition between Lacan and *L'Anti-Oedipe*. Deleuze and Guattari understand that the symbolic in psychoanalysis is the object of an appropriation. The distance from the imaginary to the symbolic, for the disciples, is the equivalent of the *itinerarium mentis ad Deum* of medieval mysticism; it establishes a hierarchy of initiates and noninitiates. *L'Anti-Oedipe* humorously mimics the essential movement of the structural analysis: "No, no, no, you're still in the imaginary, you have to reach the symbolic!"[19] But the will to appropriation that is so perfectly designated and denounced in *L'Anti-Oedipe* is not renounced by its authors. Manifested everywhere, it constitutes the book's fundamental motivation, especially with the theme of "real difference" that they accuse Lacan of situating between the imaginary and the symbolic through an error that is also an usurpation. In *L'Anti-Oedipe* the "real difference" is conveniently displaced, transported to the side of the famous desiring production and the sacred unconscious, as traffic barricades along the new itinerary of some official cortege. In the process of this relocation, the Ark of Covenant, jostled about a little too much, falls apart, and even *L'Anti-Oedipe* understands in its own manner, the manner of its misrecognition, by affirming that there never was a symbolic order and that, in any case, we must prefer the marvelous vertigo of schizophrenia, the will-o'-the-wisp of madness.

The problem for us is to know if it is here that the difference passes [between the symbolic and the imaginary]. Would not real difference lie between the Oedipus complex, structural as well as imaginary, *and* something else, something that all the Oedipus complexes crush and repress—that is, desiring production—the machine of desire that cannot be reduced to structures any more than to persons, that constitute the Real in itself, beyond and beneath the symbolic as well as the imaginary.[20]

What can be deciphered in all theoretical debates is the history of a slow sacrificial disintegration and a slow progress of mimetic desire. Desiring mimesis slowly corrodes the symbolic order, but remains structured by it for quite some time. Rivalries of all kinds continue to become more and more exasperated, but without being completely freed and disordered. This is why we always have a combination and articulation of what structural psychoanalysis calls the symbolic and the imaginary, but in variable proportions, always on the way toward the objective effacement of the symbolic order and toward the schizophrenic oscillation of the doubles.

This progression does not begin with psychoanalysis any more than it will end in delirium. To enlarge its framework—but not as much as would be suitable—we need only turn once more to *L'Anti-Oedipe*. Once we have become accustomed to the newness of its vocabulary, to "fluxes" and "desiring production," we rediscover with surprise many very familiar attitudes and themes, themes more familiar than the Oedipus complex, the very themes cultivated successively or simultaneously by the individualisms and subjectivisms of the last two centuries.

A unique subject, stranger to all laws, orphan, atheist, and bachelor, the "good" desire of Deleuze and Guattari is "held entirely within itself," like Valéry's pure self. I would say that it was entirely solipsistic if its inventors had not been shrewd enough to do away with the apprehension of "whole persons," even if only to deny their existence.

Like many exasperated individualisms, the unconscious of Deleuze succeeds in combining concrete impotence with the formidable theoretical imperialism. Like a super Pichrocole, the conquering and braggard king of Rabelais, it can assimilate almost anything, the whole universe if need be, all the while rejecting what solipsisms have always liked to reject, the existence of whole persons—including of course, you, me, and the rest of the world. But it does so very cleverly, with no obvious *ressentiment* and we are supposed to believe that no nasty *exclusion* is intended. If this unconscious acts as if I do not exist, I am not even allowed to feel rejected, the ultimate consolation of pleasurable morosity. Here is the philosophy truly suited to the anonymity of contemporary urban relations.

How can an unconscious said to be impersonal or transpersonal play a role analogous to that played by the person, self, and consciousness in the systems of the past? At the level of essences, the difference is insurmountable. But the difference of essences could mask, in the order of desire, a return of the same to which the various preachers and revivalists of desire are always firmly resolved to remain blind.

What is constant in all modern systems, whether predominantly conscious or unconscious, individualistic or antiindividualistic, is their aspect of abstract initiation, the impossible and obligatory conquest of some impalpable will-o'-the-wisp. This element reappears in *L'Anti-Oedipe*. The book is a real "trip," a new mystical quest that we must follow to the end if we are to become "successful schizophrenics." No one has yet gone "all the way," but there are those who depart and the countless crowd of those who remain. We have the impression that they were not invited. To the list of those who were traditionally excluded by modern thinkers, ostracized—perhaps I should say "disjuncted"—the wealthy, the strong, the successful, we must now add the psychoanalyst.

Once again the "horribles travailleurs" of Rimbaud, old acquaintances by now, are put to work. They are officially assigned the task of "breaking the wall of schizophrenia." It is in truth a question of inverting Freud's and turn the "wo *es* war soll *ich* werden" into the famous phrase: "where *I* was, the *id*, or perhaps the *flux*, must triumph."

The enterprise is not new, even when translated into a more or less psychoanalytical language. Surrealism is already an inversion of platonic mysticism partially applied to psychoanalysis. Any effort to situate *L'Anti-Oedipe* must certainly take surrealism into account. We can say in fact that if surrealism plunges one foot into the mystical unconscious it keeps the other one planted firmly in romantic egotism. It is thus an intermediary between the great voyage of *L'Anti-Oedipe* and all great voyages before. It carries all that we need to demonstrate that in spite of appearances all these abortive "trips" are really one and the same fiasco.

Before the arrival of individualism, the theory of imitation was present everywhere, in literature, education, and religious life. To excel in any activity was always to follow a model. The origin of individualism was not a disappearance of mimesis but its exasperation. As imitation became reciprocal everywhere, the model became an obstacle. Being conscious of its own enslavement, imitation became inadmissible. Thus, individualism arose in the context of a desire that had already reached a certain stage of mimetic exasperation, the stage where prohibitions disintegrate. This disintegration is particularly slow in our society, but rich in cultural creation of all sorts. As desire evolves, that is, as it falls deeper into the trap of its own double bind, it seems to justify itself, and these justifications only negatively reflect the real evolution of the process. The same process that I have set forth above is reproduced in our society, though in a manner at once very analogous and very different from that of primitive societies. In the primitive world, we must assume, for reasons that cannot be investigated here, that mimetic crises are very rapid and violent and that they fall quickly into the mechanism of the scapegoat victim and the restoration of a highly differentiated system.

All phenomena of "decoding" that constitute our world must be attributed to this same mimesis, a mimesis that becomes less and less regulated by prohibition, but, as if the sacrificial virtue in our society were almost inexhaustible, it is not completely unregulated because it is still ordered by its very disorder. Mimetic rivalry invades existence in forms that would be radically destructive in primitive societies, but that are incredibly productive in our own, even though they are accompanied by more and more severe tensions. Capitalism itself demands a mimetic free play that makes it inconceivable in a highly differentiated society.

The history of modern doctrines is part of this progress, of this slow evolution of desire toward delirium; hence, the rediscovery in Deleuze of many vestiges of anterior cultural forms that have been reinterpreted in terms of the delirious stance. These forms are nothing but a series of masks. When one of them successfully imposes itself, when it triumphs everywhere and becomes fashionable, it is necessarily exposed and made the object of a demystifying critique. This critique is at the same time a new undertaking of the same project, one that springs from a narrower base because it must take its own critical contribution into account. Thus, the history of the doctrines in question constitutes a series of strategic withdrawals, under the effect of a double bind that perpetually tightens because each repudiates its immediate predecessors only to propose a more implacable variant. Individualism and subjectivism chase themselves from the cultural scene. They take refuge in the most rarified layers of the cultural atmosphere or, to the contrary, they plunge into underground regions.

Then it is the "unconscious" that makes its appearance first in a critical form—psychoanalysis—then as an ideological rallying point, notably in *L'Anti-Oedipe*, where it becomes idealized as the only possible place for an ultraindividualistic claim.

I must include psychoanalysis at the heart of a process the motor of which, mimetic rivalry, is always criticized through the person of the rival, always misrecognized at the level of the observer himself. Polemics are always an effort to monopolize whatever remains of the sacred, to appropriate the sacrificial virtue that seems to belong to the other. Polemics stimulate the real displacements of sacrificial virtue, and these displacements permit psychoanalysis, as well as other forms, to play a pararitualistic role that, although more and more ephemeral and precarious each time, has never yet disappeared entirely.

L'Anti-Oedipe is visibly inscribed in this succession. Its own version of the "good" unconscious has the same air of moralizing intolerance and of terrorism that has always been characteristic of this kind of enterprise. Once vague, it seems to be growing more precise today. "Who would dare call law the fact that desire poses and develops its power?"[21] There are souls vile enough to pretend that desire could lack something. They dare "inject religion into the unconscious."[22] This discourse must be addressed to Freud himself, to Freud who, even though he invented the unconscious, is now charged with its defamation.

When they feel embarrassed by their own contradictions, the two authors raise their tone. They speak as though they had at their disposal some formidable red guard ready to go into action at their beck and call, and blindly devoted to the cause of the "molecular unconscious." All this bluster suggests that they hold what they call the *irrécupérable* in hand and will not release it. They fail to see that the *irrécupérable*, here as elsewhere, is identical to the principle of all recuperation, that is, of all ritualization. Thus, delirium would be the volcano of Empedocles itself, the supreme defiance of all attempts at "cultural exploitation." In reality, in this sort of affair there is no other cultural exploitation than that of the faithful. Human culture has not waited for *L'Anti-Oedipe* to make delirium a product of consumption. Look at the cults of possession described by Michel Leiris in his short work on the Ethiopians of Gondar.[23] It is here and not with the Ndembu of Victor Turner that we must seek the true ritual respondents to Deleuze's series of schizophrenic individuations.

All this does not lead to the conclusion that this exaggeration is purely rhetorical and that nothing is really taking place. The sacrificial virtue exhausts itself little by little and, since it is one with misrecognition, there truly is progress, but there is also a simultaneous rise in violence. We must ask which of the two progressions will overwhelm the other. The knowledge in question concerns violence and the play of sacrificial forms; it has nothing to do with an *absolute* knowledge of the Hegelian variety.

Each cultural form is founded on the repudiation of an anterior form, on the elimination of a certain positivity, that is, a misrecognition. The masks become increasingly livid, the rites more terrifying. Finally, all that remains is the infinite movement of difference deprived of all stability, the very movement of delirious polemics.

The philosophy of pure difference, without identity, pretends and effectively manages to extricate itself from certain mythic identities such as the self-identity of subject, divinity, and the Hegelian spirit. But this thought quickly exhausts its demystifying force. Being itself the result of the process we have just sketched out, it does not constitute a real rupture with the past; the authentic critical contribution still shelters a more ultimate form of misrecognition. By rejecting all identity and the principle of identity itself, Deleuze pretends to liberate himself from "western metaphysics." There were, no doubt, always metaphysical uses of identity. But can we conclude that the principle itself must be extirpated? What is metaphysical, the principle or its use? Is logic internal to metaphysics or does metaphysics attempt to perpetuate itself by repudiating all logic? Perhaps there are two sides to the exclusive emphasis on difference: the first, critical, is directed against metaphysical identities and the second is more metaphysical than ever, because it is aimed against the new use of identity made possible by symbolic disintegration, the identity with the other and not with the self, the mimetic reciprocity of the doubles.

Far from breaking with cultural tradition, the philosophy of difference constitutes its extreme and quintessential form. If there is a trait common to all cultures, from primitive religions to the contemporary counterculture, it is indeed the primacy of difference in the sense of a negation of reciprocities. For Deleuze and Guattari there is always a "real difference." From now on it must be situated in the delirium of madness, outside all cultural codes, because there is nothing else left to do, nothing else left to embrace, for all differences are dissolving, revealing their emptiness. The dying man can only appeal to the last signs of his own life, that is, the convulsions still belying death, but whose violence quickens its arrival. Everything we call *modern* is now in agony.

Thus, the schizophrenic foundations of *L'Anti-Oedipe* never stop revealing themselves as being more true, but true in the sense of the untruth of delirium. Just as we perceive in the Deleuzian unconscious the presence of elements borrowed from surrealism and German and

French Romanticism, we can easily discover in the cultural forms of recent centuries those elements already characteristic of the delirium embraced today. To appreciate this fully, we need only turn once again, not to certain thematic givens that the abstract and theoretical praises of madness often announced in embarrassing proximity of real and misunderstood madmen, Nerval next to Gautier, Artaud near Breton—and none can be sure of not repeating that misadventure—but rather, we must turn to the structural givens, to the preschizophrenic traits of exemplary personalities and portrait-models, to all the traits that are visibly shared by all the successive forms that polarize delirious mimesis.

Invariably original and spontaneous, the romantic hero alone escapes the uniformity growing heavier and heavier around him; always the hero of difference, he at times feels a deadly boredom in a universe where others so vulgarly amuse themselves. At other times on the contrary, he knows the rarest of exaltations in a world ruled by a hopeless apathy and monotony. He is always the man engaged in predictable unpredictability, in extraordinary ups and downs that give the impression of *déjà vu*. Yet he never questions the actual novelty of what he is experiencing. What is never interrogated is the modern creator's strange aptitude for generating symbols of alienation and division that become common to the multitude in the mini-rites of fashionability.

Just as delirium recapitulates the whole mimetic mechanism of which it is the outcome, *L'Anti-Oedipe* is a rather tired recapitulation of outmoded cultural forms. Thus, we must see in the reference to delirium, not an individual aberration but a predictable aberration of culture itself. It is the destiny of modern culture, of the modern end of all culture in the historical sense, to live all successive moments including delirium in relative lucidity so as to arrive at a true death of the cultural, which then should reveal its entire truth if our thought does not perish with it.

A book such as *L'Anti-Oedipe* would not be conceivable were it not for the impasse where cultural disciplines are trapped by thinking themselves unified around psychoanalysis, Marxism, or other pseudosciences, were it not for the cognitive nihilism resulting from our growing awareness of this failure. This state of affairs should be temporary. Once the mirage of the Oedipus complex is dissipated, once all illusion of difference is effaced, the identity of the doubles will become manifest and thought will be directed toward the new forms of totalization already offering themselves. Never in the movement of modern language has the enticement of incoherency overpowered the necessarily superior enticement of a new coherency.

Our intellectual fetishes conserve a semblance of reality only in function of a stabilized symbolic order, only as long as others remain who respect the prohibitions that we transgress, and only as long as there are nondelirious people who can be shocked by the dubious audacities of the Deleuzian delirium. The struggle for "real difference" still rests on the prestige of transgression, which itself depends on the ancient respect for prohibitions. The difference snatched and passed from here to there is the jewel that shines only on the innocent virgin, the forgotten Cinderella who received it from the good fairy. The beautiful treasure is transformed into ashes as soon as the rival sisters seek to appropriate it, when mimetic desire and conflictual reciprocity intervene.

For a regulated community, only a truly respected prohibition can define the sacred "beyond." Inheritor of the mythicoritual, modern thought perpetuates the "beyond." Every modern "revolt" remains metaphysical because it remains founded on valorized transgressions, the reality of prohibitions. "The stupidity of transgression," write Deleuze and Guattari most admirably, but how not to fall once more into the same stupidity, once we again begin preaching real difference, this time at the level of a sacralized delirium that we are trying to appropriate?

How to survive without prohibitions, without sacrificial misrecognition, without scapegoat victims? This is the real problem, and it is in order to *avoid* confronting it that our modern rituals of rebellion are perpetuated. To attach oneself to true diffence is to play once more the role of the great transgressor, to succumb again to false audacities; to sacrifice incipient lucidity to one more incestuous and sacred enthronement. We can hardly believe that the old machine can continue functioning much longer.

Must we convince ourselves that the prohibitions are still there, that around them powerful armies of psychoanalysts and priests stand watch, when in reality there are only lost and crippled men everywhere? Behind the ritualistic grudges against our "repressive society" is hidden the real obstacle, what we have sworn never to admit, the mimetic rival, the schizophrenic double.

NOTES

1. Gilles Deleuze and Felix Guattari, *L'Anti-Oedipe* (Paris: Editions de Minuit, 1972), pp. 137–38.
2. Ibid., p. 101.
3. Ibid., pp. 115–16.
4. Ibid., p. 87.

5. Ibid., p. 168.

6. Ibid., p. 145.

7. Ibid., p. 80.

8. René Girard, *Mensonge romantique et vérité romanesque* (Paris: Grasset, 1961); René Girard, *Deceit, Desire, and the Novel: Self and Other in Literary Structure*, trans. Yvonne Freccero (Baltimore: The Johns Hopkins University Press, 1965).

9. Deleuze and Guattari, *L'Anti-Oedipe*, p. 82.

10. Gilles Deleuze, *Proust et les Signes*, rev. ed. (Paris: Presses Universitaires de France, 1970), p. 134, note 4.

11. Gilles Deleuze, *Nietzsche et la Philosophie* (Paris: Presses Universitaires de France, 1962).

12. Deleuze and Guattari, *L'Anti-Oedipe*, p. 150.

13. Ibid., pp. 138–39.

14. Ibid., p. 167.

15. Ibid., p. 144.

16. Jacques Derrida, "La Pharmacie de Platon," in *La Dissémination* (Paris: Seuil, 1972), pp. 211–13, note 8.

17. René Girard, *La Violence et le sacré* (Paris: Grasset, 1972); René Girard, *Violence and the Sacred*, trans. Patrick Gregory (Baltimore: The Johns Hopkins University Press, 1977).

18. Luc de Heusch, *Essais sur le symbolisme de l'inceste royal en Afrique* (Brussels: Université Libre, 1958), pp. 61–62.

19. Deleuze and Guattari, *L'Anti-Oedipe*, p. 247. "Tels les jeunes chiens du palais trop prompts à boire l'eau de verset, et qui ne cessent de crier: le signifiant, vous n'avez pas atteint le signifiant, vous en restez aux signifiés! Le signifiant, il n'y a que ça qui les fait jouir."

20. Ibid., p. 61.

21. Ibid., p. 133.

22. Ibid., p. 68.

23. Michel Leiris, *La Possession et ses aspects théatraux chex les Ethiopiens de Gondar* (Paris: Plon, 1958).

6

Perilous Balance:
A Comic Hypothesis

Molière's *Bourgeois gentilhomme* is an avid seeker after culture. A wealthy man, he turns his house into his own private university. The whole affair is a professor's dream except for the tiresome presence of that good natured but incredible philistine, M. Jourdain, everybody's benefactor and only student.

At one point three teachers argue heatedly about the merits of their respective disciplines. According to the dancing master, music would not be much without dancing. According to the music master, dancing, without music, would not exist at all. According to the fencing master, even musicians and dancers need good fencing occasionally, in order not to cease to exist.

In the midst of the fracas, a fourth man appears, the philosopher in residence. The sorry spectacle presented by this interdisciplinary committee moves him to philosophical grief. With a learned reference to Seneca's treatise on anger, he steps into the midst of the quarrel to put an end to it. He is sure to succeed because all the arguments in his view are equally inane. All three crafts are really on a par, at the bottom of the scale of learning, the top of which philosophy alone is worthy to occupy.

This word from above is rejected with indignation. Now blind with rage, the philosopher comes to blows with his three colleagues. Thus, the attempted mediation turns the three-cornered dispute into a four-cornered battle, with the would-be mediator as one more participant.

I am always impressed by the similarity between this scene, so typical of a certain type of comedy, and what might be called the dynamics of tragedy, in no less a play than *Oedipus Rex*. All three masculine characters in that play, Oedipus, Creon, and Tiresias, are invited in turn to master a situation that is vaguely described as "the plague" and that we may assume to be conflictual in character. Oedi-

This essay first appeared in *MLN* 87 (December 1972): 811–26.

pus comes first; he has solved the riddle of the sphinx: no problem is too difficult for him. More modest outwardly, Creon feels no less complacent underneath. He is just back from Delphi and he brings an oracle that cannot fail to set everything right.

As for Tiresias, his resemblance to the philosopher in Molière is the most striking of all. By the time he appears, the Theban plague is truly revealed as a situation of internal dissension, notably between Creon and Oedipus himself. Tiresias is so great a prophet that he will not respond to the call unless things get completely out of hand. As he enters, the chorus chants: "Here comes the only man who carries truth in his bosom." No wonder he sounds a little pompous.

Oedipus immediately flies into a rage. He always behaves that way, we are told, when things do not come out exactly the way he wants. But the other two also fly into a rage and they are not supposed to be prone to anger. Not one, this time, but three would-be mediators are drawn into the conflict they presume to mediate. Discord seems to have a power of its own that will assert itself. especially against those who foolishly assume they can dominate its violence.

Comedy and tragedy, in these two examples, are very close to each other. The basic pattern of a presumption that rebounds against the presumptuous is constantly repeated. If this closeness is real, why are the effects of tragedy so different from the effects of comedy? When we watch the first, or more generally what is called "heavy" drama, our reaction may be such that we will shed if not real at least metaphorical tears. When we watch the second, our reaction is laughter. Laughter and tears are opposed as two contraries, as two emotions that are very different from each other.

Tears and laughter are both physical phenomena; at the physical level, the comparison is easy. It will quickly reveal that the opposition between the laughter and tears is grossly exaggerated, or rather, like so many cultural oppositions, it is founded on a common basis, a fact that is generally overlooked when considerations of literary genres and literary technique prevail. When we ask the question, "what is laughter?" outside of this narrow literary context, we must uncover that still hidden basis or else the scope of our answer will be very limited.

Physiologists would say that the normal function of tears is to lubricate the eyes. Tears are shed in quantities larger than normal on two occasions primarily. One is the emotional state just mentioned, induced by events interpreted as "sad," real or represented; the other is the presence in the eye of some foreign particle. a speck of dust, for example, that causes irritation. This purely physical crying is obviously intended to wash away the foreign invader, to expel it from the organ it has no business to irritate.

In his *Poetics*, Aristotle uses the word *katharsis* to describe the effect of tragedy upon the audience. The word means both religious purification and medical purgation. A *kathartic* medicine purges the body of its bad "humors." In the interminable debate on *katharsis*, many people hold to the view that Aristotle was oblivious to the religious and even medical uses of the word, that he was inventing a purely cultural *katharsis* that should be interpreted separately from any other mode, religious or medical, of that mysterious operation.

The question of what Aristotle "really meant" is a moot one, but it is difficult to deny that tears, as the major physical consequence of tragedy upon the beholder, provide very strong supporting evidence in favor of a stubbornly literal interpretation of the *kathartic* theory. When the human body reacts to tragic representation by crying, it seems to agree with Aristotle. The eye has nothing physical to wash away, no speck of dust to bother with, but this organ is nevertheless acting as if something had to be expelled. A demand for expulsion must exist somewhere in the mind/body complex since this organ, which is a kind of instrument, is responding to that demand. The fact that tears are not suited to do the job is no valid objection. The eye is acting *metaphorically*. When a demand is heard, the body quite frequently acts as a whole; several organs will answer the call that are really unable to perform the job but are nevertheless trying to help. The apparent overreaction may indicate something about the nature of the demand.

I am not going back to William James and his physiological theory. I do not view the body as the origin of the emotion but, more conventionally, as an *accompaniment*, almost in the musical sense. Tragic sentiment is accompanied by tears, just as a soloist, here invisible and unheard, at least by us, is accompanied by the piano.

The defenders of cultural autonomy have never come up with any interesting suggestion as to the origin and meaning of their purely esthetic *katharsis*. Not only is there no foundation for their claim, but their arbitrary separation deprives us of the only real clue we have for the interpretation of Aristotle's theory. Tears suggest that tragic emotion really has something to do with a process of purification and evacuation that is certainly present in the medical *katharsis* and that I strongly believe to be present in the religious *katharsis*. Ideas of religious purification are inseparable from sacrifice and other forms of ritual that always refer, in my view, to an original scapegoating process, to a holy lynching truly capable of restoring the order and peace of the city because it reunifies all the citizens against a single victim.[1] The ritual expulsion of this victim is the expulsion of violence itself.

Going back to laughter, now, we will note that it includes tears as an integral part of itself. That fact is often minimized or brushed aside. Our desire to oppose laughter and tears as two contraries makes us emphasize only those aspects of laughter that appear to differentiate the two. Academic considerations are less important here than what we might call the modern *praxis* of laughter. Modern man is constantly pretending to laugh when he has really nothing to laugh about. Laughter is the only socially acceptable form of *katharsis*. As a result, there is a lot that passes for laughter that is not laughter at all: polite laughter, sophisticated laughter, public-relations laughter. All that false laughter often increases the tension it is supposed to relieve and it naturally includes no genuine, involuntary physical reactions, notably tears.

Many physical symptoms of laughter are easier to mimic than tears, but they also become involuntary and compulsive when real laughter is present. The entire body is shaking convulsively; the air is rapidly expelled from the respiratory track through reflex motions analogous to coughing and sneezing. All these reactions have functions similar to crying. Here again the body acts *as if* there were physical objects to expel. The only difference is that more organs are involved.

The closest thing to a purely natural and physical laughter must be the body's response to a tickling sensation. In terms of sheer intensity, this response seems out of proportion with the feebleness of the stimulus, but it may well be appropriate to the real nature of the yet unidentified threat. In conditions of natural hostility, an urgent and deadly menace, a snake bite, for instance, might very well be preceded by no warning at all except for a little tickle. The fact that the stimulus is unknown and that it cannot be located with precision, at least immediately, increases the intensity of the reaction.

The protective nature of this reaction is also revealed by the extreme sensitivity to tickling of those parts of the body that are particularly vulnerable and/or usually protected, either by other parts of the body, like the armpits or the inside of the thighs, or by clothing, or by a combination of both, like the soles of our feet, often especially ticklish among people used to wearing shoes and socks.

Laughter, in other words, especially in its least "cultural" forms, seems to be asserting, exactly like tears, that it must get rid of something; there is more of that something, and laughter must get rid of it more promptly than mere crying. If the body is the orchestra, more instruments have joined in the accompaniment of the invisible and inaudible soloist. We may also note that when crying becomes intense, it turns into sobbing and, as such, it resembles laughter more and more. Someone whose laughter is beyond control, who is really laughing and no longer pretending, is said to be sobbing with laughter.

Between tears and laughter, therefore, the difference is not in nature but in degree. And the real paradox is in the way the pluses and minuses are distributed. Contrary to the commonsense view, the crisis element is more acute in laughter than in tears. Laughter seems closer than tears to a paroxysm that would turn it into actual convulsions, to a climactic experience of rejection and expulsion. Laughter is further along toward a total negative response to a threat considered overwhelming.

What kind of threat are both tragedy and comedy trying to ward off? What is it they are trying to expel? There are some famous answers to that question, but I will look for my own in a twin reading of *Le Bourgeois gentilhomme* and *Oedipus Rex*. In that reading, practically no difference remains between the comedy and the tragedy. Why? I emphasized a pattern that keeps recurring at the beginning of the play. I cannot do that without minimizing the differences between the characters; I can do that only at the expense of individual features that critics usually consider important. In that reading, Oedipus, Creon, and Tiresias turn out to be more or less identical, just as in *Le Bourgeois gentilhomme*, the philosopher turns out to be more or less identical to his three colleagues.

This emphasis upon recurring patterns gives *Oedipus Rex* a slightly parodic flavor, and immediately tragedy evaporates. Tragedy demands that we take the individuality of heroes seriously. Even though their "destinies" may be in the hands of the gods and their "freedom" curtailed, the individual heroes do remain the true center of reference. This is no longer so in comedy, where recurrence and other structural effects are emphasized. The vengeance of the gods, the meanness of destiny, and the malice of the "human condition" may well crush the individual in tragedy, but not to the extent they do in the case of comic patterns that are truly "structural" in the sense that they dominate individual reactions and fully account for them. Individual projects are invariably thwarted by these same patterns and individual thinking is unable to take them into account. The structural patterns of the comic, therefore, deny the sovereignty of the individual more radically than either god or destiny. As they begin to emerge, audience interest in the hero must necessarily weaken as it shifts to the pattern itself.

Is the pattern really there, in tragedy as well as in comedy? The pattern is really there; it is already there in the myths that are the common source of both tragedy and comedy. Certain myths have always been considered appropriate both to tragedy and comedy. There were comic and tragic *Amphytrions*, for instance. Many of Shakespeare's comedies play openly with patterns that are present but less visible in tragedies. Good literary criticism is often a little comic, because only half-visible patterns become fully visible in it. Great writers, great novelists in particular, often become their own parodists in their later works and they develop a comic vein because they are their own best critics. They bring out more fully the patterns of earlier work; they express their obsessions more completely, as Charles Mauron has shown so well.

Racine's tragedies deal mostly with passion. As soon as it is suggested that the lack of reciprocity in the love relationship is too constant to be due to "destiny" or to the mystery of personal choice, as soon as it appears that a law is at work, psychological or whatever, tragedy is annihilated. It is almost impossible to summarize *Andromaque* without satirical effect. The simplest enunciation of the relationship between the four major characters reveals a structural pattern. Orestes loves Hermione, who does not love him. Hermione loves Pyrrhus, who does not love her. Pyrrhus loves Andromaque, who does not love him. Andromaque loves Hector, who cannot love anymore, being dead. Were it not for that death, the chain of nonreciprocal passion might go on *ad infinitum*. And it does go on, as a matter of fact, in the other plays of Racine.

If we convince ourselves that Racine's heroes, for whatever reason, cannot experience what they call passion unless their desire is thwarted, if we see in them the dupes of some hidden mechanism, we can no longer take these passions seriously *as passions*. For one thing, all these passions have become identical; they cannot be read as the exceptional, unique sentiments that tragedy demands.

An individual is trying to assert upon his environment what he takes to be his own rule. We laugh when this pretention is suddenly and spectacularly shattered. Impersonal forces are taking over. In the crudest forms of comedy, these impersonal forces may simpy be those of gravity. The man who loses his balance on the ice is comic in proportion either to his self-assurance or to his prudence, neither of which, however extreme, succeeds in preserving *son équilibre avec sa dignité*.

There are worse obstacles than gravity to our satisfactory handling of the world. Other human beings and we, ourselves, constitute a more formidable stumbling block, the more stubborn, as a matter of fact, when it appears to have been cleared, when the road to complete mastery and graceful triumph seems to lie wide open in front of us. The Racinian heroes, for instance, may appear in a comic light. They, too, are the victims of impersonal forces that they do not perceive even though they are one with their desires. The three wise men of *Oedipus Rex* and the philosopher in Molière also fall prey to impersonal forces that, paradoxically enough, are the forces of human relations.

What does happen to all these people? We cannot attribute their downfall to a purely personal presumption. They all do the same thing. There should be an interpretation valid for all of them. We cannot talk about a "tragic flaw" in the case of Oedipus and laugh at the philosopher on the grounds that he is only acting "true to type," that he conforms to the natural pomposity of his breed.

When all our characters arrive on the stage, something already is going on that is in the nature of a conflict—the plague in *Oedipus Rex*, the dispute of the three teachers in *Le Bourgeois gentilhomme*. Eagerness to arbitrate the conflict is rooted in the illusion of superiority created by a pure spectator status. The philosopher is exposed to ridicule because of this late arrival. We must not even think of him as a philosopher first and as a latecomer second. His status as a philosopher is rooted in his status as a spectator. The philosophical attitude depends entirely on the type of observation a late appearance makes possible. Hegel compares philosophy to an owl that begins to fly at dusk. As he contemplates the wreckage left by his predecessors, the philosopher cannot help feeling superior.

The spectator's position is both one of austere moral pessimism and satiric glee over human foibles. The spectacle of human frailty has an exhilarating as well as a depressing effect upon the moralist. Even after the battle, the philosopher wants to think of his colleagues as primarily comic characters; as a vengeance against them, he plans to write a comic work, a satire "in the style of Juvenal." This spectator's position is not his only, but our own as well, since we are the spectators of the play. When we laugh at the dispute of the first three men, the philosopher is with us and we are with him; our reading of the scene is exactly the same as his.

The only difference is that our spectator status is a permanent one. We cannot step foolishly into the battle, as the three teachers have done before and as the philosopher is now doing. We are protected, not by some innate superiority but by the fact we are only watching a play. Our own illusions can never be revealed for what they are, as one more lie, as another incitement to feel "above the battle" and to volunteer as an arbitrator. We will never know if we would resist that insidious temptation because the stage is only a stage.

We are really laughing at something that could and, in a sense, should happen to anyone who laughs, not excluding ourselves. This, I believe, clearly shows the nature of the threat, unperceived yet present, that laughter is always warding off, the still unidentified object it has to expel. The man who laughs is just about to be enveloped into the pattern of which his victim is already a part; as he laughs he both welcomes and rejects the perception of the structure into which the object of his laughter is already caught; he welcomes it insofar as it is someone else who is caught in it and he tries to keep it away from himself. The pattern is never an individual one and it tends to close in upon the man who laughs. We understand, now, why laughter is more of a crisis than tears; the pattern is much more visible in the comic than in the tragic; the threat to the autonomy of the spectator is more urgent and serious. We understand, too, why the inclusion of a laughing spectator is a major procédé of comic writers. As this spectator laughs, he falls into the very trap that has already swallowed his victim and he becomes laughable in his turn.

The loss of autonomy and self-possession that is present in all forms of comic must be present, somehow, in laughter itself. Laughter, in other words, must never be very different from whatever causes it. Scenes in which the laughing spectator is included are invariably circular. The culprit is getting his just deserts. This retributive justice is no idealistic illusion; it is the reality of the structure. He who laughs last laughs best. The simplest forms of comedy show clearly this equalizing effect of laughter, which never fails to be present whenever he who is laughed at and he who laughs are not separated by some artificial barrier, such as the barrier between the stage and the audience in a theater.

A man falls on the ice; also on the ice is another man, who laughs so hard that he loses his balance and brings about his own fall. The second man is funnier than the first. A third one might be funnier still, unless of course, it is myself. As the scene keeps being repeated it reveals a strange and remarkable continuity between the essence of the comic and laughter itself. All the scenes we have mentioned so far are scenes in which the comic possibilities of laughter are already exploited, as in Molière, or readily exploitable, as in Sophocles.

I stated earlier that physical laughter is intended to repulse an aggression from the outside, to shut off the body against a possible invasion. But the near convulsions of laughter, if they continue for a while, will ultimately result in a disintegration of that self-control they are supposed to preserve. Real laughter makes us physically weak; it reduces us to near impotence.

As an assertion of superiority, in the more intellectual forms of the comic, laughter really means a denial of reciprocity. The man who makes me laugh has already tried and failed to deny reciprocity between himself and others. As I laugh, I mimic and repeat the whole process I have been watching, both the attempt to establish mastery and its failure, both the dizzy feeling of superiority and the loss of balance that comes with the dizziness, the disintegration of self-control that is always creeping upon us in the wild reactions and uncontrolled convulsions of laughter itself.

Reciprocity is reestablished through the very actions that are meant to undo it. Laughter becomes a part of the process; that is why, in itself, it can be funny. There comes a point when we no longer know if we laugh "with" or "against" the man who is already laughing. We only say, at that stage, that laughter is "infectious."

Bergson, in Le Rire, defined the comic as "du mécanique plaqué sur du vivant," as a mechanical overlay upon the fluidity and continuity of "life," as something jerky, discontinuous, and maladjusted being substituted for the perfect mobility and grace of what he called "élan vital." Bergson, of course, was the philosopher of this "élan vital." Thus, all philosophies appeared a little funny to him, except his own. Such is the case, assuredly, with most philosophers.

The Bergsonian definition of "le mécanique" includes many aspects of what has been called here "structural." What is missing, in my view, from Bergson's analysis is not a word, which has no importance whatever, but a full realization of "le mécanique" as something more than an individual or even a collective disgrace. In its major manifestations, "le mécanique" is only the outward consequence, esthetic or intellectual, of a formidable "problem" that the philosopher never really tackles. Living as he does in an age of "individualism," Bergson cannot see that the comic is rooted in the ultimate failure of all individualism, at least at a certain level. There is an element of reciprocity in human relations that will keep reasserting itself regardless of what we do; reciprocity will be there whether we welcome or reject it, for the rejection itself will be reciprocated. The reciprocity that is not welcome is the reciprocity of conflict, the unexpected reciprocity that will always have, both in its physical and intellectual manifestations, that jerky, discontinuous, and disharmonious quality that Bergson so aptly recognized in the comic.

Bergson, most of the time, seems to place the man who laughs squarely on the side of the "élan vital," on the side of the gods, in other words. But laughter itself, about which Bergson says very little in spite of the title of his book, is no less mechanical and convulsive than its own cause. The point had already been made by Baudelaire, who compares the man who laughs to a jack-in-the-box. In his few admirable pages on De l'essence du rire, Baudelaire clearly perceives the difference between the mocker and the mocked as a disintegrating and vanishing difference, as creeping identity. "What could be more deplorable," he writes, "than weakness rejoicing at weakness?"[2]

As we try to assert our independence through laughter, that laughter becomes uncontrollable and independence is already slipping away from us. This ambiguous nature accounts for the very diverse roles that laughter can play with diverse people at diverse moments in their lives. Laughter can be intelligent and sensitive as well as cruel and stupid.

Most laughter, of course, is safely ensconced in a well-protected illusion of superiority, but the slippery nature of this bizarre affection, its shaky and shaken superiority, can make it serve very different ends. It can weaken as well as strengthen the barriers that separate each of us from the others. Laughter will erupt when we see our long-cherished prejudices confirmed and also when we see them finally crumble into the dust. Baudelaire is often accused of entertaining too pessimistic a view of laughter, but he is among the few who recognize the existence of a truly superior laughter, the one that welcomes its own downfall. Unlike so many of our peevish "demystifiers," he was not building intellectual cages in which to imprison everyone but himself. He read laughter in a Pascalian light, as a sign of contradiction pointing both to the "infinite misery" and the "infinite greatness" of man.

The fact remains, however, that most people, or rather man in general, if I can still use the phrase, have very little to laugh about. If laughter is really the slippery affair I describe, if we enjoy in it our last dizzy instant of illusion before disaster strikes, why do we keep laughing as we do, why do we like laughter, why is it pleasurable?

One reason, of course, must be that we are ambivalent toward everything we call our "self," our "ego," our "identity," our "superiority." All this is both the ultimate prize we are trying to win, the most precious treasure to which we keep adding tirelessly, like busy ants, and a most frightful burden we are desperately eager to unload, preferably on the back of someone else.

Since we can never unload that burden permanently, we are constantly looking for temporary release; laughter provides some. In laughter, for a few brief moments we seem to have the best of two incompatible worlds. Our feeling of control and autonomy is increased as we see others lose theirs and slip into the pattern. And as we, ourselves, begin to "come loose," the feeling of rigidity and tension that goes with self-control is relaxed.

Laughter can be compared to a drug, and notably to alcohol, which gives at first a feeling of heightened control, of easy triumph over insuperable obstacles. A slight tipsiness is pleasurable, a little drinking will make us laugh; more will bring vertigo and nausea.

Why do we rarely if ever get that feeling of nausea and sickness, even when our laughter seems to go on forever? How can we have a "good laugh" and come out unscathed? The reason, obviously, is that our laughter is in the hands of entrepreneurs, working as amateurs or as professionals, who make it their business to make us laugh. These people provide us with exactly the right amount of the drug, neither too much nor too little. They see to it, in other words, that the exact conditions are fulfilled that make laughter possible. If there were no such entrepreneurs we would laugh very little and only very briefly.

What are these conditions? A man will not laugh, we found out, unless there is an actual threat to his ability to control his environment and the people in it, even his own thoughts and his own desires. A man will not laugh, however, if that threat becomes too real. The conditions necessary for laughter are therefore contradictory. The threat must be both overwhelming and nil; the danger of being absorbed into the pattern that has already devoured the victims of our laughter must be both immediate and nonexistent. In order to "have a good laugh," we must always come out "on top" even as we are constantly threatened to "go under."

The main recipe, of course, for fulfilling these two contradictory conditions is to have the comedian cleverly sacrifice himself on the altar of his audience's vanity. Any clown who knows something about his profession is fully aware that people will laugh only at his own expense or at the expense of a third party. But this is not enough. We discovered earlier that, in order to laugh freely, the audience must be completely cut off from the object of its laughter. If I, myself, am standing on the ice, I will not laugh freely at the man who falls on it. The isolation of the stage is only one of the protective devices that give us that pure spectator status necessary to produce laughter. The distance that separates us from foreign customs or from the distant past also makes it possible for us to laugh with impunity, therefore to laugh with abandonment.

This is not yet enough. In a culture where people have a good deal of imagination, where they "put themselves" easily in the place of others, they will not laugh unless the cancellation of personal will by impersonal forces is limited to rather minor consequences. The victim must suffer only unpleasantness; if a major catastrophe is involved, people will not laugh anymore, especially if the victim is felt to be "close."

The conditions of laughter are so complex and difficult that they would rarely be met if they were not met artificially. There are people who make it their business to meet them, sometimes through means so complex and so technical that the reality of the two contradictory conditions we have just defined becomes obvious. This fact can be verified easily in those cases where there is no sacrificial victim to spark our laughter and put the necessary distance between ourselves and the impersonal forces that are taking over, when we, ourselves, or rather our bodies, are the prime object of our amusement.

What I have in mind, here, is a particular kind of chiefly physical laughter, the one that is derived from dangers narrowly avoided, from accidents barely missed, from hairpin turns taken at speeds greater than prudence allows. All this brings joy to some people; more people, however, will enjoy such experiences only when they are simulated, in carnival rides, for instance, when they are duplicated with a great degree of realism and a reasonable degree of safety. Only when physical risks are minimal, even though they appear very great, will the fact of being violently shaken and thrown in all directions not only bring pleasure to some people but provoke their actual laughter.

We can see very clearly, here, that the production of laughter demands a threat that is both massive and nil. Thus, the two contradictory prerequisites are present both in the crudest and in the more intellectual forms of laughter. The only difference is that, in the first case, the impersonal forces that threaten the autonomy of man are purely natural and physical, whereas, in the second case, they stem from human relations themselves; they spell the inability of any individual to control these relations completely.

In tickling, which I have described as one of the most primitive, if not the most primitive form of laughter, we may discover yet another indication that the two contradictory conditions of laughter defined above may be universal. An interesting fact about tickling is that, like other forms of laughter, it can be artificially induced. When tickling is, so to speak, engineered by another human being, it produces a reaction much stronger than natural tickling and much closer to real laughter.

There is a strategy to artificial tickling that closely resembles the strategy of offensive warfare. One must not aim solely at a well-defined area of the body, however ticklish it may be. A precise aim would make it too easy for the tickled individual to locate the threat and to protect himself. In order to tickle efficiently, one must move rapidly from one area to the next, shifting targets constantly so that protection becomes impossible. In military warfare, similarly, success will go to the side with enough mobility to multiply its strikes and make them so rapid and so distant from each other that they cannot be countered.

There is a major difference, however. In tickling, no real aggressive action or intention is present. If such an intention is even suspected, laughter will not result. The threat to the body must be many-sided, the assault must be vigorous, even overwhelming, but, at the same time, there must be no threat at all, there must be no assault at all.

Tickling is mock total warfare on the other's body. The prohibition that the tickler must never transgress will usually include overtly sexual gestures, but it is not primarily sexual. It bears essentially on the *real* violence that tickling constantly mimics but never practices.

The tickling reaction is not as easy a prey for Freudian imperialism as it superficially appears. There is something definitively nonsexual about tickling, even antisexual. The sexual organs, even though they are usually protected and vulnerable, are not particularly ticklish, and properly so. Feeling tickled in response to an openly sexual initiative is normally resented, being interpreted as a form of rejection, the more deep seated for being involuntary. Tickling a potential partner for sexual purposes is, of course, a common practice. It makes it possible to break down physical resistance without incurring hostility. The nonsexual connotations of tickling make it particularly serviceable as a means of sexual seduction. Tickling will permit bodily contacts that, in spite of their intimacy, deny up to a point any immediate sexual intention on the part of the assailant.

I hope I will not be misinterpreted if I say that comedy is intellectual tickling. More than any other type of esthetic representation, it deprives us of the autonomy to which we cling and yet it does not deprive us of anything at all. When offensive thrusts are not neutralized through one device or another, they are never pursued to the bitter end. We would not laugh if we did not feel that whatever makes us laugh can be shrugged off at any time, that we can always laugh it off. A great comic writer does not avoid "ticklish" subjects, he will not stay away from "touchy" problems. He knows, however, like the tickler, that he must "use the light touch" and he alone knows how to use it. He knows where he must stop; he alone can give the rug on which we stand a tug strong enough to startle us into laughter without really pulling it from under our feet and sending us head over heels.

There is something profoundly subversive in all true comedy. One might say that Molière's laughter is anti-Cartesian, because it reveals as false the pretentions of Descartes's *cogito*. No philosophy in the classical sense can understand laughter or account for it because philosophy tries to establish our mastery as human beings or individuals on unshakable grounds.

Today we live in an entirely different world. The great modern prophets always have the same message in slightly different forms. Our actions, our thoughts, our desires are entirely dominated by patterns not of our own making, which we never read correctly. This is true of the natural scientist, this is true of the social scientist, this is true of thinkers like Marx, Nietzsche, or Freud. These last three, in particular, work in areas from which earlier comic writers drew much of their material. Before the nineteenth century, the relations between people of various cultures or different social and economic levels, the relations between servants and masters, for instance, were a staple of comedy. So were the sexual fumblings of younger and older people. Marx, Nietzsche, and Freud have certainly tried and often succeeded in taking the fun out of all that.

Nous avons changé tout cela. Freud, in particular, has introduced his fateful *slip* into former puns, jokes, *calembours*, and other *mots d'esprit*; he has turned the whole domain of wit into the object of a grave and continuous debate.

To say that this state of affairs is not "funny" does not suffice; this world attempts to take away from us all future possibilities of laughter. No illusion of human autonomy can be shattered, since none is supposed to remain. But this one-sided interpretation may well be another egotistical illusion.

Modern man's extreme humility is strangely coupled with the greatest pride of all times. As we discover the unknown forces that shape our destinies, they are supposed to come at least partly under our control. Every new discovery gives us new manipulative powers over our environment and our fellow men. We are constantly told, therefore, on the one hand that we are absolute nonentities, and on the other that a world is being created that will be entirely dominated by human will. One fact is always left out of account in these predictions, the fact that there is no such thing as a unified human will. Men are no more able to dominate their own relationships than they ever were. The formidable ambitions and realizations of modern man, thus, are extremely fragile; they are at the mercy not of nature or destiny but of those same "impersonal forces" that turn all the characters in *Le Bourgeois Gentilhomme* into puppets with no one to pull the strings.

In a sense, therefore, possibilities for comedy have never been greater. The stakes, however, are so high, and the uncertainties so great that our laughter cannot be as complacent and secure as it once was. Never before has the precarious, unstable, and "nervous" nature of laughter been so much in evidence. When we consider the type of comic we have in our contemporary world, we may well think that this age is adding, or rather revealing, a new dimension to Molière's famous words about laughter and the creation of comedy:

C'est une étrange entreprise que de faire rire les honnêtes gens.

NOTES

1. See René Girard, "Dionysos et la genèse violente du sacré," in *Poétique*, no. 3, 1970. The topic is developed in René Girard, *La Violence et le sacré* (Paris: Grasset, 1972); René Girard, *Violence and the Sacred*, trans. Patrick Gregory (Baltimore: The Johns Hopkins University Press, 1977).

2. Charles Baudelaire, *De l'Essence du rire*, in *Oeuvres complètes*, ed. Y.-G. Le Dantec (Paris: Gallimard, 1961), p. 980. My translation.

7

The Plague in
Literature and Myth

The plague is found everywhere in literature. It belongs to the epic
with Homer, to tragedy with *Oedipus Rex*, to history with Thucydides,
to the philosophical poem with Lucretius. The plague can serve as
background to the short stories of Boccaccio's *Decameron*; there are
fables about the plague, notably La Fontaine's "Les Animaux malades
de la peste"; there are novels, such as Manzoni's *I Promessi Sposi* and
Camus's *La Peste*. The theme spans the whole range of literary
and even nonliterary genres, from pure fantasy to the most positive and
scientific accounts. It is older than literature—much older, really, since
it is present in myth and ritual in the entire world.

The subject appears too vast for a brief exploration. Undoubtedly, a
descriptive enumeration of literary and mythical plagues would be of
little interest: there is a strange uniformity to the various treatments of
the plague, not only literary and mythical but also scientific and non-
scientific, of both past and present. Between the matter-of-fact, even
statistical account of Defoe in his *Journal of the Plague Year* and the
near hysteria of Artaud in *Le Théâtre et la peste*, the differences, at
close range, turn out to be minor. It would be exaggerated to say that
plague descriptions are all alike, but the similarities may well be more
intriguing than the individual variations. The curious thing about these
similarities is that they ultimately involve the very notion of the similar.
The plague is universally presented as a process of undifferentiation, a
destruction of specificities.

This destruction is often preceded by a reversal. The plague will turn
the honest man into a thief, the virtuous man into a lecher, the prosti-
tute into a saint. Friends murder and enemies embrace. Wealthy men
are made poor by the ruin of their business. Riches are showered upon
paupers who inherit in a few days the fortunes of many distant rela-
tives. Social hierarchies are first transgressed, then abolished. Political

This essay first appeared in *Texas Studies in Literature and Language* 15 (Special
Classics Issue 1974): 883–50.

and religious authorities collapse. The plague makes all accumulated knowledge and all categories of judgment invalid. It was traditionally believed that the plague attacked the strong and young in preference to the weak and old, the healthy rather than the chronically ill. Modern authorities do not believe that great epidemics really singled out any particular individuals or categories. The popular belief must have arisen from the fact that it is more surprising and shocking to see the death of the young and healthy than of the old and the sick. The scientific view, it must be noted, fits the eternal ethos of the plague just as well and better than the popular tradition. The distinctiveness of the plague is that it ultimately destroys all forms of distinctiveness. The plague overcomes all obstacles, disregards all frontiers. All life, finally, is turned into death, which is the supreme undifferentiation. Most written accounts insist monotonously on this leveling of differences. So does the medieval *danse macabre*, which, of course, is inspired by the plague.

This process of undifferentiation makes sense, obviously, and poses no special problem in the sociological sphere. The belief that a great plague epidemic can bring about a social collapse is not difficult to accept or irrational in any way; it can be based on positive observation. At the beginning of the modern age, when plague epidemics had not yet disappeared and the spirit of scientific investigation was already awakened, texts can be found that clearly distinguish the medical plague from its social consequences and yet continue to see a similarity. The French surgeon Ambroise Paré, for instance, writes:

At the outbreak of the plague, even the highest authorities are likely to flee, so that the administration of justice is rendered impossible and no one can obtain his rights. General anarchy and confusion then set in and that is the worst evil by which the commonwealth can be assailed; *for that is the moment when the dissolute bring another and worse plague into the town.* [emphasis mine][1]

This sequence of events is perfectly positive and rational. The reverse sequence is no less so. A social upheaval can bring about conditions favorable to an outbreak of the plague. Historians still argue whether the Black Death was a cause or a consequence of the social upheavals in the fourteenth century.

Between the plague and social disorder there is a reciprocal affinity, but it does not completely explain the confusion of the two that prevails not only in innumerable myths but in a good number of literary plagues, from ancient times to contemporary culture. The Greek mythical plague not only kills men but provokes a total interruption of all cultural and natural activities; it causes the sterility of women and cattle and prevents the fields from yielding crops. In many parts of the world, the words we translate as "plague" can be viewed as a generic label for a variety of ills that affect the community as a whole and threaten or seem to threaten the very existence of social life. It may be inferred from various signs that interhuman tensions and disturbances often play the principal role.

In the passage just quoted, Paré separates what primitive thought unites—the medical and social components of the mythical plague. His language, however, is interesting. The social components are described as *another and worse plague*. Anarchy is a plague; in a sense, it is even more of a plague than the disease itself. The former unity is broken, and yet it is remembered and preserved in the stylistic effect of using the same word for two distinct and yet curiously inseparable phenomena. The medical plague has become a metaphor for the social plague; it belongs to what we call literature.

Judging from the role of the plague in Western literature up to the present, this metaphor is endowed with an almost incredible vitality, in a world where the plague and epidemics in general have disappeared almost altogether.[2] Such vitality would be unthinkable, of course, if the social "plague" were not always with us, as fear or as reality, in some form or other. This fact is not enough, however, to account for the more obscure and persistent aspects of the metaphoric configuration as well as for what appears to be the real need it fulfills with a great many writers. Indeed, an analysis of significant texts reveals definite analogies between the plague, or rather all great epidemics, and the social phenomena, real or imagined, that are assimilated to them. One such text belongs to Dostoevski's *Crime and Punishment*. Raskolnikov has a dream during a grave illness that occurs just before his final change of heart, at the end of the novel. He dreams of a world-wide plague that affects people's relationship with each other. No specifically medical symptoms are mentioned. It is human interaction that breaks down, and the entire society gradually collapses.

He dreamt that the whole world was condemned to a terrible new strange plague that had come to Europe from the depths of Asia. . . . Some new sorts of microbes were attacking the bodies of men, but these microbes were endowed with intelligence and will. Men attacked by them became at once mad and furious. But never had men considered themselves so intellectual and so completely in possession of the truth as these sufferers, never had they considered their decisions, their scientific conclusions, their moral convictions so infallible. Whole villages, whole towns and peoples went mad from the infection. All were excited and did not understand one another. Each thought that he alone had the truth and was wretched looking at the others, beat himself on the breast, wept, and wrung his hands. They did not know how to judge and could not agree what to consider evil and what good; they did not know whom to blame, whom to justify. Men killed each other in a sort of senseless spite. They gathered together in armies against one another, but even on the march the armies would begin attacking each other, the ranks would be broken and the soldiers would fall on each other, stabbing and cutting, biting and devouring each other. The alarm bell was ringing all day long in the towns; men rushed together, but why they were summoned and who was summoning them no one knew. The most ordinary trades were abandoned, because every one proposed his own ideas, his own improvements, and they could not agree. The land too was abandoned. Men met in groups, agreed on something, swore to keep together, but at once began on something quite different from what they had proposed. They accused one another, fought and killed each other. There were conflagrations and famine. All men and things were involved in destruction. The plague spread and moved further and further.[3]

The plague is a transparent metaphor for a certain reciprocal violence that spreads, literally, like the plague. The appropriateness of the metaphor comes, obviously, from this contagious character. The idea of contagiousness implies the presence of something harmful, which loses none of its virulence as it is rapidly transmitted from individual to individual. Such, of course, are bacteria in an epidemic; so is violence when it is *imitated*, either positively, whenever bad example makes the usual restraints inoperative, or negatively, when the efforts to stifle violence with violence achieve no more, ultimately, than an increase in the level of violence. Counterviolence turns out to be the same as violence. In cases of massive contamination, the victims are helpless, not necessarily because they remain passive but because whatever they do proves ineffective or makes the situation worse.

In order to appreciate Raskolnikov's dream, we must read it in the context of Dostoevski's entire work, of that self-defeating mixture of pride and humiliation characteristic of Raskolnikov and other Dostoevskian heroes. The victims of the plague seem to be possessed with the same desire as Raskolnikov. Each falls prey to the same megalomania and sees himself as the one and only superman: "Each thought that he alone had the truth and looked with contempt at the others."

This desire implies a contradiction; it aims at complete autonomy, at a near divine self-sufficiency, and yet it is *imitative*. The divinity this desire is trying to capture never fails, sooner or later, to appear as the divinity of someone else, as the exclusive privilege of a model after whom the hero must pattern not only his behavior but his very desires, insofar as these are directed toward objects. Raskolnikov worships Napoleon. The possessed imitate Stavrogin. The spirit of worship must combine with the spirit of hatred. To reveal the secret of this ambivalence, we need not turn to someone like Freud. There is no secret at all.

To imitate the desires of someone else is to turn this someone else into a rival as well as a model. From the convergence of two or more desires on the same object, conflict must necessarily arise.

The mimetic nature of desire can account for the many contradictions in the Dostoevskian hero; this one principle can make his personality truly intelligible. Imitative desire necessarily generates its own living obstacles and comes to view this failure as a sign of the model's omnipotence, as convincing proof, in other words, that this model is the right one, that the door he keeps so tightly shut must be the door to heaven. Mimetic desire cannot keep its illusions alive without falling in love with its own disastrous consequences and focusing more and more on the violence of its rivals. The mimetic attraction of violence is a major topic of Dostoevskian art. Thus, violence becomes reciprocal. In the dream of the plague, the expressions "each other," "one another" recur constantly. The great Dostoevskian novels describe mimetic breakdowns of human relations that tend to spread further and further. The dream of the plague is nothing but the quintessential expression of the Dostoevskian crisis; and, as such, it must extend that crisis to the entire world, in truly apocalyptic fashion.

From Dostoevski, I would like to turn to another writer, Shakespeare, who appears very distant but is really very close in respect to the problem at hand. I want to compare the dream of the plague, a specific passage in *Crime and Punishment*, to a specific passage in a work of Shakespeare, the famous speech of Ulysses in *Troilus and Cressida*, a text that rests, in my view, on the same conception of a cultural crisis as the dream of the plague in Dostoevski.

First, it must be observed that *Troilus and Cressida* revolves entirely around a view of mimetic desire analogous if not identical to the one just detected in Dostoevski. The topic of the play is the decomposition of the Greek army stalled under the walls of Troy. Disorder begins at the top. Achilles imitates Agamemnon, both in the sense that he seriously aspires to his position (he wants to become the supreme ruler of the Greeks) and in the sense that he derisively mimics and parodies the commander-in-chief. Mimetic rivalry spreads from rank to rank and brings about a complete confusion:

> So every step
> Exampled by the first pace that is sick
> Of his superior, grows to an envious fever
> Of pale and bloodless emulation.
>   [1.3.131–34]

These lines remind us of Raskolnikov's dream: "They gathered together in armies against one another, but even on the march the armies would begin attacking each other, the ranks would be broken and the soldiers would fall on each other."

Mimetic desire also dominates the two protagonists. No less than the political and the military, the erotic aspect of the play is an affair of worldly ambition, competitive and imitative in character. We would have to call Cressida "inauthentic" if we did not suspect that the ideal of autonomous desire by which she will be judged is itself a fruit of rampant imitation. The lovers are always open to the corruptive suggestion of spurious models or to the even worse advice of Pandarus. They are really nonheroes, always caught in a game of deception and vanity that is to real passion what the behavior of the army is to genuine military valor.

No individual or psychological approach can do justice to the scope of the phenomenon. That is why the high point of the play is that speech in which Ulysses describes a crisis so pervasive and acute that it goes beyond even the most radical notion of social crisis. The central concept, degree, from the Latin *gradus*, means a step, a measured distance, the necessary difference thanks to which two cultural objects, people, or institutions can be said to have a *being* of their own, an individual or categorical identity.

> Oh, when degree is shaked,
> Which is the ladder to all high designs,
> The enterprise is sick! How could communities,
> Degrees in schools and brotherhoods in cities,
> Peaceful commerce from dividable shores,
> The primogenitive and due of birth
> Prerogative of age, crowns, scepters, laurels,
> But by degree, stand in authentic place?
> Take but degree away, untune that string,
> And hark, what discord follows! Each thing meets
> In mere oppugnancy. The bounded waters
> Should lift their bosoms higher than the shores,
> And make a sop of all this solid globe.
> Strength should be the lord of imbecility,
> And the rude son should strike his father dead.
> Force should be right, or rather, right and wrong,
> Between whose endless jar justice resides,
> Should lose their names, and so should justice too.
> [1.3.101–18]

The image of the untuned string clearly reveals that the cultural order is to be understood on the model of a melody, not as an aggregate, therefore, a mere collection of heterogeneous objects, but as a "totality" or, if we prefer, a "structure," a system of differences commanded by a single differentiating principle. Degree in the singular seems to define a purely social transcendence, almost in the sense of Durkheim, with the difference, however, that cultural systems in Shakespeare are always liable to collapse. It is with such a collapse, obviously, not with the systems themselves, that the tragic writer is preoccupied.

If mimetic desire has an object, it is degree itself; degree is vulnerable to criminal attempts from inside the structure. The thought appears irrational, but it is not. It does not mean that degree is something like an object that could be appropriated. It means exactly the opposite. If degree vanishes, becomes "vizarded" when it becomes an object of rivalry, it is precisely because it is really nothing but the absence of such rivalries in a cultural order that remains functional. The crisis, therefore, is a time of most frantic ambition that becomes more and more self-defeating. As these ambitions are mimetically multiplied, reciprocal violence grows and the differences dissolve; the "degrees" leading to the object and the object itself disintegrate. It is an ambition, therefore, that "by a pace goes backward / With a purpose it hath to climb."

As in Dostoevski's text, all constancy of purpose disappears, all useful activities are interrupted. The desire in each man to distinguish himself triggers instant imitation, multiplies sterile rivalries, produces conditions that make society unworkable through a growing uniformity. The process is one of undifferentiation that passes for extreme differentiation—false "individualism." Finally, even the most fundamental distinctions become impossible. Shakespeare writes that "right and wrong . . . lose their names," and this is duplicated almost to the letter in Dostoevski: "They did not know how to judge and could not agree what to consider evil and what good; they did not know whom to blame, whom to justify."

In both texts, though more explicit in Shakespeare, the dominant idea is that regular human activities, however reciprocal their final results, can take place only on a basis of nonreciprocity. Constructive relationships of any type are differentiated. Ulysses certainly betrays a strong hierarchical and authoritarian bias. One should not conclude too hastily that the interest of his speech is thereby diminished. The concepts with which he operates, the very notion of the cultural order as a differential system susceptible of collapse, imply the essential *arbitrariness* of cultural differences.

When the difference goes, the relationship becomes violent and sterile as it becomes more symmetrical, as everything becomes more perfectly identical on both sides: *"Each thing meets in mere oppugnancy."* It is a relationship of doubles that emerges from the crisis.

We would misunderstand this relationship if we interpreted it as a *coincidentia oppositorum*, in the tradition of philosophical idealism, or as a mere subjective reflection or hallucination, in the vein of psychological "narcissism," an approach adopted by Rank, for instance, in his essay on Don Juan and the double.

With Shakespeare, as earlier with the playwrights of classical antiquity, the relationship of doubles is perfectly real and concrete; it is the fundamental relationship of the tragic and comic antagonists. It is present among the four doubles of *A Comedy of Errors*, where it is almost identical to the relationship defined in *Troilus and Cressida* and dramatized in all of Shakespeare's plays. The fact that the doubles constantly run into each other in a desperate effort to part ways can be viewed either in a tragic or in a comic light. This is as true of Dostoevski as it is of Shakespeare. The relationship of conflictual symmetry and reciprocal fascination portrayed in the novels is fundamentally identical to what is attempted very early in the short story entitled *The Double*.

Thus, the speech of Ulysses closely parallels Raskolnikov's dream of the plague. In both these texts the authors find a way to conceptualize and generalize the same type of relationship that, in the rest of the work and in their other works, is developed in dramatic or novelistic form. The convergence of these two writers is particularly striking in view of their obvious differences of language, period, style, genre, etc. In order to be complete, the parallel should also include, on Shakespeare's side, the metaphor of the plague; and, of course, it does. In the passage quoted above, the idea of disease occurs repeatedly. Even though it does not play as prominent a role as in Raskolnikov's dream, the plague proper is not absent; it figures among the various and more or less natural disasters that accompany the crisis, as in a kind of mythical orchestration:

> What raging of the sea, shaking of the earth,
> What plagues and what portents, what mutiny
> Divert and crack, rend and deracinate
> The unity and married calm of states
> Quite from their fixture!

Looking back upon the preceding remarks, I must note that we are no longer dealing with a single theme, with the isolated plague, but with a thematic cluster that includes, besides the plague or, more generally, the theme of epidemic contamination, the dissolving of differences and the mimetic doubles. All these elements are present both in the text of Shakespeare and in the text of Dostoevski. I shall give more examples later, and they will show that this same thematic cluster

almost never fails to gather around the plague in a great many texts
that may appear to have very little in common. Some of the elements
may be more emphasized than others; they may appear only in an
embryonic form, but it is very rare when even one of them is completely missing.

First, however, I must complete the thematic cluster. Another element, which has not yet been mentioned, may be the most important
of all, the *sacrificial* element. This sacrificial element can be limited to
the assertion that all the death and suffering from the plague is not in
vain, that the ordeal is necessary to purify and rejuvenate the society.
Here is, for example, the conclusion of Raskolnikov's dream: "Only a
few men could be saved in the whole world. They were a pure chosen
people, destined to found a new race and a new life, to renew and
purify the earth." Something very similar is present in Artaud's *Le
Théâtre et la peste*: "The theater like the plague is a crisis which is
resolved by death or cure. And the plague is a superior disease because
it is a total crisis after which nothing remains except death or an
extreme purification."[4] Death itself appears as the purifying agent, the
death of all plague victims or a few, sometimes of a single chosen
victim who seems to assume the plague in its entirety and whose death
or expulsion cures the society, in the rituals of much of the world.
Sacrifices and the so-called scapegoat rituals are prescribed when a
community is stricken by "the plague" or other scourges. This thematic
cluster is even more common in myth and ritual than in literature. In
Exodus, for instance, we find the "ten plagues" of Egypt together with
the incident of Moses stricken with leprosy and cured by Yahweh
himself. The "ten plagues" are a worsening social breakdown, which
also appears in the form of a destructive rivalry between Moses and
the magicians of Egypt. Finally, there is a strong sacrificial theme in
the death of the firstborn and the establishment of the passover ritual.

The sacrificial element is sometimes an invisible dimension, something like an atmosphere that pervades every theme but cannot be
pinpointed as a theme; its status must be ascertained. An analysis not
of the entire Oedipus myth, but of the mythical elements that appear
in Sophocles' tragedy, *Oedipus the King*, may help shed some light
upon that problem.

In the opening scenes of the tragedy, the city of Thebes is in the
throes of a plague epidemic; the solution of the crisis becomes a test of
power and prestige for the protagonists, Oedipus, Creon, and Tiresias.
Each of these would-be doctors tries to place the blame on another,
and they all turn into each other's doubles. Here, too, the tragic process
is one with a worsening "crisis of degree," one with the plague itself, in

other words. The tragic conflict and the plague are in the same metaphoric relationship as in Dostoevski or Shakespeare, except, of course, that this metaphoric character is less explicit, as if the task of uncovering the element of violence hidden behind the mythical plague were initiated by Sophocles but were less advanced than in the work of the two other writers.

In the light of these analyses, the tragic conflict of *Oedipus the King* amounts to nothing more and nothing less than a search for a scapegoat, triggered by the oracle, which says, "A murderer is in your midst; get rid of him and you will be rid of the plague." How could a single individual, even the worst offender, be responsible for whatever social catastrophe may be at stake in the "plague"? Within the confines of the myth, however, not only is the significance of the strange medicine unquestioned, but its efficacy is actually verified. We must assume that the prescription works, that the discovery of the "culprit" cures the plague. The reciprocal witch hunt brings the crisis to a climax; then, the focusing of the guilt on Oedipus and his expulsion constitute a genuine resolution. The whole process is comparable to a "cathartic" purge.

A fascinating possibility arises. Even though the reasons adduced are quite mythical, the reality of the cure may be a fact. Behind the entire myth there could be a real crisis, concluded by the collective expulsion or death of a victim. In this case the oracle would be truthful in part. What is true is not that there is, as a "real culprit," a man who bears alone the entire responsibility for the plague. Such a man cannot exist, of course. The oracle is really talking about a victim who is "right," in the sense that against and around that victim everyone can unite. Oedipus may well be the right scapegoat in the sense that the accusation against him really "sticks" and restores the unity of the community. This restoration is tantamount to a "cure" if, as Sophocles himself appears to suggest, the plague is the same crisis as in Shakespeare or Dostoevski, a crisis of mimetic violence. The polarization of all fascination and hatred on a single victim leaves none for the other doubles and must automatically bring about their reconciliation.

How can the required unanimity be achieved if no one among the potential victims is likely to be either much more or much less guilty than anyone else? How can the mythical "guilt" become solidly fixed on a more or less random victim? The mimetic doubles are concretely alike; there is no difference between them. This means that at any time even the smallest incident, the most insignificant clue, can trigger a mimetic transfer against any double whatsoever. The positive effect of such a transfer, the end of the crisis, must necessarily be interpreted as a confirmation of the "oracle," as absolute proof that the "real culprit" has been identified. A faultless relationship of cause and effect appears to have been established.

The process just described implies that the random victim must be perceived as a "real culprit," missing before and now identified and punished. This random victim, in other words, will never be perceived as random; the "cure" would not be operative if its beneficiaries realized the randomness of the victim's selection.

All this goes without saying, and yet it needs very much to be said because the unperceived consequences of these facts may be decisive for the myth as a whole. I have just said that the entire responsibility for the crisis is collectively transferred upon the scapegoat. This transfer will not appear as such, of course. Instead of the truth, we will have the "crimes" of Oedipus, the "parricide and the incest" that are supposed to "contaminate" the entire city. These two crimes obviously signify the dissolving of even the most elemental cultural differences, those between father, mother, and child. The parricide and the incest represent the quintessence of the whole crisis, its most logical crystallization in the context of a scapegoating project, that is, of an attempt to make that crisis look like the responsibility of a single individual. Even today, these and similar accusations come to the fore when a pogrom is in the making, when a lynch mob goes on a rampage. The ideas of parricide and incest, and also infanticide, always crop up when cultural cohesion is threatened, when a society is in danger of disintegration. The nature of the crimes attributed to Oedipus should be enough to make us suspect that we are dealing with some kind of lynching process. And this suspicion has been present for many years; it has prompted many investigations. Unfortunately, scholars keep looking for a possible link that could be historically documented between the Oedipus myth and some particular scapegoat-type ritual. The results have been disappointing. The question of relating myth to ritual or ritual to myth is a circle that can be broken here by asking a more decisive question about the possible origin of both in a spontaneous lynching process that must necessarily remain invisible because of its very efficacy.

If the collective transfer is really effective, the victim will never appear as an explicit scapegoat, as an innocent destroyed by the blind passion of the crowd. This victim will pass for a real criminal, for the one guilty exception in a community now emptied of its violence. Oedipus is a scapegoat in the fullest sense *because he is never designated as such*. For the genuine recollection of the crisis, which allows for no differentiation whatever between the doubles, the two differentiated themes of the myth are substituted. The original elements are all there, but rearranged and transfigured in such a way as to destroy the reciprocity of the crisis and polarize all its violence on the wretched scapegoat, leaving everybody else a passive victim of that vague and undefined scourge called "the plague." A lynching viewed from the perspective of the lynchers will never become explicit as such. In order to apprehend the truth, we must carry out a radical critique that will see the mythical themes as systematic distortion of the former crisis.

The spontaneous scapegoat process now appears as the generative process of myth, the true *raison d'être* of its themes and notably of the plague, which must be viewed, I believe, as a mask for the crisis leading to the scapegoat process, not only in the Oedipus myth but in countless other myths of the entire world.

Oedipus, it will be said, is a religious hero as well as a villain. This is true, and it is no objection—far from it—to the genesis just outlined. The difference between the founding process of myth and the scapegoat processes we may know of and understand is that the first, being the more powerful, literally goes full circle from unanimous hatred to unanimous worship. The juxtaposition of the one and the other is intelligible. If the polarization of the crisis upon a single victim really effects a cure, this victim's guilt is confirmed, but his role as a savior is no less evident. That is why Oedipus and behind him the more remote but parallel figure of the god Apollo appear both as bringers of the plague and as benefactors. This is true of all primitive gods and other sacred figures associated with the mythical "plague." They are both the accursed divinities that curse with the plague and the blessed ones that heal. This duality, it must be noted, is present in all primitive forms of the "sacred."

I have already suggested that the present hypothesis bears also on ritual, that a sacrificial action or immolation is generally found, frequently interpreted as the reenactment of a divine murder supposed to be the decisive event in the foundation of the culture. In the preparatory stages of a ritual immolation, symmetrically arranged antagonists hold warlike dances or real and simulated battles. Familial and social hierarchies are reversed or suppressed. These and many other features may be interpreted as traces of some "crisis of degree" climaxed by its habitual resolution, the collective transfer on a single victim. We may suppose that ritual tries to reenact this entire process in order to recapture the unifying effect mentioned earlier. There are sound reasons to believe that this purpose is generally achieved. Being still unable to perceive the threat that internal violence constitutes for primitive society, we cannot recognize in ritual a relatively effective protection against that threat.

If the preceding and obviously too brief remarks are not unfounded,[5] the conjunction between the plague and sacrificial ritual, first in primitive religion and later in literature, becomes fully intelligible. Primitive societies constantly resort to ritual against anything they call the plague. That may comprise very diverse threats ranging from the crisis of mimetic violence and less acute forms of internal tensions and aggressions to purely exterior threats that have nothing to do with reciprocal violence, including, of course, real pathological epidemics, even the plague in the modern scientific sense.

Ritual tries to reproduce a process that has proved effective against one kind of "plague," the most terrible kind, the epidemic of reciprocal violence that never becomes explicit as such. It is my opinion that the scapegoat process, through religious myths, notably the myths of the plague, plays a major role in disguising and minimizing the danger its own potential for internal violence constitutes for a primitive community. This minimization must be viewed in turn as an integral part of the protection that myth and ritual provide against this same violence.

Certain lines of Sophocles and Euripides make it hard to believe that these writers did not have an intuition of collective mechanisms behind the myths they adapted, an intuition that is still incomplete, perhaps, but far superior to ours. These mechanisms are still well attested historically. In the Middle Ages, for instance, social catastrophes, notably the great plague epidemics, usually triggered persecutions against the Jews. Even though they have become less productive in terms of mythical lore, these mechanisms, quite obviously, are far from extinct.

We are now in a position to understand why the mythical plague is never present alone. It is part of a thematic cluster that includes various forms of undifferentiation and transgression, the mimetic doubles, and a sacrificial theme that may take the form of a scapegoat process. Earlier, I said that the plague, as a literary theme, is still alive today, in a world less and less threatened by real bacterial epidemics. This fact looks less surprising now, as we come to realize that the properly medical aspects of the plague never were essential; in themselves, they always played a minor role, serving mostly as a disguise for an even more terrible threat that no science has ever been able to conquer. The threat is still very much with us, and it would be a mistake to consider the presence of the plague in literature as a matter of formal routine, as an example of a tradition that persists even though its object has vanished.

Not only the plague but the entire thematic cluster is alive, and its relevance to the current psychosociological predicament becomes evident as soon as specific examples are produced. The continued vitality of all these themes must correspond to a continued need to disguise as well as to suggest—the one and the other in varying degrees—a certain pervasive violence in our relationships.

I will give three examples, each so different from the other two and from the texts already mentioned, at least in terms of traditional literary values, that direct literary influence cannot account for the presence of the pattern. The first is Artaud's already mentioned *Le Théâtre et la peste*. Much of this text is devoted to a strange account of the medical and social effects not of a specific outbreak but of the plague in general. In a long pseudoclinical disquisition, Artaud rejects all attempts at making the transmission of the disease a scientifically determined phenomenon; he interprets the physiological process as a dissolution of organs, which may be a kind of melting away, a liquefaction of the body or, on the contrary, a desiccation and a pulverization. This loss of organic differentiation is medically mythical but esthetically powerful because it patterns the pathological symptoms on the breakdown of culture, producing an overwhelming impression of disintegration. The apocalyptic vision is quite close to Dostoevski's dream of the plague, but this time, in keeping with the destructive ethos of contemporary art, it is a cause for fierce jubilation.

At first glance it seems that, in spite of its intensity, the process of undifferentiation does not culminate in the doubles. The doubles are there, though—less explicit, to be sure, than in Dostoevski and Shakespeare but unmistakable nevertheless—notably in those passages that hint at a purely spiritual contamination, analogous to the mimetic *hubris* of the first two examples.

Other victims, without bubos, delirium, pain, or rash, examine themselves proudly in the mirror, in splendid health as they think and then fall dead with their shaving mugs in their hand, full of scorn for other victims.[6]

The proud self-examination is *hubristic* pride, reaching out for supreme mastery, even over the plague, immediately defeated, massively contradicted by the instant arrival of the disease. Still apparently intact, the victim dies, "full of scorn for the other victims." An unquenchable thirst to distinguish himself turns the apparently healthy man into a double of all other victims, his partners in violence and death. The mirror, everywhere, is an attribute to the doubles.

The sacrificial theme is there too: first, as earlier indicated, in the rejuvenation that the plague and its modern counterpart, the theater, are supposed to bring to a decadent world, but also in more subtle touches that may be limited, at least in one case, to one single word. At one point the author imagines some kind of surgical dissection performed on the victims not with just any knife but with a knife that, for no immediately apparent reason, is described as being made of obsidian. Anthropological literature knows of knives made of this material and used on human flesh, the Aztec sacrificial knives. In the context of my analyses, it is not excessive to suppose, perhaps, that the *couteau d'obsidienne*, in conjunction with the victims of the plague, was prompted by a reminiscence of human sacrifice.

The second example is the film work of Ingmar Bergman in which the plague, the dissolving of differences, the mimetic doubles, and the sacrificial scapegoat are recurrent themes. If one particular film should be mentioned in connection with the doubles, it is certainly *Persona*. Two characters only are constantly present, a nurse and her patient, a totally silent actress. The entire work is dedicated to the mimetic relationship of these two, never a communion, really, but the same violent dissolving of differences as elsewhere. Another film, *Shame*, makes the conjunction of the mimetic doubles and of a plaguelike contamination quite manifest. A senseless civil war is being fought between two perfectly undistinguishable parties. This absurd struggle of rival doubles gradually spreads into a general infection, a literal ocean of putrefaction. Here, as in many contemporary works, the old mythical plague literally merges with such positive threats as radioactive fallout and industrial pollution, both of which "function," of course, exactly like the plague and constitute disturbingly appropriate "metaphors" of individual and social relations in a state of extreme degradation.

One may single out *The Seventh Seal* as one film of Bergman in which the interplay of all the elements in the thematic cluster is quite spectacular. The mimetic doubles are there, and death is one of them. So is a real medieval plague with its cortege of flagellants. In the midst of all this comes the brief suggestion of a mob scene, a collective transfer against a very random and at the same time quite significant scapegoat, an actor, a mime, the very personification of mimesis.

The third example is both literary and cinematic. It is the famous short story by Thomas Mann, *Death in Venice*, which was made into a film by Luchino Visconti. My own comments are based on the short story, which remains, I believe, the more striking of the two in the present context.[7]

An older and famous writer, Aschenbach, goes to Venice for a rest. As he arrives, he notices another elderly man who clings desperately to a group of younger people. His modish attire and the rouge on his cheeks turn this pathetic figure into a monstrous mask of pseudoyouthfulness. Later, the protagonist will permit a hairdresser to paint his face and dye his hair, which makes of him the exact replica, the perfect double, of the grotesque vision encountered at the beginning.

In the meantime, at the hotel and on the beach, the artist has come under the spell of a Polish adolescent. The differences of age, language, and culture, as well as its homosexual character, make this silent attachment more than a mere transgression; it is really a destruction and a disolution of the old man's entire life.

The sense of decay is heightened by the plague and the rumors of plague that are abroad in the city. The sacrificial theme is present, of course, first in the hero's dream of a primitive bacchanal during which animals are slaughtered and, no less decisively, in his sudden death the next morning, which seems a retribution for his surrender to the forces of cultural disintegration. The writer has become the very embodiment of the plague. He literally sides with the epidemic when he chooses not to inform the Polish family of its presence in Venice, thus increasing their exposure to danger. He delights in the plague, and the plague will literally die with him since, as he dies, everybody is leaving Venice and the drama is resolved.

In these three contemporary examples the plague and associated themes are all present; the entire cluster is strikingly intact. It even has more thematic consistency than in Sophocles, Shakespeare, or Dostoevski. The plague is a less transparent metaphor in Thomas Mann and Artaud than in *Crime and Punishment, Troilus and Cressida,* and even *Oedipus the King.* This very opacity confers to the plague a great evocative and esthetic power. The doubles, too, appear in a light of romantic mystery, in contrast with the unadorned severity of the tragic rapport.

Such opacity, it must be noted, belongs to myth—distinguished, of course, from its tragic adaptations—as well as to modern literature. If we limited ourselves to these chronological or cultural extremes, which is what recent investigators tend to do, the conjunction between the plague, the doubles, and the sacrificial scapegoat would remain unintelligible. Many specialists, of course (for instance, the psychoanalysts), have all sorts of answers. Unfortunately, these ever ready answers shed no real light on the texts. As for the literary critics, they usually reject not only these superficial answers—which is good—but also the question itself—which cannot be good. In a misguided effort to protect the integrity of literature against all possible enemies, they refuse the open and equal dialogue between literature and anthropology they themselves should promote. We should not cut off literature from the vital concerns of our age. We should not divorce esthetic enjoyment from the power of intelligence, even from scientific investigation. We cannot simply "enjoy" the plague and be quiet, like old Aschenbach, I suppose, awaiting in pure esthetic bliss whatever fate may lie in store.

I find Shakespeare more bracing than Aschenbach. One reason is that he does not despair of the truth. If I had not turned to him earlier,

I could not have made sense out of the thematic cluster. The brightest
light available is still there. Shakespeare does not use the plague as
verbal violence against an indifferent world. He is not interested in
words as shields or weapons in the dubious battle of individual *ressentiment*. What concerns him most is the myth and the truth of his own
language.

In these contemporary examples, the thematic elements of the cluster are juxtaposed a little like colors on the flat surface of a modern
painting. It takes Shakespeare to realize that these themes are not
really on a par, that they are not really even themes, and that it is a
misnomer to call them so. The plague is less than theme, structure, or
symbol, since it symbolizes desymbolization itself. The doubles, on the
contrary, are more than a theme; they are the unperceived reciprocity
of violence among men. They are essential to the understanding of
sacrifice as a mitigation, a displacement, a substitution, and a metaphor
of this same violence. The closer the writer gets to the fundamentals of
that process, the more the plague and other metaphors become transparent. Sacrificial values disintegrate, disclosing their origin in the
unifying and reconciling effect of a spontaneous scapegoat. If the
scapegoat process described above is the resolution of the crisis and
the source of mythical meaning, it must also be the end of tragedy and
the restoration of degree. Shakespeare does not simply repeat; he reveals the entire process.

In *Romeo and Juliet*, for instance, it takes Shakespeare no more than
six words to suggest the entire pattern of metaphoric and real interaction. The famous cry of the dying Mercutio, "A plague on both your
houses," is not an idle wish. It is already fulfilled in the endlessly
destructive rivalry of these same two houses, Montagues and Capulets,
who turn each other into perfect doubles, thereby bringing the plague
upon themselves. At the end of the play, the prince equates the death
of the two lovers with the plague of their families: "See what a scourge
is laid upon your hate." The two statements are really the same. Both
are uttered *in extremis*, as a revelation of the truth: the first by a dying
victim; the second as the last judgment of the sovereign authority,
always a sacrificial figure in Shakespeare, and a potential scapegoat.

The death of the lovers is the entire plague, in the sense that it
represents the climax of the scourge, the plague finally made visible
and, as a consequence, exorcised by its very excess; the plague is both
the disease and the cure. A sacrificial death brings about the end of the
crisis and the reconciliation of the doubles. Talking to Capulet, Mon-
tague aptly calls the victims "poor sacrifices of our enmity."

Thus, a scapegoat mechanism is clearly defined as the solution to the
tragic crisis, the catharsis inside the play that parallels the catharsis

produced by that play, the catharsis twice announced and proposed to the spectators at the very opening, in an enigmatic little prologue that contains literally no other idea: Romeo and Juliet, we are told,

> Do with their death bury their parents' strife.
> The fearful passage of their death-marked love,
> And the continuance of their parents' rage,
> Which, but their children's end, naught could remove,
> Is now the two hours' traffic of our stage.
>
> [1.1.8–12]

The word *catharsis* originally refers to the purifying effect of a particular sacrifice. Shakespeare needs no etymology to see through Aristotelian estheticism and to reveal in the most concrete and *dramatic* fashion that all drama is a mimetic reenactment of a scapegoat process. In his tragedies, Shakespeare reproduces the cathartic mechanism of all tragedy; but he underlines it so forcefully that he lays it bare, so to speak, forcing us to ask questions that run counter to the cathartic effect, questions that would tear the entire dramatic structure asunder if they were seriously asked.

In his comedies, Shakespeare openly derides the sacrificial pattern. The Pyramus and Thisbe episode of *A Midsummer Night's Dream*, the play that comes immediately after *Romeo and Juliet*, parodies the cathartic system of this first play. He comes closer to a full revelation of the sacrificial values hidden behind the plague and other mythical or tragic metaphors than our contemporaries, including those like Artaud, whose frontal attacks against sacrificial values ultimately regress into the crudest forms of sacrifice. Contrary to what we believe, we may not be in a position to criticize Shakespeare. He may be the one who criticizes us. Rather than trying to judge him from above, from a necessarily superior "modern" viewpoint, we should try to recover some major intuitions of his that obviously escape us. We must have lost them somehow and somewhere, unless, of course, they have yet to be grasped.

NOTES

1. Quoted in Johannes Nohl, ed., *The Black Death: A Chronicle of the Plague,* trans. C. H. Clarke (London: Unwin Books, 1961), p. 101.

2. Concerning the symbolic significance of disease in modern literature, see Gian-Paolo Biasin, "From Anatomy to Criticism," *MLN* 86 (December 1971): 873–90.

3. Fedor Dostoevski, *Crime and Punishment,* trans. Constance Garnett (New York: Random House, 1945), pp. 528–29.

4. Antonin Artaud, *Le Théâtre et son double*, in *Oeuvres complètes* (Paris: Gallimard, 1964), 4: 38–39.

5. For a more complete exposition of the collective transfer and single victim process as mythical genesis, see René Girard, *La Violence et le sacré* (Paris: Grasset, 1972); René Girard, *Violence and the Sacred*, trans. Patrick Gregory (Baltimore: The Johns Hopkins University Press, 1977).

6. Artaud, *Le Théâtre*, p. 29. My translation.

7. A paper on "The Plague in *Death in Venice*," by Ruth Ellen Perlman, a student at SUNY at Buffalo (Spring 1972), first made me aware of the short story's relevance to the present investigation.

8

Differentiation and Reciprocity
in Lévi-Strauss
and Contemporary Theory

The conclusion of Claude Lévi-Strauss's *L'Homme nu*, entitled "Finale," asserts that myth embodies a principle of differentiation identical with language and thought.[1] Ritual, on the other hand, tries to retrieve an *undifferentiated immediacy*. It tries to undo the work of language. Fortunately, Lévi-Strauss adds, this perverse undertaking will never succeed. The "undifferentiated" of ritual can only be made up of objects already differentiated by language and artifically pieced together.

Unlike "immediacy," about which I will speak later, the notion of "undifferentiated" certainly corresponds to part of what goes on in rituals all over the world: promiscuous sexual encounters, the overturning of hierarchies, the supposed metamorphosis of the participants into each other or into monstrous beings, etc. One cannot agree, however, that rituals are committed to this "undifferentiated" once and for all. All great traditional interpretations, notably the Hindu and the Chinese, attribute to ritual the end that Lévi-Strauss would reserve to myth alone: differentiation.

Before structuralism, no anthropologist had expressed a different view. Lévi-Strauss would reply that in all the examples that seem to verify my objection, language has been reintroduced and a secondary effect of differentiation has occurred, alien to ritual as such. Yet, there are innumerable instances of ritual differentiation visibly independent from the words that may or may not accompany them. In all *rites de passage*, for instance, the temporary loss of identity, or whatever ordeal the postulant may undergo, fits very well the undifferentiated conception of Lévi-Strauss but only in a first phase that, rather than being an end in itself, is a means, paradoxical no doubt but constantly reas-

This essay appeared under the title "Differentiation and Undifferentiation in Lévi-Strauss and Current Critical Theory," in *Directions for Criticism*, ed. Murray Krieger and L. S. Dembo (Madison: University of Wisconsin, 1977), pp. 111–36.

155

serted, toward the ultimate goal of ritual. This goal is obviously (re)differentiation, because it consists in a new and stable status, a well-defined identity.

The same is true of sacrifice, singled out in *La Pensée sauvage* for a preliminary skirmish against ritual.[2] Frequently, the victim must be carved along rigorously defined lines that correspond to the structural subdivisions of the community. Each piece goes to its own subdivision. Here again, the first phase belongs to the undifferentiated that culminates in the immolation where it turns into its opposite. The communion aspect of sacrifice coincides not with the undifferentiated, which is invariably conflictual, but with the end result, which is the regeneration of differences.

If ritual is no less committed to differentiation than myth, the converse is true: myth is no less involved with the undifferentiated than ritual. A cursory examination will reveal that it is the same involvement; it occurs in the same manner and probably for the same reasons. The undifferentiated presents itself as preliminary to (re)differentiation and often as its prerequisite. The original chaos of the Greeks, the *tohu wa bohu* of Genesis, Noah's flood, the ten plagues of Egypt, and the companions of Ulysses turned into swine by Circe are all examples of mythical undifferentiation.

In order to achieve this undifferentiation, myths, as well as rituals, resort to make-believe. They, too, piece back together entities that, "in reality," are already distinguished by language. Monsters are nothing else. We have a typical variation of this in a myth analyzed in *Le Cru et le cuit*. At the beginning, according to Lévi-Strauss's reading of that myth, living creatures were so numerous and so compressed that they could not yet be distinguished. Later on, one single component is removed and the compactness of the mass is reduced. Interstices appear that make the necessary distinctions possible. Lévi-Strauss has a diagram showing that the space provided by the removal of even a small fragment can be distributed along a continuous line in such a way as to produce a number of separate segments, with no change in the total length of the figure. This myth and others are read by Lévi-Strauss not as differentiated solely, as any text would be, but as differentiation displaying itself. Myth is not simply structured, it is structuralist. It is not a mere product of symbolic thought, it is the process of symbolization made visible as process.

Lévi-Strauss also says that myths are able to think each other as myths. The formula has been most successful but its real meaning is not explained. It cannot mean only that many variations of the same myth are found. In nature, many varieties of the same species are found, many varieties of ants, for instance, but we would not say that these different ants think each other. In order for myths to think each other, it is necessary that each myth, up to a point, think itself as myth. And myths appear to think themselves because they provide the mirror in which they reflect their own process. Since the process is one of pure differentiation, the only appropriate mirror is the undifferentiated. This mirror is identical with the "primordial stuff" the myths are supposed to carve up. It is the presence in myths of the undifferentiated that allows Lévi-Strauss to say that they "think each other as myths."

In myth as well as in ritual, this undifferentiated can only be a *representation*. There is no difference and yet myth and ritual are treated quite differently by Lévi-Strauss. Ritual is severely rebuked for entertaining artificial representations of something language cannot really express. In myth, the same representations are praised, at least implicitly, since we would not even know without them that the myth intends to distinguish certain objects. We must have that first moment when these objects are supposed to be stuck together. In reality the undifferentiated plays the same role everywhere. Is it reasonable to describe the incentive for plunging a postulant into the undifferentiating waters of baptism as "a nostalgia for the immediate"? The postulant will not stay in there forever; he will drown only symbolically in order to reach the shore of a new differentiation.

The facts contradicting Lévi-Strauss are so massive that he cannot disregard them entirely. The combination of the undifferentiated plus differentiation is so commonplace that Lévi-Strauss grudgingly acknowledges its presence but he views it as no less unnatural and perverse than ritual. He explains it by the existence of bastardized myths that are primarily the account of some ritual. They should not influence the theoretical perception of the problem. The truth of the matter is that Lévi-Strauss is going to tortuous extremes of scholasticism to defend his assimilation of myth with differentiation and of ritual with the undifferentiated, but it cannot be done. The two are always present together and their juxtaposition produces the standard profile of both myth and ritual. This profile has been identified and described in various languages and terminologies since time immemorial. To recognize this is to recognize a structural fact of life that Lévi-Strauss has always implicitly denied in his analyses and that he denies explicitly in the "Finale" of his *Mythologiques*. It must be possible to recognize that fact without compromising with the spiritualist exploitations of myth.

If the useful categories of the undifferentiated and differentiation are not manipulated in order to fit a preconceived formula, these categories help us understand the structural parallelism of myth and ritual. There are no anthropological reasons to cast myth as the hero and

ritual as the villain in a drama of human intelligence. The reverse
formula has already been tied, at least up to a point, with equally
unsatisfactory results. The reasons for this anthropological supreme
court are not anthropological. A major one, of course, is the structuralist commitment to the so-called "model" or "pilot" science of
linguistics. Ritual uses language extensively but not exclusively like
myth. This really leaves no choice. Since Lévi-Strauss is almost as eager
to castigate religion as to extol language, he can assimilate the non-
verbal means of ritual to the hard core of religious behavior and kill
two ideological birds with the same stone.

There is still another bird from whose back Lévi-Strauss likes to
pluck a few feathers once in a while, and it is philosophy. This third
bête noire is also assimilated to ritual. The definition of ritual as "a
nostalgia for the immediate" has a curiously philosophical ring for an
anthropologist. One of the reasons could be that it is also Lévi-Strauss's
definition of philosophy.

When we read such phrases as "l'immédiateté du vécu," we are inevitably reminded of the philosopher who dominated the French scene
during the formative years of Lévi-Strauss: Henri Bergson. If we keep
Bergson in mind as we read the "Finale," we cannot fail to discover
many more Bergsonian expressions, and they are far from limited to
those things Lévi-Strauss detests and assimilates to philosophy and
ritual. His references to the structural principle he espouses are also
couched in phrases borrowed from that philosopher, such as "discon-
tinuité," "découpage," "schématisme de la pensée," etc. Lévi-Strauss is
convinced there is not an ounce of philosophy in him, especially
Bergsonian philosophy. We can readily understand the cause of that
belief. He and Bergson are literally poles apart. The two poles, however, are those of Bergson's metaphysics. If you turn these poles
around, you understand better why the undifferentiated and differentiation mean so much to Lévi-Strauss, why he hates to find them in
conjunction. Everything Bergson embraces Lévi-Strauss rejects; everything Bergson rejects Lévi-Strauss embraces.

One single sentence in Lévi-Strauss's text says more than a long
exegesis: "La fluidité du vécu tend constamment à s'échapper à travers
les mailles du filet que la pensée mythique a lancé sur lui pour n'en
retenir que les aspects les plus contrastés" (p. 603). If we had to guess
the author, we would certainly name Bergson. It does more than sound
like Bergson, it gives us his whole metaphysics in a nutshell. Bergson
hoped that a more advanced science, led by biology, would understand
the inadequacy of rigid differentiations and move to his side. Recent
discoveries, especially that of the genetic code, have convinced Lévi-
Strauss that the opposite must happen. Thanks to the genetic code,

Lévi-Strauss can now put a name, he says, on that principle of discontinuity that governs the works of nature as well as of culture; this principle moves the entire universe and finally becomes conscious of itself, first in a crude mythological form, later in the works of science.

This association between genetics and mythology has an unexpected result; it permits a reappropriation by Lévi-Strauss of none other than the good old *élan vital*, which needs only a slight adaptation before it can reappear as an *élan différenciateur*, perhaps, or *codificateur*:

En suivant des voies auxquelles on reproche d'être trop exclusivement intellectuelles, la pensée structuraliste recouvre . . . et ramène à la surface de la conscience des vérités profondes et organiques. Seuls ceux qui la pratiquent connaissent, par expérience intime, cette impression de plénitude qu'apporte son exercice, et par quoi l'esprit ressent qu'il communie vraiment avec le corps. [p. 619]

The specific and generic consequences of the genetic code do not resemble the mythical representations of the undifferentiated and differentiation. This is equally true of language, of course, which operates through a smaller number of already discrete elements, not through the physical partitioning of some more or less homogeneous underlying substance. This is an objection that Lévi-Strauss himself brings up (p. 605). Myth represents only in a very imperfect fashion the process of intelligence and life. Between myth and the universal life force, there is nevertheless a communication, a reciprocal affinity that is all the more remarkable for lacking the proper means of expression. Thus, Lévi-Strauss explicitly admits that even in myth there are representations of the undifferentiated that do not correspond to the "real" metaphysical drama he thinks modern science has uncovered. But this inadequacy becomes one more cause for admiration, whereas in the case of ritual the very same thing becomes an irritating artifice, a deplorable phoniness.

The similarities between Bergson and Lévi-Strauss are more than an amusing paradox; they reach down to the core of structuralism. The fact that Bergson privileges one pole of the metaphysical dualism and Lévi-Strauss the other makes little difference. The important thing is that, in each case, both reality and the mind have been replaced by a metaphysical principle. These two principles appear closely interrelated but are really independent. Reality's being assimilated to a pure undifferentiation does not suggest in what manner it should be carved. It provides no guidelines to the differentiating principle that operates in the void. Any mode of differentiation is as good or as bad as any other.

When Lévi-Strauss becomes aware of the metaphysical substitutions

I have just detected, he attributes them to mythology itself, he views them as a brilliant intuition of mythical thought and the end result is the same. If we examine still another facet of the structural practice, we will realize that the reading of mythology depends even more on metaphysics than my previous remarks have already made clear.

Take the myth that is dominated until the end by a character defined as the jaguar-woman. If this monster belonged in a ritual, she would probably appear as a mask, worn by one or several participants, and we could dismiss her as the artificial piecing together of two creatures already differentiated by the language of myth, the jaguar and the woman. If she appeared only at the beginning of a myth, we could see her as a representation of the undifferentiated once more, but a legitimate one this time, a stepping stone to the differentiation that is to follow and reconfirm the mutual separateness of jaguars and women. Neither of these two solutions is available, since the jaguar-woman has decided to stay around until the bitter end of the myth. This monster, it would appear, is not playing by the rules. She is no less perverse than ritual. She should be kicked out of the structuralist classroom. What is Lévi-Strauss going to do?

Lévi-Strauss remains imperturbable. He keeps on playing his binary game as if the jaguar-woman were an object like any other object. Why should it matter if the pawns are jaguars, if they are women, or if they are jaguar-women? Lévi-Strauss does not have to take such trifles into account. His structural principle has nothing to do with a real perception that discovers real objects in the real world. It is a pure differentiating principle that operates on a pure undifferentiated. He does not have to apologize, therefore, because the machine turns out jaguar-women from time to time rather than women that are only women and jaguars that are only jaguars. Who has ever said the products of differentiation should be the same for everybody? Who knows if we are not the victim of an ethnocentric fallacy when we look condescendingly at the jaguar-woman? Can't we object, as in the case of ritual, that the jaguar and the woman are already distinguished by language? Possibly, but it is also possible that the original language of the myth treats the jaguar-woman as a genuinely independent entity. The combination of a horse and a human being is something like the jaguar-woman but we call it a centaur, don't we? We do not say a horseman or, when we do, we mean something quite different.

The layman is lost in admiration. There must be something vastly scientific, he assumes, about a method that can disregard so superbly the questions that keep nagging our little minds. Why is *le fantastique* on the same footing with the real? The question cannot be asked any more because the real has disappeared. For all practical purposes the real is assimilated to the undifferentiated and human thought is explicitly assimilated to the principle of pure differentiation.

Le fantastique has been dissolved all right, but in the most unscientific fashion. If the preceding observations are correct, le fantastique is divided into three fragments, and structuralism disposes of these fragments separately. Only in the case of ritual is le fantastique at least indirectly acknowledged as a disturbing question and unceremoniously discarded as contrary to the principles of human thought. The old anthropologists would have said that it was "irrational." Two fragments are left, and they both belong to myth. They are both incorporated into the process of differentiation. The second one is swallowed up by the machine and it comes out looking like everything else; the first one provides the indispensable background for differentiation as a self-displaying process. In this dissolution of all fantastic elements, the dissolving agent is always the same; it is the metaphysical dualism borrowed from Bergson.

We have philosophical and ideological motivations for the one-sided treatment of both ritual and myth. These motivations are paramount but they operate within a context shaped by the history of anthropology. A brief glance at this history may be in order. At the beginning of the twentieth century, Lucien Lévy-Bruhl was led to postulate the existence of a "primitive mentality" unable to distinguish entities and categories that mature human thought can and must distinguish. Emile Durkheim reacted against this view. The association between the kangaroo and a group of human beings does not signify a confusion between the two; rather it signifies a distinction between this first group and a second one that is associated, perhaps, with the wallaby. Symbolic thought demands both conjunction and disjunction. If the observer is not familiar with the conjunction, he is likely to concentrate unduly upon it; failing to perceive its disjunctive role, he will mistake it for a complete assimilation. Americans use animals for their political symbols; they do not confuse one another with real elephants and real donkeys.

Following the lead of Durkheim, Lévi-Strauss shows that much that formerly appeared senseless in primitive cultures really makes sense. The sense is made through binary networks of symbolic conjunctions and disjunctions that can be methodically mapped out. If there is a "manifest destiny" of structuralism, it is to extend as far as possible the area of meaningfulness in the structural sense. In Le Totémisme aujourd'hui, Lévi-Strauss reaches the conclusion that the whole problem of totemic institutions is not only wrongly labeled but unreal.[3] The illusion that the so-called totemic cultures do not think like us and need to be set apart rests entirely on ethnocentric fallacies of the type I have outlined.

Lévi-Strauss speaks of his surprise when he found that Bergson had anticipated his own elegant dissolution of the totemic problem. Such a coincidence, Lévi-Strauss speculates, must come from the very primitiveness of the philosopher's thinking, from an emotional empathy that puts this creature of instinct directly in touch with *la pensée sauvage.* The same intuition can only reappear at the other end of the intellectual tunnel, fully articulate this time, in the cold scientific glare of structuralism.[4]

We might have anticipated this miraculous agreement. Focusing as he does upon "la continuité du vécu," Bergson shows little interest in the various ways in which this continuity can be broken. If you bring to his attention something like totemic institutions, he will immediately realize that they are as far from his cherished immediacy as Socratic dialectics or medieval scholasticism. All modes of articulate thought allow this immediacy to slip from their grasp. Bergson will be inclined, therefore, to lump totemism with all the other modes as, of course, Lévi-Strauss also does.

Let us see, now, what happens with an investigator who is not Bergsonian in any form, not even in reverse. As a critic of the ethnocentric fallacy and an initiator of structuralism, Durkheim is especially appropriate. In some respects, his view of totemic names as "emblems" is even more destructive of the problem than that of Lévi-Strauss. At no point, however, does he substitute a metaphysical undifferentiated for the perception of the real world. As a consequence he finds himself asking concrete questions about the so-called undifferentiated. What can it be? What may have caused it?

Human experience is never such as to suggest the combinations and mixtures we find in totemic institutions. From the perspective of sense observation, everything is diverse and discontinuous. Nowhere in nature do we see creatures mix their natures and metamorphose into each other. An *exceptionally powerful cause must have been present, therefore, to transfigure the real and make it appear under aspects that do not belong to it.*[5] (translation and italics mine)

Because he does not confuse the undifferentiated and differentiation with the two poles of a Bergsonian metaphysics, Durkheim *must* ask himself why primitive thought can have at the same time so many monsters and so many distinctions that are sound. Durkheim does not say that the Australian aborigines cannot distinguish a man from a kangaroo, but he does not say either that the proliferation of kangaroo-ancestors and jaguar-women poses no problem whatever. His position avoids both the extreme of the so-called primitive mentality and the other extreme represented by structuralism and its various offspring. Durkheim's position may look at first like a timid compromise between two valorous knights-errant of anthropology who fearlessly radicalize the problematic. In reality, Durkheim's perspective is the only one from which the problem of culture, or the problem of language, or, if you prefer, the problem of symbolic thought, becomes concrete.

Durkheim speaks of an *extremely powerful cause* that must make reality accessible to man and at the same time partly transfigures it; he suggests the same origin for primitive religion and for symbolic thought itself, a volcanic origin that makes reality appear both under aspects that belong to it and under aspects that do not belong to it. This view of the problem may well be the most precious legacy of Durkheim that later developments have obscured and pushed aside.

Lévi-Strauss perceives that the origin of symbolic thought is a legitimate theoretical question. He denies, however, that this question can be concretely investigated. As a proof of this, he mentions the failure of those who tried, the Freud of *Totem and Taboo* and Durkheim himself, who were unable, in the hypotheses they formulated, to divest themselves of the cultural rules and symbolicity for which they were trying to account. These failures are real but they do not mean the undertaking is meaningless. There is a lot to learn, anyway, both from Durkheim's idea of a collective *effervescence* and from Freud's idea of a primordial murder, even if neither idea is an acceptable solution of the problem.

In my view, the achievements of Lévi-Strauss himself make more meaningful a new attempt at solving the same problem. His specific contribution, I believe, lies in these two categories of differentiation and undifferentiation that he has developed but that he cannot fully utilize because he turns them into metaphysical absolutes. When he insists on equating differentiation in myths with the process of "human thinking," he does not do justice to the conjunctive elements in his own symbolic network; we must not follow him when he says that myth alone is "good to think," when he excommunicates ritual from anthropology, and when he equates the undifferentiated with ritual.

Can the undifferentiated be equated with the fantastic elements in primitive religion? Not quite, but the two questions are closely related to each other. We have already suggested that mythical monsters, those conglomerates of differences, must be in some respects the verbal equivalent of the bizarre actions demanded by rituals such as incest, sex inversions, and reversal of social hierarchies, which have the undifferentiation of the community as their common denominator. We can consider all these phenomena as accidents of differentiation that suggest a real social crisis. If the undifferentiated cannot be a perverse "nostalgia for the immediate" or a legitimate allusion to some genuinely presymbolical no man's land, it can only allude to some kind of disorder, to a crisis of differences.

The structuralists would say that such speculations are idle talk because the nature of primitive societies and the absence of documents precludes any historical investigations. The possibilities I have in mind have nothing to do with a historical investigation. The only investigation that makes sense is still a structural one. There are many features in ritual behavior and in the fantastic elements of both myth and ritual that suggest the same type of crisis everywhere, a pattern of disintegration that transcends the historical uniqueness of specific incidents.

If we want to understand the nature of the ritual crisis, we must pay heed, I believe, to those aspects of rituals and prohibitions that suggest fierce mimetic rivalries and a reciprocal alienation that is constantly reinforced by a feedback effect until separate perceptions become jumbled together. If we observe the constant fascination with mirror effects and enemy twins, in primitive ritual as well as in primitive mythology, we will have to conclude that the undifferentiated has something to do with the symmetry of conflict, with a circular pattern of destructuration that must constitute a real threat. This would explain why primitive societies are almost as loath to think these matters through as structuralism itself. Their purpose is the same as Lévi-Strauss's—to redifferentiate the identical twins, to stop the crisis, and to replace the fearful symmetry of mimetic rivalry with the reassuringly static and manageable binary patterns to which structuralism limits its understanding of the religious text.

The possibilities I am trying to explore are often suggested by the myths and rituals that rarely speak of themselves as if they constituted an absolute beginning. Lévi-Strauss takes note of these suggestions but he rejects them as ridiculous. How could disorder generate order? he explicitly asks (p. 607). Not directly, of course, but why should the generative process be direct? Lévi-Strauss himself has often acknowledged, notably in *Anthropologie structurale I*, the key role played by some very ambiguous figures, such as the North American trickster upon whom all the contradictions inherent not only in disorder but in the improbable conjunction of disorder and order appear to converge and to settle. These figures are highly exalted as mythical heroes, founding ancestors, even savior gods, but they may also be debased as cheats, transgressors, and criminals. At the least, there will be something anomalous in them that bespeaks great misfortune as well as a high destiny.

If we assume that the mimetic crisis can be resolved through a still mimetic but unanimous transfer against an arbitrary victim, we can also be sure that the arbitrariness of the deed will escape the reconciled community. The victim should therefore acquire in retrospect all the features that are ascribed to the ambiguous mediators of mythology. In the eyes of the community, that victim will appear responsible both for the violence that raged when it was alive and for the peace that is restored by its death. It becomes the signifier of all relations between the members of the community, especially the worst and the best. We can understand, then, why all religious prescriptions can be referred to that ambiguous mediator—the prohibitions because their purpose is to avoid a recurrence of the crisis that the victim embodies, the rituals because they are a reenactment of the crisis not for its own sake but for the sake of the sacrificial resolution and the greater communal unity it is supposed to achieve. We can understand why a notion such as the sacred, with its omnipotence both for the best and for the worst, can develop from such episodes of "victimage."[6] If we only assume that the original transfer is effective, the interpretation of both conflictual and harmonious relations, inside and outside the community, must focus on the victim; all features of religious systems and religious behavior become intelligible.

The religious transfer is the fundamental fact that each religious community must interpret in its own way within the structural constraints that stem from the type of collective delusion it cannot fail to be. Far from being rigidly reductive, the hypothesis accommodates all the variants of religious systems, as well as their invariants. The element of victimage often remains half-visible, but it normally assumes only a secondary role, as if the game were dominated by the victim rather than the victimizers. The structuring power of victimage remains hidden.

An examination of myths reveals that, at the moment of resolution, whenever it remains perceptible, a diversity of oppositions tends to give way to an *all against one* pattern that is treated, of course, by the structural analyst as one more binary differentiation of the usual type. This pattern recurs so frequently that the observer should suspect it may have a structural relevance. Even if the structuralists did isolate this pattern, their formalistic and metaphysical assumptions would prevent them from grasping its real power both as a peacemaker and as a symbol maker.

If we look at the two myths mentioned in the preceding pages, we will see that both can be interpreted as the mythical surfacing of structurally misunderstood scapegoat phenomena. In the first myth, the overcrowding and confusion that prevails at the beginning is resolved by the elimination of a single element. Lévi-Strauss offers a purely logical interpretation of this process. This is what he does, too, in *Le Totémisme aujourd'hui*, with two other well-known myths. The genesis of "totemic" classifications is accounted for by the elimination of something in excess; *more space* is thus provided. In the case of each of these two myths, however, he acknowledges the presence of a greedy and indiscreet divinity, analogous to the Scandinavian Loki, whose ill-advised and pernicious action triggers the process of elimination. The god himself, in each case, is either the sum total or part of what is forcefully expelled.[7] Obviously, an interpretation that would not be purely logical and spatial is possible; if this interpretation runs along the lines I propose it will make fully intelligible all the elements that structuralism is forced to leave out of account. The same is true, of course, of the jaguar-woman, that resilient monster who is finally brought to a sad end. After much mischief, she is thrown into a fire and burned to death by all the other characters united against her. This is the end of the myth, and we must presume that order is (re)established.[8]

Collective victimage is a *hypothesis* regarding the origin of both primitive religion and symbolicity. The unanimous transfer and victimage to which all directly and indirectly observable religious systems can be traced must be the distant descendants of more elementary and unimaginable phenomena from which symbolic thought itself originates. The word *hypothesis* must not be interpreted as a precaution or a hesitation in the face of the current climate of opinion. The structuring power of victimage is necessarily *hypothetical* because no continuous line of empirical evidence, no linguistico-structural analysis will ever lead directly to it. This does not disqualify it at all, because all religious themes are brought back to a single structural delusion that necessarily transfigures or eliminates its own generative mechanism.

Let us return to the text at hand, which is the "Finale" of *Mythologiques*. If my hypothesis is correct, if the origin and structure of symbolic forms are such as I claim, this text too should fall somehow under its jurisdiction, however remotely and mediately.

First, let me consider the problem of the text from a purely rational and scholarly perspective. I said that the "manifest destiny" of structuralism was to extend further and further the frontiers of meaning in the structural sense. The gist of my remarks is that the reach of structuralism has exceeded its grasp. Many disciples, direct and indirect, would deny this, of course, but Lévi-Strauss himself knows better. His "Finale" is a long-postponed encounter with those phenomena that do not respond properly to the structuralist method.

If a methodology is not universal, it must at least state unambiguously to which objects it does apply and to which it does not. If there are rebellious phenomena, it is imperative to show that they are not spread throughout the anthropological corpus; they must belong to some well-defined area easily separated from the rest. Lévi-Strauss must also show that these phenomena do not amount to some impenetrable mystery, or worse still, to some enigma that could be solved by means other than his method. Ideally, therefore, he must find a unique center of willful and sterile resistance to his structural reason.

In the "Finale" of L'Homme nu, Lévi-Strauss announces that in ritual he has found precisely what he needed; this institution is a senseless revolt against the very essence of human intelligence, and those who insist on taking ritual seriously can only share in the same delusion. His conclusion is untenable. It cannot be defended unless the data are seriously distorted. In order to validate the claims of his structuralist method, Lévi-Strauss needs this conclusion badly. If we look at these distortions, however, they do not suggest anything like a conscious manipulation or even careless expediency. They have a coherence of their own; they form a pattern systematic enough to be both less visible before we detect it and more visible afterward than a calculated falsification or an accidental error could be.

Let me summarize that pattern once more. Lévi-Strauss takes all differentiation away from ritual and gives it to myth. He does the same thing with the undifferentiated, but in reverse. What is taken away from ritual, myth must receive; what is taken away from myth, ritual must receive. The redistribution is symmetrical, with one small but essential exception. In order to turn myth into the sacred temple of differentiation, some of the undifferentiated must be kept there, acknowledged as such, or almost as such.

How can we account for this remarkable pattern, and especially for that crucial ambiguity at the center of it, for the dual nature of the undifferentiated that is evil in bulk, so to speak, but becomes good and indispensable in smaller amounts at the beginning of myth? If we view the excommunication of ritual as the intellectual equivalent of the ritual expulsion, if we reread our text in the light of the anthropological hypothesis I have outlined, we will find that the systematic distortion of the antropological data becomes intelligible. This application of the hypothesis will appear more appropriate if we think of the arbitrariness that characterizes the treatment of ritual and that duplicates exactly the arbitrariness of the victim in the hypothesis. Ritual, philosophy, and even what Lévi-Strauss calls "structuralisme-fiction" are not really what Lévi-Strauss says they are, nor can they all be found together—or even separately—in the place where he seeks them.

Ritual is expelled as the sole and complete embodiment of the un-differentiated. This expulsion is supposed to rid us once and for all of this "evil mixture," as Shakespeare would call it. And yet, a small quantity is needed to insure the transfiguration of myth. It is no longer the "evil mixture" but a most crucial component in the presentation of myth as an exemplary manifestation of human thinking. How can this transfiguration take place? If we confer the generative role upon the expulsion of ritual, we will see that the circulation and metamorphosis of the undifferentiated works exactly like the *sacra* of primitive reli-gion. The victim appears to embody the violence of the crisis, inter-preted as a bad and disruptive *sacrum* but metamorphosed by the expulsion into something still dangerous but beneficial and construc-tive, provided it is used in the right place, at the right time, and in precisely measured quantities. Only priests or initiates can practice this delicate operation.

The undifferentiated is viewed as an infection that would contami-nate the whole anthropological body if the affected limb were not speedily amputated. Since the undifferentiated is supposed to be en-tirely contained in ritual, it is entirely expelled by the expulsion of ritual. What we have at the beginning of myth is not some of the old stuff left over, even though, at the same time, it is still exactly the same thing, but the result of an alchemy that coincides with the "kathartic" effect of the expulsion. The deadly fermentation that threatened the whole body is gone; in its place is a pinch of yeast that causes the whole textual dough to rise. Left to itself, the undifferentiated is pure disintegration; once transmuted by the expulsion, it holds the key to the structure of myth as a self-organizing system. In this expulsion of the various *bêtes noires*, a negative force is partly spent and partly channeled into the directions required for the reorganization of the text on a basis acceptable to structuralism.

The undifferentiated of Lévi-Strauss works exactly like the *phar-makon* in Plato's *Phaedrus* as explicated by Derrida.[9] It is the drug that is both bad and good at the same time: in large amounts it acts like poison; in the right doses prescribed by the right doctor, it be-comes the medicine that restores health. The reference to Plato is especially appropriate. The most striking parallel to the expulsion of ritual comes in *The Republic* with the treatment of the poet, who is adorned as a sacrificial victim before being ordered to leave. To Plato, most poetry—and mythology—is a mimetic loss of differentiation and the concomitant production of undifferentiated monsters. All art is closely related to the undifferentiation of orgiastic rituals. The fact that philosophy and mythology are on opposite sides of those particular fences is unimportant; the scapegoats cannot fail to be arbitrary. The purpose of the expulsion remains constant. Plato, like Lévi-Strauss, wants to make his perfect city safe for differentiation. Knowledge and differentiation are the same thing. We must not be surprised if the inverted Bergsonism of Lévi-Strauss sounds like a Platonism right side up.

Ritual, contrary to what Lévi-Strauss believes, is an earlier effort to expel the "evil mixture" and make culture safe for differentiation. Paradoxically, therefore, the Lévi-Straussian expulsion of the undifferentiated, just like the Platonic expulsion of mimesis, pursues the same objective as ritual. This observation can be generalized. The horrified recoil from primitive ritual and religion stems from the same impulse as religion itself, in the new circumstances brought about by this very religion. We must abandon the linear logic that sees the antireligious text as independent from the religious text it pretends to "demystify." In reality the religious text is a first violent recoil from crude forms of violence; it is also a complex economy in which this same violence is in part assuaged by sacrifice, in part camouflaged, ignored, and transfigured.

Contrary to what Lévi-Strauss believes, ritual is a first effort to expel the "evil mixture." Thus, the Lévi-Straussian text is generated by a new expulsion, in many respects identical to the ritual one; what is expelled is the expulsion itself, but so it is already in the religious forms. The truth of the expulsion is the essential taboo of human culture; far from transgressing it, the second-generation expulsion reinforces this taboo. This explains why this metaphysical operation produces effects structurally similar to the religious expulsion; these effects generate a new text, a duplicate of the religious form in which the metaphysical notions, and more specifically the undifferentiated, display the same paradoxical qualities and function exactly as the former *sacra*.

All postritual institutions are generated, it appears, by these second-generation expulsions that expel the former agent of expulsion. This is true of the theater, of philosophy, and also of the judicial system, political institutions, etc. In all these forms, the process of "expelling the expulsion," of effacing the traces, is a continuous one that takes these forms farther and farther away from their origin. They are more and more estranged from their real subject and yet they can never really take leave of that subject.

The greatness of modern anthropology is that indirectly, no doubt, unknowingly, and still unsuccessfully but nevertheless significantly, it reaches back toward those cultural forms that can throw the most decisive light upon the generative process of all cultural texts. The discipline of anthropology was fascinated at first by primitive religion. In recent years, however, that fascination has subsided. The history of that discipline seems to repeat the history of all postritual institutions or texts. With structuralism, that evolution has accelerated and it is, so to speak, legitimized. The great religious questions are out. By purging anthropology of its "evil mixture," Lévi-Strauss tries to rid it of those elements that still remain intractable after a century of speculation. It is true that these speculations, so far, have not produced the expected results. But it is better to acknowledge the failure than to declare the problem meaningless.

The problem was certainly badly formulated, and the Lévi-Straussian purge, perhaps, can contribute to a better formulation. The greatness of Lévi-Strauss is that his text still bears the marks of this arbitrary purge. At least indirectly, therefore, the text still communicates with everything it disallows. This will not be true, I am afraid, of the anthropological "discourse" Lévi-Strauss has made possible. This discourse can go on endlessly without being interrupted by any disturbing questions. From now on, we will learn everything there is to learn about the contrasted significance of "rare," "medium rare," and "well done" in the cannibalistic feast, but of cannibalism itself there will be no question. As with prejudice against the jaguar-woman, refusal to eat human flesh will be treated as an ethnocentric fallacy we must learn to overlook.

This process of anthropological neutralization closely resembles what has happened to a great deal of literary criticism in the last thirty years, both in this country with the great war against "the intentional fallacy" and in the French-speaking countries with the so-called "thematic," then with the "structuralist," criticism. As Leo Bersani observes of Georges Poulet:

> The image of a circle may be recurrent in literature, but no interesting literary work can be adequately discussed in terms of its metaphors of "centers" and "circumferences." And even the categories of time and space in, for example, Proust can themselves be made intelligible only if they are placed in relation to other things in the work (jealousy and snobbery, which Poulet doesn't even mention), that is, considered as metaphorical terms of a larger system in which affectivity is infinitely more than geometric.[10]

It is supremely significant, of course, that the themes eliminated from the reading of Proust be jealousy and snobbery. These themes are the equivalent of ritual in the anthropological text; erotic and social discrimination are the specifically Proustian modes of expulsion. Once more it is a former agent of expulsion that is expelled, and this expulsion generates a critical discourse free from all traces of "evil mixture," totallly sheltered from potentially disruptive questioning.

One can show, I believe, that the parallelism between the transmutation of literary criticism and that of anthropology stems from a second-generation expulsion that drowns all decisive questions in some form of metaphysical idealism. What is unique with Lévi-Strauss is the scrupulous exactness of his Bergsonism in reverse. The dualism itself, in forms that may vary with the individual borrower, is the common denominator for all those combinations of philosophy, ideology, literary criticism, and social science that, under diverse labels, have dominated the French scene for many a year.

Sartre undoubtedly played a pivotal role in this affair. His well-known misreading of Heidegger, that famous *contresens* to which we owe *Being and Nothingness*, truly amounts to a first and historically decisive relapse into Bergsonian metaphysics, disguised by the Germanic terminology. It does not really matter if the earlier "flux" freezes into a motionless *en-soi*. It does not matter if the agent of differentiation becomes the negativity of a *pour-soi*. The important point is that the relationship between the two poles remains indeterminate, behind an appearance of determination. Sartre is the only one who ever explicitly recognized this indeterminacy. He calls it *freedom*. He almost gave the whole game away even before it started, and he has been rebuked for this ever since.

As long as this indeterminacy is clearly understood, only avowedly subjective idealists will be attracted to the metaphysical dualism. And it is, indeed, in a mood of avowedly subjective idealism that *Les Temps modernes* was launched. The indeterminacy, however, is likely to remain unperceived. The relationship between the two poles is always expressed in pairs of terms that do not make sense if they are employed separately, such as the *pour-soi* and the *en-soi*, the *découpage* and the *non-découpé*, differentiation and the undifferentiated. These pairs of words make us feel that the relationship must be very close, even inextricable. It looks like a serious matter, something that cannot be taken lightly. In reality this relationship is one of undefined and undefinable distortion on both sides, even of complete betrayal. Even if we wanted to, we could not take it into account. Structures can be studied as if they were completely autonomous, which is the only manner, of course, in which we can study structures and even conceive of such things as structures.

Social scientists are always on the lookout for a position that will reconcile their awareness fo cultural relativism with their belief in the unity of knowledge, a belief they cannot discard without discarding the scientific enterprise itself. As long as its real nature is not clearly understood, the metaphysical dualism inherited from Bergson and Sartre appears to square that particular circle. Singularities do not have to be silenced and yet oppositions do not have to be resolved. It does not

matter if the stuff on the outside is solid, liquid, or in between. It does
not matter if it is lumpy, grainy, or smoothly homogenized. What really
matters is that it gives no indication whatever of how it should be
carved; it provides no guidelines to the process of differentiation. With
Sartre, for instance, as in the Lévi-Straussian mythology, the *en-soi* is
perfectly meaningless until it is given meaning by the *pour-soi*. This
meaning is already a structure that is called the *project*. We cannot
even ask, in the last analysis, if some projects are better than others.
Some people see their colleagues as colleagues when they get to the
office in the morning, others see them as jaguar-women. Everybody is
entitled to his own project and *honni soit qui mal y pense*.

The shift from the *existential* to the *phenomenological* and to the
structural corresponds to a gradual move away from the first pole, a
move led by Sartre himself, who soon gave up the nauseous embrace of
the *en-soi* for analyses of the *pour-soi's* projects. The structural label
has less to do with a specific method, or methods, than with the fusion
of the second pole with some social or anthropological discipline. This
combination gives the second pole the added "weight" needed to tip
the scales in its favor. Instantly, the borrowed discipline seems to
achieve a high degree of autonomy and scientific maturity. Thus,
Gestalt psychology, ethnology, and structural linguistics together with
a constantly revamped Freudianism and Marxism were successively or
simultaneously brought into play.

All the loudly advertised "revolutions" of the past thirty years have
never changed anything essential; they simply tend to eliminate the
first pole entirely and to widen in the extreme the definition of the
second. The evolution itself and its effects are both entirely predictable. It is obvious, for instance, that there cannot be any *subject*
but the structure itself. As long as the arbitrary *découpage* that determines the structural field remains under the influence of classical
philosophy, or literature, the individual will appear omnipotent because the structure will extend no farther than his reach. When the
emphasis shifts to the social sciences and to language, the structure
exceeds anything we can call individual, and the impotence, even the
inexistence, of the individual subject follows as inexorably as its total
omnipotence in the previous phase.

We can also expect that, in due time, the whole mood of the enterprise is going to change. As the disciples contemplate the works of their
masters, enthusiasm gives way to lassitude, even to a spirit of rebellion,
to a desire for new expulsions. All these solipsistic structures lined up
on the cultural shelves of *la modernité*, be they books, paintings,
myths, entire cultures, or anything else, begin to look and to taste like
canned goods on the shelves of a supermarket. When all the sublimely

"unique" "worlds" of countless individual writers are neatly stashed away in the pages of critical anthologies, each occupying roughly the same amount of space, the undivided worship briefly granted to each in turn cannot fail to evoke the treatment reserved to tourist-class passengers on a fully loaded commercial airplane. We have better reasons than we think to be vociferous in our dislike of the *société de consommation*. We are an integral part of it. We cannot respect all differences equally without in the end respecting none.

To a Lévi-Strauss, the infinitely diverse products of the symbolic function testify to the unlimited power of man to create order out of chaos. To others, this same diversity testifies to man's inability to reach even a stable illusion, a permanent fiction, let alone any ultimate truth. In this disenchanted and subversive mood, the temptation will be irresistible for the investigator still faithful to the method to turn it into a weapon against the whole Western industry of knowledge and finally against itself. To the Michel Foucault of *Les Mots et les choses* each period in the old "history of ideas" is a structure floating in the void, like the Lévi-Straussian structure or the Sartrian project here called an *episteme*. When the analysis reaches down to the observer's own time and to his own structuralist *episteme*, the scholar's enterprise vacillates on its pedestal to the obvious delight, this time, of this particular scholar who seems primarily intent on a most scholarly burial of scholarship itself.

An illusion of long standing is now dissolving, the illusion that a reconciliation has been achieved between the autonomy of "structures" and the requirement of a universally valid context in which to study these structures. The conditions of a genuine science have never been met. Foucault clearly perceives this fact but he does not seem to perceive that the failure is that of a metaphysical system only. To conclude as he does that no science of man is possible, that the very idea must be a passing phase, is an illegitimate extrapolation. And that extrapolation obviously results from a continued belief in the old metaphysics. Foucault correctly appraises the limitations of this system but he confuses them with the absolute limits of human language and of our power to know.

Lévi-Strauss deplores this nihilism: he attributes it to "structuralisme-fiction," a loose application of his method (p. 573). As a response, in the "Finale" of *L'Homme nu*, he hardens all his previous positions; his differentiating principle becomes more isolated and abstract than ever. He reinforces in his own work the very features that lead to the attitudes he deplores. The same epistemological nihilism moves the later work of Gilles Deleuze. His fluxification of all differences, in *L'Anti-Oedipe*, is a parodic mimicry and a confusion of the structural gesture par excellence: the differentiation of the flux.[11] Differentiation itself, this time, turns undifferentiated, and the two together, more sacred than ever, are supposed to herald the schizophrenic liberation of our structuralist and capitalistic society.

The all-purpose differentiating machine is beginning to look like a played-out toy, a primitive noisemaker, perhaps, that must be agitated more and more wildly to keep the public and even its own users at least mildly interested. The metaphysical dualism is disintegrating from the inside but it still holds sway. It is natural for the entire venture to end up in the current solipsistic idealism of the linguistic structure.

We are constantly told these days that each interpretation is a new text and that for every text there is an unlimited number of interpretations, each no more and no less valid than the next. We are constantly told of the irremediable loss that occurs even in the most careful translation from one language to another. Everybody says so; no one ever says anything else. Everybody by now should be convinced and there must be some other reason than our need for enlightenment in these sempiternal objurgations. There can be only one reason. We live in a world more unified every day by science and technology. The weight of evidence against the current view of language is so formidable that it needs no spokesman to be heard. Our unanimous chorus is not really able to cover the unacknolwedged voice.

It is interesting to note that Lévi-Strauss, in theory, wants no part in this chorus. Only the natural sciences flourish, he says, because *in them only, the symbols and the referents are really adequate to each other.* The sorry state of the social sciences comes from their inability to emulate that ideal (p. 574). This adequacy is not an exclusive monopoly of advanced science with its highly mathematized language. It must obtain in large areas of even the most primitive cultures; otherwise, techniques would not be successful and could not be transmitted from generation to generation. The people would simply perish. From the technique of irrigation in ancient Egypt to the recipe for *boeuf bourguignon,* there is an immense linguistic domain whose practitioners never experience that titillating *glissement du signifié sous le signifiant* that is quite real, no doubt, in some domains, but that cannot be presented as characteristic of all language.

Lévi-Strauss acknowledges this fact too. Unfortunately, these healthy theoretical views have no effect on the practice of structural analysis. Even if it is legitimate at some stage in the analysis of a myth to place side by side all the entities it differentiates, jaguar-women and all, it cannot be methodologically sound to assimilate, once and for all, those objects that can have a real referent and those that cannot. The sciences Lévi-Strauss admires did not reach their present state of eminence by disregarding the difference between real percepts and hallucinations.

When we turn language into a prisonhouse, to use an expression of Fredric Jameson's,[12] we ignore its true mystery just as much as when we take it for granted, when we assume it is always perfectly adequate to its task. The true mystery is that language is both the perfectly transparent milieu of empiricism and the prisonhouse of linguisticism. Sometimes it is the one, sometimes it is the other; often it is an inextricable mixture of both.

No wonder some philosophers tried, and failed, to separate the linguistic wheat from the linguistic chaff. Even after we get rid of jaguar-women and other monsters—and the achievement should not be underestimated, since it makes the natural sciences possible—our power to distinguish real objects, to fashion symbols that are adequate to their referents, seems to weaken as we turn back upon ourselves, as we try to understand the distinctions we make in the social, cultural, and religious fields. The hypothesis I propose makes these difficulties understandable. If the power of man to distinguish anything is rooted in the most arbitrary of all our distinctions, in the sacralization of collective victims, if residual forms of victimage and sacralization are still operative among us, it is inevitable that objectivity will be most difficult to achieve as we reach closer and closer to the source of all symbolicity. Logical and philosophical means alone will never solve the problem. This does not mean a solution cannot be achieved, but the only hope to achieve it lies in the discovery of the origin and true nature of symbolicity. The problem is one with the enigma of primitive religion and the solution lies in a theory of the spontaneous scapegoat victim as the original symbol.

From the standpoint of the various trends that dominate the intellectual scene at the present time, this hypothesis inevitably appears marginal, eccentric. There are signs that it may not remain so forever, but these signs are still scattered in works of very different inspiration and their unity is difficult to perceive. Among the more recent signs, all those critical works should be included that suggest some relationship, however indirect and tenuous, between human conflict and the principle of form or structure. I read some texts of Jacques Derrida as such a sign. Another one, in my view, is the *pharmakos* archetype in the criticism of Northrop Frye.[13] A third and most remarkable figure in the present context is Kenneth Burke. He anticipated some of the most interesting intuitions of recent years on the nature of symbolicity, yet he never succumbed to the seduction of the metaphysical dualism that limits the scope of these intuitions, on the other side of the Atlantic

Ocean. As a consequence, Burke effectively encounters problems that remain invisible in the context of the free-floating solipsistic structure. Burke asserts that a "principle of victimage" is implicit in the nature of drama. He takes it for granted, legitimately I believe (but surprisingly, in view of the general tenor of Aristotelian criticism), that the notion of *katharsis* refers to a process of victimage. In *Coriolanus*, Shakespeare consciously provides his hero with all the ambiguous qualities that make a good scapegoat.[14] These qualities are those enumerated by Aristotle in his *Poetics* and they are really a transposition of the requirements for a good sacrificial victim. Since tragic heroes normally come from religious myth and ritual, one would like to see the Burkean reading of tragedy expanded into a theory of these religious institutions that are based on explicit forms of victimage, like the *pharmakos* ritual of the Greeks.

In the eyes of Burke, violence and victimage result from a desire for a form too perfect and therefore from an abuse of the formal principle; they are not essential to that principle itself. Victimage follows from the form, in other words, but the reverse is not true: the form does not follow from victimage. Even if the principle of victimage is present in Burke's definition of man, that "symbol-using and mis-using animal," it will be there only as a "codicil."[15] Its position remains marginal, eccentric. Massive evidence from the anthropological data demands, I believe, that it be moved to the center, that it be made the origin of symbolicity.

NOTES

1. *L'Homme nu* (1971) is the last volume of Claude Lévi-Strauss, *Mythologiques* (Paris: Plon, 1964–71). The other volumes are *Le Cru et le cuit* (1964), *Du Miel aux cendres* (1966), and *L'Origine des manières de table* (1968). Subsequent references to the "Finale" of *L'Homme nu*, indicated in the text in parentheses, will be to this edition.

2. Claude Lévi-Strauss, *La Pensée sauvage* (Paris: Plon, 1962), pp. 295–302.

3. Claude Lévi-Strauss, *Le Totémisme aujourd'hui* (Paris: Presses universitaires de France, 1962).

4. Ibid., pp. 132–49.

5. Emile Durkheim, *Les Formes élémentaires de la vie religieuse* (Paris: Presses universitaires de France, 1968), pp. 337–38.

6. See René Girard, *La Violence et le sacré* (Paris: Grasset, 1972); René Girard, *Violence and the Sacred*, trans. Patrick Gregory (Baltimore: The Johns Hopkins University Press, 1977).

7. Lévi-Strauss, *Totémisme*, pp. 25–37. For a more detailed reading of these myths, see Chapter 9 of this volume.

8. Lévi-Strauss, *Du Miel aux cendres*, p. 313.

9. Jacques Derrida, "La Pharmacie de Platon," in *La Dissémination* (Paris: Seuil, 1972), pp. 71–197.

10. Leo Bersani, "From Bachelard to Barthes," in *Issues in Contemporary Literary Criticism*, ed. Gregory T. Polletta (Boston: Little, Brown and Co., 1973), p. 97.

11. Gilles Deleuze and Felix Guattari, *L'Anti-Oedipe* (Paris: Editions de Minuit, 1972).

12. Fredric Jameson, *The Prison-House of Language* (Princeton: Princeton University Press, 1972).

13. See René Girard, "Lévi-Strauss, Frye, Derrida and Shakespearean Criticism," *Diacritics* 3, no. 3 (1973): 34–38.

14. Kenneth Burke, "Coriolanus—and the Delights of Faction," in *Language as Symbolic Action* (Berkeley and Los Angeles: University of California Press, 1966), pp. 81–97.

15. Ibid., p. 16.

9

Violence and Representation in the Mythical Text

Many myths pretend to account for the birth of the cultural order to which they belong. According to Lévi-Strauss this claim is necessarily spurious, since even modern anthropology must give up the search for origins. As a result, the dramatic elements of mythology do not interest Lévi-Strauss as such. He has little patience for the students of mythology who focus their attention on those aspects. He is aware, however, of the obvious similarities between myths even very distant from each other. In order to fulfill his project of a scientific theory of myth, he must somehow account for these. In his famous article on the Oedipus myth, he developed a view of the hero as a mediator between contradictory propositions. This view has become extremely popular even though or perhaps because it is only a Hegelianized version of the nineteenth-century conception of mythology as *philosophie sauvage.*

Obviously less satisfied with this theory than his followers, Lévi-Strauss, in *Totemism*, attempts a second synthesis, which in my opinion is no more successful than the first but is much more interesting even though, to my knowledge at least, it has received almost no critical attention. This second treatment rests primarily on two examples. One is the Ojibwa myth from which modern anthropology has borrowed the word "totemism." The second comes from Tikopia, in Polynesia, and it also deals with the alleged origin of a so-called totemic system. In *The Raw and the Cooked*, the whole interpretation is reworked and completed apropos of a Bororo myth.

Here is the summary of the Ojibwa myth in the English translation of Rodney Needham:

A myth explains that the five "original" clans are descended from six anthropomorphic supernatural beings who emerged from the ocean to mingle with human beings. One of them had his eyes covered and dared not look at the Indians, though he showed the greatest anxiety to do so. At last he could

This essay appeared in *MLN* 92 (December 1977): 922–44.

no longer restrain his curiosity, and on one occasion he partially lifted his veil, and his eye fell on the form of a human being, who instantly fell dead "as if struck by one of the thunderers." Though the intentions of this dread being were friendly to men, yet the glance of his eye was too strong, and it inflicted certain death. His fellows therefore caused him to return to the bosom of the great water. The five others remained among the Indians, and "became a blessing to them." From them originate the five great clans or totems.[1]

This summarizes the second myth, the one from Tikopia:

A long time ago the gods were no different from mortals, and the gods were the direct representatives of the clans in the land. It came about that a god from foreign parts, Tikarau, paid a visit to Tikopia, and the gods of the land prepared a splendid feast for him, but first they organized trials of strength or speed, to see whether their guest or they would win. During a race, the stranger slipped and declared that he was injured. Suddenly, however, while he was pretending to limp, he made a dash for the provisions of the feast, grabbed up the heap, and fled for the hills. The family of gods set off in pursuit; Tikarau slipped and fell again, so that the clan gods were able to retrieve some of the provisions, one a coconut, another a taro, another a breadfruit, and others a yam. Tikarau succeeded in reaching the sky with most of the foodstuff for the feast, but these four vegetable foods had been saved for men.[2]

The two myths have several points in common, and the essential one is defined as follows:

In both cases, totemism as a system is introduced as *what remains* of a diminished totality, a fact which may be a way of expressing that the terms of the system are significant only if they are *separated* from each other, since they alone remain to equip a semantic field which was previously better supplied and into which a discontinuity has been introduced.[3]

In *The Raw and the Cooked*, this logical or, more precisely, topological interpretation becomes more explicit. Differentiation, the essential process of human thought, can only be represented as a spacing-out of the entities that must be differentiated. All these myths, Lévi-Strauss speculates, posit a *totalité originaire* so compact, a mass so crowded with elements, at the beginning, that human thought cannot penetrate. So many entities are packed so tightly in a space so small that differentiation cannot take place. In these circumstances, the removal of a few elements, even a single fragment, will provide enough free space for differentiation to take place. Continuity will give way to the discontinuity of "human thought":

In each case, discontinuity had to be achieved by the radical elimination of certain fractions of the continuum. Once the latter has been reduced, a smaller number of elements are free to spread out in the same space, while the distance between them is now sufficient to prevent them from overlapping or merging into one another.[4]

Thus, to Lévi-Strauss, the mythical drama really boils down to an allegorical dramatization of the thinking process itself, the production of differences. Myths are not merely structured; they are already structuralist. Unlike Lévi-Strauss, however, they can conceive of intellectual operations only as real events that take place "at the beginning" and that they regard as the "origin" of the cultural system.

The observations of Lévi-Strauss are correct. Something like a "radical elimination" does really constitute the high point in the mythical drama and it is supposed to play a crucial role in the establishment of the cultural order. The common denominator is real, and it belongs not only to the two myths analysed in *Totemism* but to many others. But the topological model invented by Lévi-Strauss does not account for that common denominator; it does not even always agree with the mythical data.

The eliminated fragment must belong to the so-called *totalité originaire*, otherwise its elimination will not provide more space than was available at the beginning. If the fragment is extraneous, if it enters the totality after it is constituted, its elimination will cure, perhaps, whatever disturbances the presence of that foreign body may have caused but it will not modify the situation that prevailed originally *as far as space is concerned*; it will merely restore that original situation.

In order to find out if the eliminated fragment truly belongs to the *totalité originaire*, we must know, of course, what this fragment or fragments consist of. In his analysis of the Tikopia myth, Lévi-Strauss seems to refer to those unspecified totemic goods that Tikarau manages to steal away. But what about Tikarau himself? He, too, is radically eliminated. The general make-up and vocabulary of the so-called structural analysis suggest a world of inanimate objects but this is somewhat deceptive because, in the case of the Ojibwa myth, the only possible candidate for the role of eliminated fragment is the god sent back into the deep as a punishment for lifting his veil and killing one member of the community. Lévi-Strauss himself underlines the similarities between the two gods; in both myths, a greedy and indiscreet action by one of these gods triggers the elimination, which, in turn, triggers the totemic differentiation. In each myth, the god himself is eliminated.

If we assume, as we must, that the *totalité originaire* signifies whatever ensemble or community comes first in the mythical sequence it is evident that neither one of our divine malefactors belongs to it. In the Ojibwa myth, the human community comes first. The six supernatural beings may well form another totality but they are defined as outsiders; they come into the human community as visitors from another world. In the myth from Tikopia there is only one totality and we are told quite explicitly that Tikarau does not belong to it. Lévi-Strauss himself describes Tikarau as "un dieu étranger." Rodney Needham translates this as "a god from foreign parts." The phrase reminds one of Lévi-Strauss's own source, Raymond Firth, in *Tikopia Ritual and Belief*: "Tikarau came to the land of Tikopia from foreign parts."[5]

It is not my purpose to prove that the "eliminated fragment," as a rule, does not belong to the original totality. In some cases it does, in other cases it does not; still other cases are ambiguous or handled in such a way as to make the spatial reduction of the mythical drama unlikely at best. Oedipus, for instance, can be defined as an "eliminated," even twice-eliminated fragment. He really does belong to the *totalité originaire*; he was born, in other words, in the city of Thebes, but it would be absurd, obviously, to reduce his comings and goings in and out of that city to their spatial consequences. In many myths, ambiguity prevails and makes it impossible to equate the real message of the myth to the neat space-producing device imagined by Lévi-Strauss.

Even if all textual data agreed with it, the space-producing device would still be unsatisfactory. The problem is not that it does away with all the moral, existential, or psychoanalytical values or intuitions that many people attach to mythology and that Lévi-Strauss regards with great contempt. The problem is that it does not even account for all the features that Lévi-Strauss himself recognizes as common to the two myths he analyzes. Here is one of these features: "The same opposition will be noted between individual and collective conduct, the former being negatively regarded and the latter positively in relation to totemism."[6]

Why should the god—who happens to coincide in both myths with the eliminated fragment—appear as a threat to the community if the only problem is to provide a little more elbow room by unloading some excess baggage? According to Lévi-Strauss, the topological scheme that is the real message of the mythical drama is imaginary; it can only be a representation therefore. Why should a representation so bland and so harmless be obscured behind a bizarre indictment of the "eliminated fragment" who also happens to be a god?

The paradox of divine misbehavior and "radical elimination" affects not only the two supernatural heroes in the two myths of *Totemism* but countless other heroes in countless myths all over the world. It is this paradox, really, that reappears even in Aristotle's *Poetics* under the famous label of *hamartia*, the tragic flaw that justifies the demise of the hero in the eyes of the crowd and of Aristotle himself, thereby providing us with an exact literary equivalent of the "structure" isolated by Lévi-Strauss, a collective action that is positively qualified because it radically eliminates the individual responsible for an action that is "negatively qualified."

Lévi-Strauss himself seems to acknowledge the scope of the problem in the passage immediately following the last one I quoted: "In the two myths," he writes, "the individual and maleficent conduct is that of a greedy and inconsiderate god (a point on which there are resemblances with Loki of Scandinavia, of whom a masterly study has been made by Georges Dumézil)."[7]

The paradox of divine transgression is still with us. The central enigma of mythology is no less relevant and mysterious than ever for being dressed up in the titillating novelty of a "topological model."

This does not mean there are no sound observations in the analysis of Lévi-Strauss: even though it is not really satisfactory, the topological model touches upon a representation that is almost invariably neglected and that is truly central not only to the two myths analyzed by Lévi-Strauss but to mythology as such. And it is, of course, that "collective action" that is also a "radical elimination" of a threat to the collectivity. If we give up the topological model and retain the observations for which it cannot account, we will realize that the radical elimination truly amounts to collective violence against the delinquent divinity, a kind of lynching. In the Ojibwa myth, we have five individuals acting together in order to get rid of a sixth one, presumably by drowning. In the Tikopia myth, a furious mob hunts down a presumed thief. Why and how should Tikarau fall, since he also flies up into the sky? Lévi-Strauss towers over such undignified and illogical detail but the question may be answered if we turn to Raymond Firth's *Tikopia Ritual and Belief*, a book published too late to be used in *Totemism*.[8]

According to Firth, Tikarau fell on the crest of a hill, overhanging a cliff. This can mean, I suppose, that, from the perspective of the myth itself his pursuers caught up with him and *made him fall*. Still, he "bolted to the edge of the cliff, and being an *atua* launched himself into the sky and set off for the far lands with his ill-gotten gains."

In many societies with no judicial system, the favorite mode of ritual execution is identical with an action that is not really represented in our myth but only suggested or alluded to. The Tarpeian rock in Rome is one particularly famous example of this action. The plunge over the cliff has important features in common with other widespread modes of ritual execution such as collective stoning, abandonment of the victim in the middle of a desert or in a bark at sea, . . . etc.

All these methods permit a community to get rid of an anathematized individual with little or none of the direct physical contact that might be dangerous in view of the contagiousness of violence. Participation is minimal and at the same time it is collective. The responsibility for the death of the victim rests upon no one in particular and this is an added advantage: the chances of further division in the community are diminished.

In the case of the cliff, the community's role can be almost entirely passive. It consists in blocking all avenues of escape except over the cliff. Quite frequently the victim will become so panicked that he will not have to be pushed. Like Tikarau, he will appear to hurl himself into the sky of his own volition. As with Tikarau, we do not know what happened but we may assume that the victim, were he not an *atua*, meaning spirit or a god, would meet his death rather than fly away. Even if the first fall were not fatal, the second one inevitably would be. This point is crucial, I believe, and it does not really matter if the myth blurs it; the blurring itself fits very well with the ominous context that the whole scene cannot fail to evoke.

Like the sacred interpretation of mythology by mythology itself— Tikarau flying into the sky—the space-producing device of Lévi-Strauss is another transfiguration of the collective violence at the heart of the myth, half visible and half hidden, it seems, in all major interpretations. Lévi-Strauss is much closer than he thinks with his "radical elimination" to a text he believes completely alien to his thought, the fourth essay of *Totem and Taboo*, closer, no doubt, than any of the current psychoanalytical readings of mythology, but not close enough to acknowledge his kinship with the best Freud.

Lévi-Strauss thinks he is "scientific" because he reifies the representation of a human process: he reduces men to inanimate objects, mere elements and fragments in a purely spatial field. This dehumanized language of which he is so proud makes it impossible for him fully to perceive the representation that must be revealed, at the center of mythology, in order to make a truly scientific theory possible.

If we test the "topological" model on a still mythical but more explicit representation of lynching than the two examples analyzed in *Totemism*, we will immediately perceive the perfect homology between the two. The Pentheus episode of the Dionysiac cycle, in the dramatic adaptation of *The Bacchae*, constitutes one such explicit representation of lynching. King Pentheus commits all kinds of impious actions; he spies on the bacchantes. As a result of this "negatively qualified" action he becomes the wretched "fragment" that is unceremoniously but quite "radically" and efficiently "eliminated" by the

united bacchantes. This elimination is "positively qualified" in the sense
that it fulfills the will of the god and brings order back to the city of
Thebes.

I do not say that the so-called structural analysis of *Totemism* must
be applied to *The Bacchae*. I say that *The Bacchae* must be applied to
structuralism. The superior intuition of Euripides may finally force the
structuralist to understand what he is talking about. Thanks to
Euripides and *The Bacchae*, we can relate to each other the two very
pertinent observations that I have utilized and that remain unrelated in
Lévi-Strauss. We can understand why the eliminated fragment must
commit some action negatively qualified; the elimination is really
murder and even the most hysterical murderers do not kill without a
motive. The "negatively qualified action" really consists of an alleged
threat or crime that the collective murder is intended to ward off or
punish.

Lévi-Strauss correctly observes isolated features of the representation central to mythology but he cannot integrate these features
because he cannot arrive at the lynching process itself. Only through
this lynching process will all the isolated features so aptly observed by
him crystallize into a single coherent picture. We must not believe that
a solution is scientific simply because it presents itself as a "model" or,
better still, as a "topological model." To be scientific is to choose the
path that will account for the greatest number of mythical features in
the most simple and obvious way. In order to be scientific, therefore,
we must first of all acknowledge the representation of lynching that
lurks behind the topological model. My purpose is the same as the
purpose of Lévi-Strauss. It has nothing to do with a "mystique of
violence" or other such nonsense. It is certainly impossible to elaborate
a scientific theory of myth unless we acknowledge the true nature of
the mythical representations. We must now find out if this acknowledgment can help fulfill the goal of Lévi-Strauss.

First I will turn toward the murder and its motivation. Tikarau is
accused of stealing the totemic goods, the whole cultural system in
other words. His action threatens the community as a whole and, as a
result, justifies or seems to justify the collective nature of the retaliation, the apparently unanimous participation in murder. The same is
true of the Ojibwa god, really. Thanks only to the rapid intervention of
all the other gods, the murderous glance of their indiscreet companion
kills no more than one member of the community. Potentially at least,
the whole community is threatened, as in the case of Tikarau.

It is impossible to steal the cultural order; it is impossible to kill
people simply by looking at them. These accusations are fantastic and
they reappear constantly in mythology. Students treat them from a

rationalistic viewpoint as products of religious superstition, from a literary and esthetic viewpoint as products of a gratuitous imagination,
from a psychoanalytical viewpoint as symbols of an individual or collective unconscious.

No one, to my knowledge, has ever investigated the sociological
implications of these same accusations. It is probably felt that they are
too fantastic to appear in a real sociological context. This assumption is
erroneous. Even today, in communities or milieux that sociologists do
not yet hesitate to call "backward," especially if they belong to the
Western world, there exists an equivalent of the mythological power to
kill at a glance or to inflict disease and other kinds of misfortune, and it
is called the "evil eye." In certain regions of Italy, for instance, belief in
the "malocchio" of certain individuals is still common.[9]

Once it has been suggested that someone has the evil eye, every
misfortune that befalls the community as a whole or any of its members can be read as added evidence that the accusation is justified. The
tremendous scope and overwhelming vagueness of the "evil eye" make
it a formidable charge indeed, which no rational refutation can
counter. The exercise of this power does not even have to be voluntary.
The good intentions of the Ojibwa god do not save the Indian upon
whom his glance happens to fall. The good will of King Oedipus
toward the city of Thebes and the involuntary nature of his crimes do
not prevent him from spreading the plague among his citizens. *The
discovery of the victim's evil power always comes from the crowd and
never from the victim.*

Why and in what circumstances should such monstrous accusations
appear and take hold among human beings who are no more monstrous, presumably, than others? With the advent of the new primi-
tivism it is now fashionable to assume, at least implicitly, that in
primitive societies, disruptions of the social order do not occur or that
these societies are somehow better able to deal with them than we are.
This belief is probably wrong unless we agree that accusations like the
evil eye and whatever consequences follow from them constitute the
most satisfactory means to solve certain social problems.

If a community is deprived of political and legal means to deal with
internal divisions and agitations, there will be an irresistible tendency
to pin the responsibility for whatever ails it on some individual or
individuals close at hand. The specific type of the fantastic that characterizes the accusations against Oedipus, or against the two central
characters in the two myths discussed in *Totemism*, corresponds
perfectly to what may be expected when an unmanageable and even
undefinable social malaise or crisis is turned into the responsibility of a
single individual.

Do we have reason to believe that the preceding considerations could be relevant to mythology? Do we have mythical representations that suggest the social circumstances in which accusations such as the evil eye are likely to arise? According to structuralism, of course, we do not. Lévi-Strauss describes as a *primordial* absence of order the state of affairs that prevails at the beginning of many myths. According to him, this state of affairs is characterized by an "undifferentiation" that constitutes a purely logical if not a historical starting point for the deployment of human thought.

Although it is nonhistorical, this view remains obviously influenced by the creation myth in Genesis and its theological interpretations in the Judaeo-Christian world. It takes no account of the conflictual aspects in the narrative elements at the beginning of many primitive myths. These elements suggest violent disorder rather than a mere absence of order, primordial or otherwise. We often have a confused struggle between indistinguishable antagonists frequently defined as identical twins. If there is enough space for these antagonists to exchange blows, there should be enough too for the differentiation process of human thought. In *La Violence et le sacré*, I have tried to show that this lack of differentiation is no mere logical starting point, but reflects the vicious and undecidable nature of the revenge process; the world of reciprocal violence is one of constant mirror effects in which the antagonists become each other's doubles and lose their individual identities. It is true, of course, that at the beginning of myth the whole classification system and, as a result, the whole natural as well as the whole social order appear to be inexistent or in shambles. All I say is that if the emphasis is placed on the conflictual and therefore social aspects of these representations they will provide the type of context in which accusations like the "evil eye" or the "theft" of the entire cultural order by one individual are likely to occur.

The theme of conflictual undifferentiation or intense competition is not too explicit in the two myths of *Totemism*. In the myth from Tikopia, nevertheless, these aspects are recognizable in those "ordeals of speed and strength" to which Tikarau is supposedly "invited" and that result in his lynching.

The festival that turns into a lynching party is another theme common to the myth from Tikopia and *The Bacchae*. It constitutes, I believe, a partial ritualistic reframing of the type of social crisis that leads backward communities to seek relief through a polarization against a single individual, the very polarization that is represented in the myth as an objective qualification of the victim. Since the crisis is social, it necessarily transcends all individual responsibility and can only be expressed in that form we find in mythology. The victim is endowed with a truly fantastic and superhuman power to harm the community.

We have now three types of representation that dovetail perfectly: (1) intimations of a social crisis, (2) the attribution of something like the "evil eye" to some individual, and (3) the collective murder of that individual. We have, in other words, the social circumstances likely to induce collective violence juxtaposed with an accusation typical of those societies in which collective violence is endemic, and all this is immediately followed by an act of collective violence against the victim of this accusation.

When I define the "evil eye" or any other version of the victim's fantastic power for evil as an "accusation," I am not true, of course, to the explicit message of the myth. In the perspective of that message, the "evil eye" is not a simple accusation; there is nothing conjectural or hypothetical about it; it is presented as an unquestionable fact, an unshakeable truth. It could nevertheless be an accusation because it is surrounded by other representations that suggest it is neither a fact nor the fruit of a gratuitous imagination, but the kind of collective delusion that appears in the circumstances to which our myths seem to allude, always likely to end up in the collective violence that is also represented by those same myths.

Between the explicit message of our two myths, therefore, and the implicit or indirect clues we have gathered from an analysis of that message, there is a contradiction.

The Ojibwa victim is presented as the only god in the myth who unleashes the terrible power of his "evil eye." Tikarau, in the myth from Tikopia, is presented as the only thief. In both myths, therefore, the malefactor and victim is presented as someone very special. He is the only individualized character in the myth; the only proper name in these two myths belongs to one of these victims, Tikarau. This is the message of the myth; it proclaims the extreme difference, even uniqueness of the victim. If, instead of that message, we listen to the indirect clues, the lynching of the victim will suggest a collective mechanism of projection that must be understood in reference not to the victim, of course, but to the unmanageable and incompletely formulated problems of that collectivity.

This means that far from being uniquely differentiated, the victim must be regarded, if not necessarily as random, at least as arbitrary in regard to the real problems of the community. Since nobody, absolutely nobody, can have the "evil eye" or steal the totemic system, there is no significant reason why one individual rather than another would become the target of this accusation.

This contradiction is not something that is limited to my two examples or even to a few other myths; it is a basic feature of primitive mythology and its resolution cannot fail to be crucial for the elaboration of the scientific theory of myth that is the unfulfilled ambition of structural ethnology.

If we believe the explicit message of the myth, or even if we question that message in the manners now traditional, if we regard it as merely "superstitious" in the style of the rationalists, if we regard it as fantasmatic in the sense of the Freudian unconscious, or if we regard it as an allegory of human thought as Lévi-Strauss does, we will always end up once more at the impasse to which these methodologies inevitably lead. Does it mean that this contradiction will always remain unintelligible and that no scientific theory of myth can be formulated? It means nothing of the sort. The explicit message of the myth can still be questioned and criticized from a standpoint that has never been tried and that should be the first to be tried since it is suggested by the myth itself. We know very little about the spontaneous mechanisms of collective violence, but we know enough to realize that these mechanisms do generate the type of collective delusion that these myths represent as an unquestionable fact. It is very easy, therefore, to reconcile the thematic elements in mythology that suggest an arbitrary lynching with the thematic elements that assert that whatever happened is fully justified, that the victim is truly endowed with a supernatural power for evil. All we have to do to account for everything is to assume that *the lynching is represented from the standpoint of the lynchers themselves.*

We can be absolutely sure that this perspective will produce all the significant structures detected by Lévi-Strauss, all the narrative common denominators between the two myths analyzed in *Totemism.* When the lynchers look back at their own lynching they will certainly present it as a positive action, and they will present the behavior of their victim as a threat. Only the perspective of the lynchers will tie together the various observations of Lévi-Strauss and account for the fact that the oppositions characteristic of the mythical drama, unlike so many others, are not really reversible when you shift from myth to myth. Even though the victim turns out in the end to be the divine benefactor of the community, he remains first of all a malefactor; he remains always guilty, in other words, and the lynching is always justified.

The perspective of the lynchers recording their own lynching solves every problem, but this perspective cannot arise without real lynchers, of course, and a real lynching. In order to account for the nature and organization of the mythical themes, we are led to postulate that the mythical text is rooted in an extratextual event. Until now I have been

very careful to treat the mythical representations as purely representations, but their analysis has logically led me to the hypothesis that some
of them at least must have a real referent, as the linguist would say. In
order to arrive at a truly concrete and efficient theory of the myth we
must face the possibility that some of its representations are trustworthy, the ones that suggest the lynching itself, the ones taking place
in the circumstances that are likely to trigger that kind of collective
violence.

If we go back and examine the steps that led me to postulate a real
lynching, we will observe that all the arguments are textual; at no point
did I transgress the most valid rule of modern criticism, the one that
demands that the *signifié* of a text not be confused with a referent in
the real world. The conclusion that the lynching must be real is nothing
of the sort; it is a hypothetical conclusion forced upon us by the results
of the purely immanent analysis. This hypothesis is powerful because it
and it alone can solve the textual enigma that structuralism and the
other theories cannot solve.

This hypothesis, I repeat, does not merely consist in saying that
because lynching is represented in an enormous number of myths it
must somehow take place in the real world. This hypothesis is no
illegitimate assimilation or confusion of the *signifié* with the real world.
It is prompted by the constant juxtaposition in mythology of representations that strongly suggest and of representations that explicitly deny
a mimetic polarization of violence on an arbitrary victim. It is the text
itself, therefore, that demands that hypothesis. Only through that
hypothesis does the contradiction woven into the very texture of
mythology become not only intelligible but necessary. Only through
that hypothesis do the contents and organization of the mythical
themes become understandable and coherent.

In the present climate of opinion, however, it is almost impossible
for the arguments I advance to be heard. A valid methodological principle has been espoused with such fervor that it has turned into a
metaphysical dogma. As attempts to elaborate a scientific theory of the
sign have given way to more and more radical critiques of such attempts, the principle of a textuality entirely closed upon itself and for
which no extra textual referent and origin can be reached has become
an unchallengeable absolute. Like all true believers, the devouts of this
absolute are deaf to anything that views their assumptions merely as
assumptions. Whatever disturbs their negative faith in the ultimate self-
referential nature of all texts will automatically be perceived as a regression toward the old empirical confusion between a sign and its
referent.

Can I avoid a direct clash with this metaphysical prejudice? Could I

not retain the gist of my hypothesis and yet accommodate myself to the
current dogma, perhaps by defining the perspective of the myth as one
of approval and endorsement vis-à-vis a mere representation of lynching rather than the perspective of the lynchers themselves?

It cannot be done. A perspective of mere approval would inevitably
entail that the opposite attitude is also possible, that implicitly at least,
it is already part of the mythical perspective. If the myth merely approved, it might also disapprove of the lynching it represents. This is
the perspective of a detached spectator or of a reader confronted by a
text that is already written; it implies a distance from the scene that is
obviously absent in the case of the mythical elaboration. The striking
thing about primitive mythology is the constant juxtaposition of
thematic elements that suggest entirely different interpretations. Some
of these, we found, firmly pin upon the victim the responsibility for
whatever misfortunes or catastrophes beset the community; others
suggest a vulgar episode of collective violence, a mindless crowd carried away by the mimetic power of its own hysterical paranoia. The
only way to account for this constant juxtaposition is to suppose that
the elaboration of the text takes place under the continued influence of
this mimetic power. Only the lynchers themselves can believe enough
in their own lynching to read it as the emergence, in supernaturally
troubled circumstances, of an all-powerful demonic figure threatening
to destroy the entire community and only prevented from doing so by
this community's timely violence. The fact that this violence may be
presented as the action not of a human but of a divine community that
parallels the community of human ancestors, as in the Ojibwa myth,
may correspond to the beginning of a distanciation, but it does not
truly modify the perspective of the myth, the perspective of the lynchers themselves, which was inherited by the community of believers.

We cannot renounce the definition proposed above. The perspective
of the lynchers implies a real lynching, and it must be that real lynching that is represented not only in the two myths discussed in *Totemism* but in countless other myths. We cannot accommodate the
hypothesis to current dogma. We will have to challenge that dogma,
but we are not going to do it on purely theoretical grounds. A purely
theoretical discussion is always a philosophical discussion in disguise,
and it can be avoided by introducing into the debate another category
of texts that is really very close to the myths I have discussed, but that
is not acknowledged as such.

The texts I have in mind could be defined as texts of mystified
persecution. These texts range from the documents of medieval and
modern anti-Semitism, including violent pogroms, to the records of the
Spanish Inquisition and the trial of witches down to the primarily oral

text of modern racism, the lynching of blacks, for instance, in the American South.

Let us consider the accounts of medieval violence against Jews as they were recorded from the perspective of the Christian majority. We all know so well which thematic elements must be there and how they are organized that there is no need, really, to mention any specific examples. Let me briefly enumerate these elements:

1) Something is wrong with the community. Many people become ill and die mysteriously. The most sacred rules are transgressed; differences are erased; chaos reigns.

2) The Jews have the "evil eye." The Jews commit the most unnatural actions, such as parricide, incest, etc. Hostile as they are to the true faith, the Jews must be responsible for whatever ails the community—a real plague, social agitation, etc. Rumor has it that some Jews have been seen tampering with the water supply.

3) Some Jews are killed or driven out.

4) Tranquillity and order return to the community.

We can easily see that these elements duplicate almost perfectly those in the mythical text. That is why the formulas of the structural analysis in *Totemism* will apply perfectly. There is a *radical elimination*, of course, and the *eliminated fragment* or fragments are guilty of a *negatively qualified action*. The elimination itself is *positively qualified* and it is *collective* rather than *individual*. We begin with *undifferentiation* and we end up with *differentiation*. The representations are the same in both categories of texts. No one would suggest, however, that the texts of mystified persecution should be read in the Lévi-Straussian key of a topological mode; no one would suggest that these representations must be some kind of allegory for the virgin birth of "human thinking."

The reason why we treat the two kinds of texts differently is that, in the case of mystified persecution, we immediately realize that we are dealing with real victims in a real episode of lynching. We understand that whenever lynching is reported from the perspective of the lynchers themselves, *the victims can and must be fantasized without being unreal.*

The accusations against the Jews are no less fantastic than the nefarious properties attributed to mythological heroes. The two, in fact, are exactly the same: they include the evil eye, the plague, parricide, incest etc. The circumstances are the same and the sequence of events is exactly the same. It is the same contradiction between the explicit message that singles out the victims as the only cause of the community's problems and the numerous indications that suggest a sudden and brutal outburst of arbitrary violence.

Even a superficial examination of the text will confirm what our
common sense has already told us: the Jews' supernatural power for
evil is imaginary, but it is not the fruit of an imagination purely gratuitous or determined solely by psychoanalytical drives. The delusion
plays a social function and it is specific of that function. The evil
powers of the Jews constitute permanent beliefs of the Christian community; these beliefs may remain dormant for a while in periods of
relative social harmony but they will be quickly reactivated in times of
crisis, when the problems of the community become unmanageable
and even undefinable. Whenever the tensions become acute, the society will turn toward the Jews. We acknowledge the fact when we say
that the Jews are the favorite scapegoats of Christian society. The word
scapegoat is the English translation for the designation of the victim in
an Old Testament ritual, the ritual described in the twenty-first chapter of Leviticus. In modern usage, this word has acquired a very special
connotation, which constitutes at least an implicit interpretation of the
ritual itself. It refers to the process of really arbitrary victimage, unperceived as such, which provides a key to the interpretation of the
quasimythical texts I am now discussing, the texts of mystified persecution. We would not interpret these texts as we do, if we were not able
to *de*mystify them. And we demystify them when we realize they are
structured on the scapegoat process itself: they reflect the delusion that
inevitably accompanies that process. The "best" scapegoats, the only
"good" scapegoats, really, are the scapegoats who are not recognized as
such. We cannot read the text of persecution correctly unless we become able to rehabilitate the victims, to realize that the accusations
against them are groundless. It is very important to observe, at this
point, that the demystification of the quasimythical text, the text of
mystified persecution, is inseparable from a certain ethical attitude.
The only scientific reading of the text certainly coincides with the
fulfillment of an ethical exigency.

I do not claim that there are no objective differences between the
text of medieval persecution and mythology proper. Differences are
certainly there, but they may not be such as to preclude a similar
referent and origin for the two types of text. This is really the gist of
my hypothesis. Mythology is so similar in themes and structure to the
texts of mystified persecution that it could also be rooted in a scapegoat
process of which we would be the dupes like the believers themselves,
a scapegoat process that we have not yet been able to decipher, perhaps because it is culturally too distant from us, perhaps because it is
better concealed, perhaps because of these two reasons combined, perhaps because of other reasons still invisible to us.

You can see now how useful it is to introduce into the debate those documents I call texts of mystified persecution, now demystified by modern interpretation. These texts should make my hypothesis entirely clear. Their interpretation does not provide a metaphor or a model. It is the thing itself. What I really assert, in other words, is that the enigma of mythology can be solved and everything can become intelligible—even the divinization of the victim, diminished but not absent from the texts of persecution—if we regard the process of mythical elaboration as a process similar, but more powerful than, the one we assume is really present behind such documents as the Christian account of a medieval pogrom or accounts of lynchings by lynch mobs themselves, wherever they are and whoever their victims may be.

Because the texts of mystified persecution have been demystified for a while now, because their interpretation has been settled once and for all along the lines that I propose to adopt in the case of mythology, these texts make my hypothesis obvious. They also have another advantage, which cannot be spurned in the contemporary climate of intellectual opinion. Even the most rabid exponents of a textuality detached from any referent and entirely closed upon itself will relent when confronted with the texts of persecution. They will not only confess that a referent is in order, but they will identify that referent if asked to do so; and it will be, if not exactly the same, at least analogous to the one I propose for mythology proper.

The same people who will not even listen to my arguments when presented in a properly mythological context, will quite willingly surrender to them, or rather they have already surrendered in the case of the quasimythical texts, the texts of mystified persecution. This fact reveals that the antireferential dogma is as inconsistent really as it is vociferous, and it does not have to be taken too seriously. The only reason why this bizarre attitude can express itself with confidence comes from the exclusively mythical and literary context in which its exponents operate. They themselves, it appears, have not really considered the consequences of their own views. They do not think of what would happen if the dogma were seriously applied to all texts indiscriminately. The amazing thing is that these people can see themselves as "revolutionary"; even the most timid doubt regarding the legitimacy of their subjective nihilism is regarded as "reactionary."

Let us see what would happen if the texts of mystified persecution were treated in strict conformity with the dogma currently fashionable in the best intellectual circles. In the text of medieval anti-semitism, many representations are clearly spurious and unbelievable. No historian worth his salt, however, will conclude from this fact that all representations are equally spurious and unbelievable, that it would be "naively empirical" to trust any of them. The truth is just the opposite.

The representations that describe an episode of collective violence taking place at the height of a social crisis are made more rather than less trustworthy for being juxtaposed to the most fantastic accusations against the victims. If a historian well versed in structuralist and post-structuralist thought concluded that no real event, no extratextual referent could be deduced from any representations, he would be considered either as an *agent provocateur* or as a fool, more probably still as both.

Texts of mystified persecution are the primary source for the treatment of persecuted minorities. And no one would deny the certainty of these persecutions, even if it is of a very different nature from the mathematical certainty of the natural sciences. No one has yet suggested that this certainty must be another myth, the specific myth of a modern and humanistic era.

What the current dogma really amounts to is really a blanket dismissal of all representations. This treatment seems poles apart from the blanket faith in all representations that characterizes religious faith, but it really is the closest thing to it, its modern equivalent, the greatest obstacle to a real penetration of the mythical text.

What has prevented that penetration so far is precisely what religious faith and the current antireferential skepticism have in common, the one-sided treatment of all representations. The same people who see very well the need not to treat all representations identically when they read a text of mystified persecution are blinded by their false radicalism to the possibility that a diversified treatment may also be needed in the case of mythology. We can see at what point exactly the valid methodological principle gives way to the blind theoretical faith.

Between our two categories of text, the similarities are simply too striking for anyone to assert that the solution universally acknowledged for one category can be excluded out of hand for the other. Even if the parallel in the end turns out to be sterile, no one can say a priori that it must not be attempted, especially in view of the continued enigma presented by the mythical text. To assert a priori once more that this enigma will never be solved or that it does not really exist constitutes a surrender to the most oppressive dogmaticism, the one that wants to stifle not certain attitudes only, but the very spirit of research, the belief that decisive results can be achieved, that significant truths can be ascertained. This skeptical dogmaticism pretends to dominate the social sciences by legislating all their interesting questions out of existence.

If we surveyed other texts of mystified persecution already acknowledged as such, we would find that most of them, if not all, come from the same historical world, ours. This fact is certainly related to our ability to demystify these texts. In each and every case, the victims of persecution are easily acknowledged because they bear some unmistakable sign of what we might call their "scapegoatability." These signs, of course, are just as arbitrary as any other signs; they are not transcultural; we are able to decipher them because they are signs of our society, because the code that provides the key to these signs is never really unfamiliar to us.

In the case of mythology we know of no such clear cultural signs to help us understand that the victims might be real. This can mean one of two things. Either the signs are present but we are unable to decipher them because we have not yet cracked the code or the signs are really absent. The possibility that there are no cultural signs at all cannot be excluded. Most myth-producing societies are too small and too homogeneous to possess the religious or ethnic minorities that usually provide the large and heterogeneous "civilizations" with their reservoirs of scapegoat victims.

We should not hurry to conclude, however, that the absence of cultural signs necessarily means the absence of all signs. Other signs of scapegoatability do exist. As a matter of fact, they are very easy to ascertain because they are really transcultural; everybody is aware of them and can verify for himself that they correspond to the constantly recurring features of worldwide mythology.

In order not to miss these signs, we must turn once more to the backward societies questioned earlier, the ones that are addicted to such things as the "evil eye," or to children in groups, perhaps to the type of communities children will form when they are left to their own devices in disintegrating societies.

When there are no ethnic minorities, when there is no one in a community who can be defined as a "stranger," aggressive tensions tend to polarize against those people who, for some reason or other, are still maladjusted to the ways of the community, notably the people who are physically crippled or deformed or who have some other kind of infirmity, like a speech impediment. When all the cultural signs are gone, in other words, or not yet available, very crude but highly visible physical signs tend to become the rallying point for the collective transference of anxiety and hostility.

Tikarau walks with a limp. So do Oedipus, Hephaistos, the biblical Jacob, and countless others in the entire world. When the "evil eye" is not otherwise impaired, it may be a single eye, and the missing eye is the equivalent of the limp.

These facts have been observed long ago and no theory of mythology can dispense with their interpretation. The interpretation of Lévi-Strauss must be consistent, of course, with his interpretation of the mythical drama as a spatial allegory of the differentiation process:

In all these instances, [the myths discussed in both *Totemism* and *The Raw and the Cooked*] a discrete system is produced by the destruction of certain elements or their removal from the original whole. In all these cases, too, the originator of the reduction is himself in a sense reduced: the six Ojibwa gods were blind from choice and exiled their companion who had been guilty of removing the bandage over his eyes. Tikarau, the thieving Tikopia god, pretended to limp in order to be better able to get possession of the banquet. Akaruoio Bodokori also limped. Mythological figures who are blind or lame, one-eyed or one-armed, are familiar the world over; and we find them disturbing, because we believe their condition to be one of deficiency. But just as a system that has been made discrete through the removal of certain elements becomes logically richer, although numerically poorer, so myths often confer a positive significance on the disabled and the sick, who embody modes of mediation. We imagine infirmity and sickness to be deprivations of being and therefore evil. However, . . . "negativized being" is entitled to occupy a whole place within the system, since it is the only conceivable means of transition between two "full" states.[10]

Very much in the style of a certain literary criticism, Lévi-Strauss reads the crippled victim as a formal *mise en abyme* of his topological allegory. The only difficulty with this interpretation is that the theme of the organ in excess or enlarged—the hunchback, for instance—is almost as frequent as the theme of the organ missing or shrunken. When lameness itself is defined as a "swollen foot," it must belong to the first type of disablement rather than the second.

The Freudians, of course, can deal with both sides of the coin. Wherever castration will not do, the good old phallic symbol will, and vice versa. Psychoanalysis is no more satisfactory than structuralism, however, because its theory of symbolization demands that the object symbolized be out of sight. We may still believe that such is the case with Pulcinello; in many myths, however, the object is simply too much in evidence to be comfortably defined as repressed. In many North American trickster myths, for instance, the object is so inordinately long and cumbersome that its possessor must carry it wrapped around his neck or shoulders, like a fireman does his hoses, until he can dispose of it more permanently by having it cut off; an operation that seems deplorably explicit from the standpoint of a castration *complex*.

Contemporary Freudians are too wise, of course, to be put off by my objections. They have whole arsenals of distinctions specifically designed to counter them. At this point, for instance, they would probably reproach me for ignoring the formidable difference, the gaping abyss Jacques Lacan has discovered between the symbolic phallus and the human penis. . . .

The last phase of great theories that have almost exhausted their creative power is usually marked by the proliferation of subtle and ultimately sterile readjustments. It is a phase of *préciosité*, really, immediately followed by the absolute skepticism that is now gaining all around us. To those raised in such a climate, the truly revolutionary intuitions that are about to take over appear too direct and simple to be of any value.

The search for interpretations more and more refined can only mislead us, blunt our sensitivity to the crude forms of victimage that are really at work behind mythology. If we could learn common sense, once more, without forgetting what we know, we would realize that the infirmities and disabilities of so many mythical heroes merely designate them to the crowd as potential victims; they are signs even less ambiguous, really, than the sign of "scapegoatability" in the texts we can already acknowledge as texts of mystified persecution, membership in an ethnic or religious minority.[11]

In the passage just quoted, the desire of Lévi-Strauss to read the *radical elimination* of the crippled hero as a purely logical game brings him very close to the truth, too close for comfort, perhaps, judging from his curious recommendation to the reader that he should not find any of this "disturbing." Is mythology the still misunderstood record of countless Cains killing countless Abels? Can cultural differentiation be founded on murder? Can it be the same thing as *the mark of Cain?* The consequences of a positive answer would be "disturbing" indeed. We prefer to believe the question is not genuine. It must not be asked in good faith. It is obviously not "scientific" but "impressionistic," and even "mystical." There must be a vast ideological plot behind it, a "reactionary" plot, *bien entendu.* How could a question be "scientific" and "disturbing" at the same time?

In such a climate of opinion, it is interesting to show that even and especially the analyses of Lévi-Strauss, when they are submitted to the slightest scrutiny, immediately produce the problematic that seems most alien to them and that compels us once more to ask the question that is most inimical: can we always avoid facing that disturbing question?

NOTES

1. Claude Lévi-Strauss, *Totemism,* trans. Rodney Needham (Boston: Beacon Press, 1963), p. 19.

2. Ibid., p. 25–26.

3. Ibid., p. 26.
4. Claude Lévi-Strauss, *The Raw and the Cooked*, trans. John Weightman and Doreen Weightman (New York: Harper and Row, 1969), p. 52.
5. Raymond Firth, *Tikopia Ritual and Belief* (Boston: Beacon Press, 1976), p. 230.
6. Lévi-Strauss, *Totemism*, p. 26.
7. Ibid.
8. Firth, *Tikopia Ritual and Belief*, p. 230.
9. Please note the similarity between the "evil spying" attributed by the bacchantes to Pentheus (which is the proximate cause of his death, of course, according to the story) and the "evil eye" of the Ojibwa divinity (the "negative action" that triggers his "radical elimination"). Evil spying is really the same thing as the evil eye; it is an evil eye emptied in part of its supernatural power, "desacralized" in *The Bacchae* to the same extent that other mythical themes are desacralized. We should also note the similarity between this "evil spying" and the "peeping Tom" complex always widespread in those cultural areas where collective violence is still simmering beneath the surface.
10. Lévi-Strauss, *The Raw and the Cooked*, p. 53.
11. Another and even more essential difference between mythology and the texts I have already acknowledged as texts of persecution is the sacralization of the victim: always present in the former, almost completely absent in the latter. In order to prove my point, I must show that the scapegoat process, in certain conditions, can also generate all sacred representations. This analysis is not possible within the limits of the present essay. See René Girard, *Violence and the Sacred*, trans. Patrick Gregory (Baltimore: The Johns Hopkins University Press, 1977). See also *Des Choses cachées depuis la fondation du monde* (Paris: Grasset, 1978).

10

An Interview with René Girard

Diacritics: Your work displays a fundamental continuity resulting from the focus upon the sociocultural process that relates order and disorder, stability and violent upheaval. Yet we can also detect a shift, in your recent writings, in the function of the literary work: whereas in your earlier writings literature appeared to be the scene or agent of demystification, it now seems to be more symptomatic in its relation to sociocultural processes, that is, to the scapegoating mechanism that you have systematically highlighted during the past few years. How, then, would you characterize the development of your work from *Deceit, Desire, and the Novel* to *Violence and the Sacred?* Do you see the latter as an extension or extrapolation of the former, or does it mark a fundamental rupture with the earlier (and extraordinarily influential) analysis of mimetic desire? Does the resolute emphasis on the scapegoating process signal a crucial change in your view of the literary text?

René Girard: There is a kind of "rupture," I believe, but it results from the continuity of my interest not merely in the literary treatment of mimetic phenomena but in these phenomena themselves. Unanimous victimage, in a sense, is only one mimetic phenomenon among others. At the time of *Mensonge romantique*, this mimetic nature of victimage did not escape me, but its enormous potential in regard to primitive religion certainly did. When my attention turned to anthropology this potential finally dawned on me. I remember these days as the most exciting intellectual experience I ever had. The "essayistic" nature of *La Violence et le sacré* reflects that excitement too much and fails to convey as systematically and successfully as, I am sure, it can be conveyed the massive evidence that designates unanimous victimage as the generative mechanism of all religious and cultural institutions.

I still regard not literature as such, not the novel as a genre, but certain exceptional works as agents of a very special demystification

This essay appeared in *Diacritics* 8 (1978): 31–54.

that bears on the hidden role of mimetic effects in human interaction. If *Mensonge* were written today it would be written differently, of course, but it would remain a less problematic book than *La Violence* because it deals with writers who, as a general rule, do not reach the unanimous victimage mechanism any more than I could reach it myself at the time. My only vital "literary" interests, now, concern those writers who do reach that mechanism and, above all, William Shakespeare.

Diacritics: The strength of your work derives, in part, from its refusal to allow itself to be conveniently located within a single discipline. It bears decisively on several traditional canons—history, philosophy, sociology, anthropology, literary criticism. Before considering our questions concerning your interests in these various disciplines, could you reflect on the level of generality at which your work operates? How do you now conceive the *extent* of its claims to validity?

R.G.: My claims are scandalously out of proportion with the general temper of the times and with my literary background, which must be regarded by almost everybody as the worst possible recommendation for the type of research that interests me.

In order to show the inevitability of these claims I will explain how they arose. It is natural to try to make mimetic phenomena manageable by inscribing them in some kind of theoretical framework. I cannot remember a critic of mine who did not think he had the right framework—almost never the same twice in a row—and I understand this temptation because I almost succumbed to it myself on several occasions.

First, there was a neo-Marxist and Lukacsian temptation embodied in the late and lamented Lucien Goldmann, for whom mimetic desire was the monopoly of a specific literary genre, the novel, belonging to a historically dated social milieu. Then came a psychoanalytical temptation that presented itself in an orthodox Freudian as well as in a Lacanian version. To the orthodox Freudian, it must be possible to distribute mimetic phenomena between the Oedipus complex and narcissism. I was never told how. To the Lacanian, whatever I call mimetic in human interaction must correspond to the vaunted but mysterious "capture par l'imaginaire" and be rooted—where else?—in "le stade du miroir." No one ever told me how the "capture par l'imaginaire" can really operate.

There is also a poststructuralist and philosophical temptation that is especially alive at the present time, and to it many of my remarks will be directed. One formulation can be found in "Typographie," an essay by Philippe Lacoue-Labarthe (in *Mimesis des articulations* [Paris: Aubier-Flammarion, 1975]).

My first objection is that the author does not see the real basis for my "quarrel" with Plato. Plato's problematic fails to mention the domain of application where imitation is inevitably conflictual: appropriation. No one has ever perceived that failure. Everybody always imitates Plato's concept of imitation. As a result of this curious mutilation, the reality of the threat imitation poses to the harmony and even to the survival of human communities has never been correctly assessed. The omission by Plato of acquisitive mimesis as a source of conflict is paradoxical because Plato still shares but cannot justify the universal terror of primitive communities for mimetic phenomena.

Thus, the dynamics of mimetic rivalry are rooted in a disputed object and not in that "Hegelian desire for recognition" that I have always viewed as derivative—insofar as it resembles Hegel's—of more elementary mimetic interferences over an object. At that elementary level the word desire is not appropriate.

My early utterances on the subject are contaminated, at times, by the Hegelian climate of the fifties as well as by the literary nature of my analyses, but even then all subsequent mimetic effects are ultimately brought back to the radical simplicity of that primordial mimetic interference. When any gesture of appropriation is imitated, it simply means that two hands will reach for the same object simultaneously: conflict cannot fail to result.

In order to perceive the disconcerting simplicity and elementariness of that starting point, one must realize that mimetic rivalry is not even specifically human. There must be a mimetic element in the intraspecific fighting of many animals, since the absence of an object—the flight of the disputed female, for instance—does not always put an immediate end to the fighting. Eventually, however, the fighting comes to an end with a kind of submission of the vanquished to the victor. The dominated animal always yields to the dominant animal, who then turns into a model and guide of all behavior, *except appropriation.*

Unlike animals, men engaged in rivalry may go on fighting *to the finish.* To account for this by a *violent* instinct, in contradistinction to an *instinctual* inhibition of intraspecific murder in animals, results in an impasse. It is more productive, I believe, to assume that an increased mimetic drive, corresponding to the enlarged human brain, must escalate mimetic rivalry beyond the point of no return. Far from hypostatizing violence and murder, I see both as that part of the mimetic process that escalates beyond the animal and must have caused, when it first appeared, the breakdown of societies based on dominance patterns.

Excessive rivalries make human societies problematic. The increased

intensity of intraspecific conflicts obviously results in a new and infinitely more complex form of society rather than in the annihilation of
the hypermimetic primate. The emergence of more and more complex
symbolical societies must somehow correspond to the catastrophical
breakdown of the earlier forms. The mechanism of symbolicity must be
triggered by the murderous exasperation of mimetic rivalry.

It is commonly observed that the intensification of rivalry produces a
shift of the mimetic attention from the disputed objects to the rivals
themselves. This shift accounts for the efficacy of the so-called "scapegoat effect," still insufficiently studied but readily observable. The same
mimesis that is conflictual and divisive as long as it focuses on objects
of appropriation must become reunitive as the very intensity of the
escalation substitutes one single scapegoat for many disputed objects.
Why one scapegoat only? Once two or more antagonists have joined
against any given one, the mimetic attraction of their common target
must increase with the number of individuals thus polarized. When the
snowball effect of this antagonistic mimesis has reached every individual, a de facto reconciliation is achieved, at the expense of the single
scapegoat.

If we look at the prohibitions and rituals of primitive religion we
must realize that both could stem from that strange resolution. The
object of the prohibitions is always some likely object of mimetic strife
or mimetic strife itself, either directly or indirectly as in the case of
images, twin brothers, etc. The rituals obviously reenact the mimetic
escalation the prohibitions try to prevent. That is why the conjunction
of the two has always eluded rational interpretation. All difficulty disappears if we assume that, in the rituals, the escalation is mimicked
only for the sake of the immolation it is supposed to trigger. We can
understand why the communities saved from mimetic strife by unanimous victimage would try to prevent a relapse both by prohibiting
whatever may have caused such strife in the first place and by reenact-
ing the actions that brought an end to it.

In order to be effective, the reconciliation must not be perceived as a
mimetic phenomenon. The only good scapegoats are the ones we are
unable to acknowledge as such. Religious belief is founded on "scapegoat effects" so powerful that the victim seems omnipotent not only as
a troublemaker but as a peacemaker as well. Ignorance of the mimetic
effects that have caused all successive changes in the collective mood
turns the scapegoat into the sole agent of the rivalry first, then of the
"miracle" that puts an end to it. Ignorance of the mimetic cycle
amounts to a dual collective transference that accounts for the duality
of everything designated as "sacred," "numinous," "mana," etc. Victimage thus becomes the sacred epiphany of the founding ancestor, or

divinity, who was the first to transgress the laws he also brought to the community. He came first to chastise, then to educate and reward by showing how to practice ritual, how to kill substitute victims, in other words.

The classical structuralists repress conflictual mimesis as much as anyone ever did. That is why the poststructuralists, beginning with Derrida, could turn mimesis into a weapon against the structuralist theory of the sign. They make a purely critical use of mimesis, however. They do not believe that one can ever achieve on the basis of mimesis what structuralism has failed to achieve on its own basis. If structuralism can be undermined with mimesis, any system based on mimesis can be undermined by showing it must presuppose difference, representation, etc. Neither problematic can exceed the other sufficiently to become the basis for an *inescapable* system. In order to conceive a project such as structuralism, or such as mine, one must be unconsciously one-sided, they feel, in one's choice of philosophical concepts; one must unwittingly recommence an adventure that has already run its full course and failed somewhere in the accumulated writing of Western philosophy.

This is Philippe Lacoue-Labarthe's critique of my thesis in "Typographie." In order to sustain his position the author must show there is no departure from philosophy in my conception of mimesis. He has no difficulty reaching his goal and defining mimetic *desire* as Platonic and Hegelian because he, himself, even as he confronts my text, remains blind to the mimetic interferences that constitute my real non-Platonic and non-Hegelian starting point, at the more primitive level of appropriation common to all primates.

The non-Hegelian starting point changes everything. If there is a conflictual mimesis before anything definable as human, in animal life itself, how can we say that mimesis does not precede representations and sign systems? If this conflictual mimesis comes "before" sign systems, it also comes "after," in the sense that it can disintegrate all cultural systems. The new problematic of mimesis exceeds the problematic of signification in all directions. Lacoue-Labarthe and poststructuralism see mimesis as a factor of undecidability, and this is not radical enough. As a result, they never reach the other side of mimesis already perceived by religion but in a purely religious and fantastic light. They do not understand that mimesis can also play the crucial role in the genesis and practical stabilization of cultural differences.

A close examination of religious structures shows that mimetic escalation in men must reach what should be the point of no return almost as a matter of routine, but this point, in reality, turns out to be the point of all returns and of all new "beginnings."

Lacoue-Labarthe tries to show that the unanimous victimage hypothesis must be one more philosophical *decision* analogous to Plato's. This philosophical decision should be something absolute, good for all times and all circumstances. My generative hypothesis is nothing of the sort. All it says is that, if mimesis is undecidable and worse than undecidable, there must be a mechanism of self-regulation somewhere and it must be mimetic too. Through that mechanism, cultural forms can appear and stabilize to such an extent that philosophers can make mimesis safe for philosophy. The cultural stabilizations are not absolute but relative, of course, not universal but local; they are destined to last not forever, but for a time only, for the historical duration of specific institutions.

The "apocalyptic" character of a world in which the mimetic doubles threaten each other and mankind with nuclear weapons is the same thing, for me, as a full revelation of human violence beyond the tearing apart of sacrificial screens, a reassertion of conflictual mimesis in a world forever deprived of these screens by its superior knowledge, not of natural forces only, but of cultural forces as well, of the generative mechanism itself. Either I "decide" mimesis in order to flee the supposed nightmare of philosophical "undecidability" or I play up a more uncanny version of the same nightmare in my apocalyptic "visions." I cannot be doing these two things simultaneously.

My interest in mimetic phenomena, in and out of literature, led me to the victimage mechanism. I now understand that the anthropology based on the victimage mechanism is the first to do away with the metaphysical postulate of absolute human specificity, still present in Marx and in Freud, without espousing the simplistic assimilation of man and animal practiced by the ethologists. Mimetic phenomena provide the common ground between animal and human society as well as the first concrete means to differentiate the two, concrete in the sense that all observable analogies and differences between the two types of organization become intelligible.

My last book, written in collaboration with J.-M. Oughourlian and G. Lefort, makes a more systematic attempt to deal with all these questions and show that the fundamental institutions of mankind— funeral rites, the incest taboos, the collective hunt, the domestication of animals—become structurally and genetically intelligible as products of unanimous victimage.

Diacritics: Your own historical narrative postulates a moment of violent crisis at the beginning—the plague of conflictual undifferentiation—that is then arrested by the sacrificial mechanism of the scapegoat, whose role is to institute hierarchies and to determine differences, to impose values, where before there was only arbitrary conflict, through the dialectical play of the mimetic rivalry. The memory of the violence and of the expulsion is preserved yet concealed under the distorting veils of ritual sacrifice, which both falsifies the nature of the crisis and moralizes the scapegoat mechanism. At later stages in culture the function of ritual is taken over by literature, which reproduces the mystifications, but in certain instances—the great texts of Sophocles, Euripides, Shakespeare and the Bible—lifts the veil enough for you to glimpse the long-hidden historical truth that lies at the origin.

It has been suggested that your project resembles most closely that of Durkheim. Like him, you place social and cultural processes at the center of your optic; for both of you the origin and constitution of culture are situated in a universal explanatory matrix marked by a struggle between order and disorder, and that origin serves to generate a historical or at least a sequential narrative. How would you situate your project in relation to Durkheim?

R.G.: Durkheim rejected the idea common to Lévy-Bruhl, Frazer, and others that there is a fundamental opposition between primitive religion and other kinds of human thinking. He was the first to show that certain incongruous conjunctions in primitive classifications really play a disjunctive role, that they amount to an intellectual discrimination quite analogous to ours. The moieties of the black and white cockatoos do not confuse themselves or each other with these birds any more than we confuse Democrats and Republicans with donkeys and elephants. All these animals play similar disjunctive roles between human groupings. They form a sign system.

The best of structuralist ethnology is right there and Lévi-Strauss acknowledged the fact in *Totemism*. He learned the lesson too well, however, and implicitly, at least, he concluded that all ethnological problems are created by our "ethnocentric" blindness in the face of inhabitual disjunctions. It may appear, at times, that Durkheim is making the same mistake, in his reading of totemism, for instance, but Durkheim usually pulled back from the brink and never forgot that, to his Australian worshipers, the sacred kangaroo ancestor is *something* that the elephant is not to the Republicans. In his imperialism of significance, Lévi-Strauss implicitly cancels out all difference between differences, treating fantastic monsters exactly the same as if they were real objects, when he analyzes mythology. This treatment greatly facilitates the elimination of religion as a significant problem, but how did the exact sciences Lévi-Strauss professes to admire reach their present state of eminence? Certainly not by assimilating monsters to real objects and throwing common sense to the winds as Lévi-Strauss constantly does.

In order to maintain at all costs the purity of mythology as a repository of "human thought," Lévi-Strauss is finally obliged in the last chapter of *L'Homme nu* to dump anything intractably religious into the lap of ritual, which is then dismissed and anathematized as unworthy of "human thought." A strange gesture, to say the least, on the part of an anthropologist who was supposed to "rehabilitate" primitive thought! As far as ritual is concerned, Lévi-Strauss reverts to the pre-Durkheimian view of religion as an unforgivable confusion of data that *should be distinguished* (!) This treatment of ritual is the hidden side of a structuralist imperialism that turns mythology into a slightly more rustic version of Valéry's *La Jeune Parque.*

Durkheim lacked the concrete means of showing that religion, far from being merely parasitic, as we have believed since Voltaire, is really the generative force behind human culture. It is unfair to dismiss Durkheim either as a man who "reduces" religion to the social, or as a "mystic" who reduces the social to the religious. Durkheim will always remain vulnerable to these symmetrical charges, however, because *something* is needed to fulfill his program that he himself lacked. In my opinion, of course, this *something* is the mimetic cycle and unanimous victimage mechanism.

Diacritics: A reader of contemporary textual theory is made somewhat uneasy by the assurance with which the historical narrative to which we alluded in our preceding question enables you to control so rigorously the displacements from one cultural stage to another. The underlying truth of the historical process remains intact through all its metamorphoses. It appears that nothing is ever lost through those displacements; the truth is merely shrouded in deeper veils awaiting the moment, in your text, when it can be fully uncovered. How do you account for your own discovery of the truth that has so long been hidden? From what standpoint, or through what form of privileged insight, or as a result of what historical conditions, have you been able to grasp and state the underlying truth at once hidden and displayed by the movement of history?

R.G.: How can an "insight" be defended, if not as "privileged"? The only difference between the various insights of those who write books is that some have greater consequences than others.

Especially at the beginning of a scientific development, amateurish approaches are the more likely to yield genuine discoveries. Even in the most favorable conditions, however, the chances of anyone's ever discovering anything new are remote at best. Very little risk is involved, therefore, in dismissing out of hand any claim such as mine. From this very little risk, however, only a very little gain can be expected. My own intellectual life operates on the opposite principle.

The risks must not be exaggerated but they are more real, nevertheless, than if I embraced the fashionable skepticism. The potential gains, as a result, are also more real, however great the odds against them. I prefer this second kind of game, but I did not deliberately choose it. It was forced upon me by the insight, true or false, upon which I have stumbled.

In order to reassure those who fear a touch of megalomania in my behavior, I must add that I do not consider my insight as truly personal. It is "in the air," I think, and if I had not stumbled upon it myself, someone else, rapidly, would have. I view this insight as a minor part of that complete disintegration of sacrificial protections it is our misfortune and privilege to witness.

Your interpretation of my mechanism as a "historical narrative" reflects the usual structuralist assumption that synchronic structures will never yield diachronic information. In his first articles on "symbolic thought" of *Anthropologie structurale I*, Lévi-Strauss observes that, from the perspective of the life sciences, the origin of symbolic thought is a meaningful problem but one that will never be solved, *in the absence of the proper historical information.*

I am not trying to make up that missing historical information through some fanciful story. I say that the aspects of religious forms dismissed as nonsensical by a still narrowly differential ethnology could be traces of a mimetic destructuration or crisis plus mimetic restructuration through unanimous victimage. If you confront that possibility with the reality of mythical and ritual forms you quickly realize that, everywhere and always, everything does correspond to one or another of the innumerable combinations of distorted and also relatively undistorted representations that can be expected from such a process. My thesis is based entirely on structural inferences and it becomes compelling through the sheer number and variety of examples that can be exhibited. It is not the truth of some historical narrative that remains intact through the vicissitudes of cultural evolution, it is the efficacy of the unanimous victimage effect or scapegoat process. How could I avoid postulating the reality of that event, since its effects can still be verified down to this day, in the inability, for instance, of psychoanalysts to realize that the parricide and incest of Oedipus are typical scapegoat accusations throughout the entire world.

If the unanimous victim truly reconciles a community, he will be turned into a transcendental model of differentiation and the mimetic forces destructive or preventative of symbolicity during the mimetic crisis that triggered the victimage will be rechanneled in differentiated and nonconflictual directions. All evidence suggests that this process is not limited to the examples of primitive religion that have reached us.

It must be as old as humanity itself, since it makes the passage intelligible from the nonsymbolical dominance patterns of animal societies
to the complicated systems of ritual and symbolical exchange that
make up the religious and cultural systems of mankind. Once you
realize that the representations and actions you can expect from scapegoat delusions, at the climax of a mimetic free-for-all, perfectly fit
every single feature of mythical themes and ritual actions, you cannot
fail to postulate the reality of the victimage phenomenon whose effects
make it possible for the first time to bring such coherence and intelligibility.

This is a far cry from the historical fable of *Totem and Taboo* and
yet, up to a point, it means the rehabilitation of a work that has been
unfairly treated and literally scapegoated by the whole intellectual
community. In the last analysis, the ultimate object of scapegoating,
even when we selectively denounce it, as we always do in our historical
world, is scapegoating itself.

Diacritics: You systematically insist on the historical reality of the
original crisis, for which, by definition, there can be no direct docu-
mentary evidence within the culture. Why, in your system, must the
crisis be considered to have been historically actualized? How do you
discover the *fact* of the historical crisis, i.e., how, in methodological
terms, do you establish it as fact? What is to be gained by arguing for a
historical event that cannot be represented? What would be lost, to
your system, if the crisis were posited as a transcendental origin, a
necessary explanatory fiction comparable, for example, to the status of
Rousseau's state of nature? Does the historical or "eventful" status of
the originary scapegoating process not serve to restrict the claims to
universality that we normally expect from a rational construction of the
universe?

A great deal of contemporary anthropology has turned its back on
the whole project, beginning with Frazer, of discovering universal explanations of phenomena such as sacrifice and scapegoating. How do
you respond to the charge from those quarters that, in your eagerness
to posit a general theory, you neglect the specific historical and cultural
context—the concrete details and precise structures—of your anthropological materials?

R.G.: Anthropology has, indeed, turned its back on the whole
project. People as different as Evans-Pritchard, Dumézil, and Lévi-
Strauss speak with a single voice against it.

When a problem remains unsolved for too long, it is legitimate to
question its relevance as a scientific problem. Anthropologists have
good reason to challenge the relevance of religion as a single problem.

The results of the challenge, however, have been just as inconclusive, so far, as the efforts to solve the problem. Anthropology cannot claim, therefore, that it has disposed of this problem.

In spite of current fashion, all signs point to the continued relevance of the problem. If you read monographs on individual cultures, you find that they are incredibly awkward and repetitive in all matters religious, through no fault of the authors, simply because no one can agree on the definition of even such basic terms as ritual, taboo, sacrifice, etc., and yet no one can dispense with them. What kind of a science is it that cannot define any of its terms? All the religious systems taken together constitute a combination of constants and variables that the modern scientific spirit is irresistibly tempted to turn into some kind of puzzle or riddle, something, in other words, that it should be possible to untangle. Sooner or later, the pendulum will swing the other way once more, and interest in religion per se will perk up again.

Those who charge me with neglecting the concrete details and precise structures of my anthropological material are guilty themselves of that very neglect. They take one brief look at my hypothesis and they say, "It does not look right to me," or, "If it were true, we would already know it." Most of my critics simply do not understand what I am talking about. When they maintain, for instance, that it is impossible to "reduce" institutions so diverse as the religious ones to a single "concept," they do not realize that, for me, religion is "always already" interpretative and its interpretations cannot fail to be diverse because by definition they must wander away from the truth of the scapegoat mechanism. This "toujours déjà" is somewhat different from Derrida's but close enough, nevertheless, for me to place more hope in the readers of *Diacritics* at this early stage, in spite of the inevitable misunderstandings, than in professional anthropology.

As I shift from the overall genetic and structural scheme of my hypothesis to the specific institutions of specific cultures, I find variables that correspond exactly to what can be logically expected from the misinterpretation of scapegoat effects. Founding ancestors, gods, and sacred kings can be shown to be alternate solutions to the same problem of interpretation. Once a culture has launched into one of these directions, it can be expected to follow it to the end and to diverge more and more from those that made a different choice, in complete unawareness, of course, that they were actually choosing. The most impressive sign that my hypothesis cannot be a mere "effect of truth" is that it accounts both for the variables of religious systems and for such constants as the universal existence of prohibitions, rituals, and the belief in something like the "sacred." The presence of such

constants is incompatible with the now popular tendency to see each
culture as an almost absolutely singular phenomenon.

Why in my system must the crisis—and victimage—be considered to
have been historically actualized? Because the efficacy of unanimous
victimage alone can account for the nature and organization of the
mythemes and "ritemes" in all of primitive religion. This nature and
organization coincide too well with the foreseeable distortions of victimage in countless myths and with its reenactment in countless rituals
to authorize the slightest doubt.

In order to show that the preceding is not mere presumption, all that
is needed is some attentiveness, on the part of my readers, in following
the successive steps in the parallel I am about to make. This parallel, I
believe, can answer all your questions satisfactorily: *What is to be
gained by arguing for a real event? What would be lost by turning that
real origin into an explanatory fiction?*

Let us think of the texts most crucial in the modern awareness of
"scapegoating" as a structuring mechanism for representational *distortion*. The notion of distortion, here, must probably give way, at least in
principle, to a specific combination of representations that are *true* in
the sense of being generally faithful to the event they represent and of
representations that are *false* in the sense of being generally unfaithful
to these same events or to the roles played by the principal actors.

Let us think of those texts that relate episodes of anti-Jewish persecution during a medieval plague, the notorious Black Death, for instance. They are often contaminated by the perspective of the
persecutors in the sense that they tend to describe the Jews as inhuman
monsters. These texts are unreliable, therefore, and yet we all assume
that they are reliable in one fundamental respect, in the assertion that
the persecution really took place. This assumption is just as *hypothetical* as my *hypothesis*, since we are usually unable to match specific
texts with instances of persecution that would be documented by independent sources. The historian's view that the persecution must be real
has ethical implications, no doubt, but they are not primordial. The
conclusion of the historian is based on textual or "immanent" considerations.

In the text of persecution—as in most etiological myths—we have
two kinds of themes. First, we have unbelievable themes, such as the
magical power of the Jews to harm the community, as a result of their
unnatural acts similar to those of Oedipus. Second, we have themes
that are more or less believable, such as conflictual undifferentiation
(the plague), persecution, and redifferentiation (the restoration or
establishment of order).

Unlike the mythologist, the historian does not feel that the unbelievable character of some themes invalidates the entire text as far as extratextual information is concerned. Just the opposite. The more unbelievable the accusations against the likely victims, the more believable the persecution itself becomes, and the reality of the social disturbances that must have triggered it. Once the distortion introduced by the perspective of the persecutors is perceived, everything becomes clear; the genesis and structure of all textual features are too well matched and convincing to escape the perceptive reader. The "hypothesis" of real persecution is just about as certain as any historical occurrence can be and it is adopted as a matter of course. This "hypothesis" is much more than one possible reading among countless others, all equally "interesting" and equally relative. No one can say that it should be on the same footing as the perspective of the persecutors. To the question of what is to be gained by postulating the reality of the persecution, the answer is clear: the complete coherence and intelligibility of the text, the one and only *true* interpretation.

Innumerable myths resemble the texts of persecution in regard to the nature and combination of believable and unbelievable features. The similarities are such that even if my explication turned out to be false, still no one could exclude it a priori, on purely theoretical grounds. In the last analysis, this hypothesis amounts to treating mythology as if it were a text of persecution. If we agree that there must be real persecution behind the text of medieval anti-Semitism or the text—oral as well as written—of Southern racism in post–Civil War America, the same *can* be true, inevitably, in the case of those mythical texts that organize very much the same material along similar lines. In the case of mythology, just as in the case of persecution already acknowledged as such, the thesis accounts perfectly not only for the presence of unbelievable and believable features, but also for their constant juxtaposition. For the first time, a theory of mythology explains not some features abstracted from the myth as a whole, but all of them, around their dramatic core whose perpetual recurrence is also explained.

The hypothesis that the victimage must be real does not originate in the old confusion between signified and referent that it is correct to reject. It is demanded by an analysis that must finally transgress the rule of immanence, not unthinkingly but quite deliberately, because the respect of that same rule, up to that point, has demonstrated that the structuring power of real victimage is the only means to make complete sense, not of the collective violence alone, but of all the other features of the myth as well, the one and only solution that brings to mythology the kind of coherent intelligibility no rational mind can dismiss.

In the case of the text of persecution, no one ever asks "what is to be gained" by supposing that the victims are real? The answer is obvious, but the question should be asked because it is a textual question even before it is an ethical one. The answer gives the lie to the interpretative nihilism of our time. It is true that many interpretations of the same mythical text are possible, but they are all false; one interpretation alone is true, the one that reveals the structuring power of the persecutors' standpoint, to which all the others remain blind. It is not true that no decisive advance is possible in the understanding of texts, since the text of persecution is not really a separate category, but a myth that failed, and the myth that fails is a conquest of interpretation, a conquest of the worlds that come under the active influence of the Biblical texts, as we shall see later.

I am not oblivious to the difference between the text of persecution and mythology, and I will say a word about it later. For the time being, let me point out the relevance of the preceding remarks in regard to *representation*, a point on which I am supposed to be especially weak. Structuralist and poststructuralist theorists assume that I fall naively into the trap they denounce. I seem to move directly from the representation of victimage to its reality.

All theories of representation have something in common; whether religious or antireligious, they make all representations equivalent and they blind us, inevitably, to the analogies between persecution and mythology. The religious theories hold that all mythical representations are equally trustworthy and fully adequate to the sacred reality they represent. Antireligious theories hold that all representations are untrustworthy and unreal. These two opposites differ as far as a superficial conception of religion is concerned, but they are really the same in regard to structuring scapegoat effects. They make their detection impossible. They make it impossible to see my point about the unbelievability of certain representations' reinforcing the believability, then ultimately, as the evidence accumulates, the certainty of others. The a priori equivalence of all representations cannot remain unchallenged in the case of mythology, since it has been successfully challenged already in the case of persecution.

You understand, I hope, why it is important for me to show that the point I am trying to make apropos of mythology has already been made apropos of other texts; the only reason why these other texts appear different from myths is precisely that this point has been made and that it has been so decisively won. In the long run, I believe, the same point cannot fail to win everywhere.[1]

All a priori theories of representation, whether religious or philosophical, constitute obstacles in the path of a radical demythification.

The belief that there cannot be any advance except in the direction of more cognitive nihilism is erroneous. Cognitive nihilism plays in our world the role formerly reserved to religious faith. It makes all discovery impossible in the religious and anthropological field.

Far from being an end, the current disenchantment can be viewed as the precondition for a more scientific stage in the study of man. Earlier hopes to reach that stage, being based on dogmatic methodologies, were bound to fail. The present cognitive nihilism is rooted in a purely philosophical idea of truth and of the means to reach that truth. All established methodologies, such as structuralism, are dogmatically bound to the idea of truth. The sciences of man in their past and present state still share in an ideal of direct mastery and immediate evidence that is the epistemological dimension of what Derrida calls "the metaphysics of presence." This avaricious ideal dominates both empiricism and phenomenology, which are never abandoned without a fight because their practitioners cannot see any other possibility of knowledge. As a result, most people feel today that the end of all certain knowledge has arrived. The only intellectual activity they conceive is the interminable and solemn burial of "Western philosophy."

I believe the opposite to be true. When the failure of all dogmatic methodologies is fully acknowledged, the scientific threshold is close. We are about to give up that grasping and avaricious ideal that makes it unthinkable for the researcher to move away from the data and, in his despair, humility, craftiness, or mere idleness, look for possible clues in areas distant enough from these data to have been left unexplored until then, clues that obviously cannot yield the kind of direct evidence sought by dogmatic methodologies.

This is the threshold of hypothetical knowledge. Any knowledge henceforth will be hypothetical in the sense that it will never stem directly from empirical observation or phenomenological intuition alone. This, of course, is true of the unanimous victimage hypothesis, which has not been taken seriously so far by those who do not feel "in their hearts" that it can be right; the direct empirical evidence we can provide is marginal and it bears only on residual phenomena.

To the dogmaticists of pure empiricism, or empiricophenomenological structuralism, the *gap* between the data and the victimage hypothesis is perceived as a purely negative factor. As soon as they perceive that gap, they turn away and they dismiss the hypothesis as "farfetched." All good scientific hypotheses are by definition *farfetched*. They are so farfetched that it is impossible for those who find them to retrace the steps of their discovery. Only dogmatic methodologies can tell you which steps must be taken at all times and in what order. This is precisely the reason for which Michel Serres rightly observes that dogmatic methodologies never have and never will discover anything new.

The sciences of man have been dogmatic and philosophical for so long that they have lost sight of what scientific knowledge is really about. In an English review of *La Violence*, a charming gentleman of the *Times Literary Supplement* did explain to his readers that my thesis could not be taken seriously and that the author, fortunately, was aware of the fact since he called it a *hypothesis*. Scientific thought, for Lévi-Strauss, is called "la pensée des ingénieurs." The fact that engineers work on *hypotheses* provided by pure science is never mentioned.

Far from spelling the end of all knowledge, as the dogmaticist takes for granted, the *gap* between the hypothesis and the data becomes the space of verification, which remains unconceivable to dogmatic methodologies. By space of verification, I simply mean that the victimage mechanism looks different enough from any existing religious practice, such as a specific sacrifice, in a specific cultural context, or a specific sacred monarchy, etc., to cause the dogmaticist to shrug his shoulders and throw away the book in despair. But this very lack of resemblance is the sole reason for which the hypothesis can be concretely tested against an enormous variety of data. Either it will be possible to move from unanimous victimage to the specific data through fully intelligible steps or it will not. If these steps can really be taken in the case of one institution first, then a second, then a third, a fourth, a fifth, etc., the moment must come when the hypothesis becomes inescapable. It has proved its power as a generative mechanism of primitive religion.[2]

How could science reject this genetic mechanism out of hand, on a priori theoretical grounds, since it is the same mechanism, really, that is universally acknowledged as genetically relevant to texts almost homologous with the type of myths I focus upon, the texts of persecution. Either the structural and poststructural interpreter will confront the possibility I am trying to explore or he must reject the now standard reading of the text of persecution on the same a priori theoretical grounds. The fact that this alternative is never perceived clearly demonstrates that the antireferential stance of current theory is no genuine "radicalization." It is an unwarranted philosophical extrapolation of valid methodological principles.

The current theoretical phantoms will have their day and when their day is gone the commonsensical force of the point I am trying to make will reassert itself. Once you really understand this point, you realize it amounts to more than one theory of myth among others; it is the inevitable extension to the whole planet, including the cultural texts most distant from us, of a power to demystify persecution that is already effective within the confines of our own culture, at least to a certain extent.

Almost no one has ever looked at the evidence I have tried to utilize, with great awkwardness so far, I will admit. People immediately jump from my scientific hypothesis to what they regard as my ideological and religious prejudices and they automatically conclude that the first is dictated by the second. I am fully aware that the misunderstanding is inevitable and it may go on for quite a while, but not forever, because there is a lot of genuine research too. The type of coherence I am trying to establish will come more and more within our reach as the sacrificial resources of our culture become exhausted and the mythical compartments of Western knowledge further disintegrate.

You will say that my theory has philosophical implications and it is susceptible to a philosophical challenge. No doubt. The very idea of distortion, of representations that are false and of representations that are true implies that perception is intrinsically trustworthy as soon as you can disentangle it from the most proximate effects of its origin in victimage, and these effects are always social and religious. Discrimination in English means religious, ethnic, and social discrimination on the one hand and, on the other, the most fundamental operation of the human mind, the one that does indeed prove enormously reliable insofar as it can be kept separate from the other kind. This must be the reason why the first science to achieve spectacular results was astronomy. Today, the human power to discriminate can finally turn back against itself and reveal its own origin in victimage.

The epistemological assumptions behind all this are vulgarly commonsensical and I welcome them as such because they are the assumptions common to all the durable achievements of Western thought. No beginning science, in particular, has ever been able to dispense with them. These epistemological assumptions can be challenged in the abstract, but so can the general consensus in favor of real persecution behind the text of medieval anti-Semitism. Who would fail to see the ridicule of such a challenge?

Diacritics: Vis-à-vis the logical and semiological investigations that characterize one strand of contemporary philosophical inquiry, you reject out of hand what we might term, using a now conventional shorthand, the *epistemological* question—a question that eventually points to the problematic status of any discourse of truth and knowledge. In pragmatic terms, we can, of course, readily appreciate your stance here, since it amounts to refusing a form of reflection or reflexivity that often appears stultifying or crippling, doomed to the endless rediscovery of the elemental paradoxes or aporia that invariably haunt thought about thought, discourse on discourse, knowledge of knowledge, and so forth. In theoretical terms, however, the rationale behind your position is perhaps not quite so clear. Does the logic of the scapegoat mechanism as you have unraveled it not have some bearing on the conception and theory of knowledge? Has the development of your theory of culture not reached a point at which, in its very resistance to the critique of language and language use pursued by some of the "contemporary" schools of analysis and interpretation that you have sometimes seen fit to deplore, a certain implicit epistemology has begun to assert itself and thus deserves to be elaborated? Do you feel, for example, an imperative for a theoretical *reprise* comparable to the one that informs Foucault's *Archeology of Knowledge?*

R.G.: You can now see, I hope, that I do not reject the epistemological question. I refuse the frame of current theory and I deliberately reintegrate the banal and traditional framework of scientific research. Until recently, the essential thing for me was to protect what you call my insight and what I call my hypothesis from being intimidated out of existence by the great theoretical steamrollers of our time. The danger has decreased both because more and more implications of my work are slowly becoming visible, at least to a few people, and because the theoretical steamrollers, for all their huffing and puffing, have not progressed very far. The day is approaching, I am afraid, when the real but limited achievements of these great machines will have to be maintained in the face of a new unthinking rejection by the same forces of mimetic snobbery that espouse them so unthinkingly at the present time, I will then be regarded as too close an ally of views from which many people now feel I artificially try to distinguish myself.

I take the death of philosophy seriously, I repeat, but to me this death can only mean once more what it has already meant in the other areas from which philosophy and the philosophically inspired dogmatic methodologies have been successfully dislodged: the crossing of a scientific threshold. Questions these methodologies cannot successfully answer will be answered in a scientific framework. This does not mean the science of man about to be born will correspond to the expectations of the old scientistic ideology. If I am right about victimage, if not only mythology and ritual but hominization itself are dependent on this process, the consequences are no less shattering for modern than for traditional beliefs and it might be prudent to postpone the final theoretical reprise for a while. This is a task that I will never complete, I am afraid.

Judging from past history it can already be seen that the old effort to turn the study of man into a science is far from dead and ultimately it will triumph. This statement sounds preposterous, no doubt, in a certain intellectual climate. But this climate has changed in the past and it will change again in the future. The next change is going to affect even those figures that are likely to retain the importance they now have, Freud, for instance. The emphasis will shift from the linguistic and psychoanalytical Freud to the later Freud of the totally misunderstood and gigantic last essays in both *Totem and Taboo* and *Moses and Monotheism*.

The gradual shift to later and later achievements is fairly typical of what happens to the works that are too far ahead of their time and, in a sense, of themselves, to be readily intelligible. These two works are objective failures, no doubt, but their failure must be ascribed not to their excessively hypothetical nature, as most people believe, but to the very opposite, to the insufficiently hypothetical nature of their major thesis. Far from being merely "speculative," these two works are already *more* hypothetical in the truly scientific sense than all their predecessors and they represent an enormous advance over them.

To dismiss them as "speculative" is what everybody does and the error of that dismissal cannot become visible until the greater validity of the even more hypothetical solution I propose has been recognized. My hypothesis, too, is dismissed as speculative, of course, but other people will come who will further refine it and prove more successful than I am in demonstrating its efficacy. There will be scientific studies of mimetic conflict among animals and men. Some day the evidence will become so overwhelming that the dogmatic slumber of the specialists will be interrupted.

If I am not mistaken, therefore, the victimage hypothesis represents a higher stage in a process already well under way when Freud wrote about his primordial murder, the discovery he himself regarded as his greatest achievement. There will be still higher stages. Once the process is completed, people will realize that it runs parallel to what has always happened in the past each time a still impressionistic discipline has been able to cross the all-important threshold of hypothesis. No philosophical challenge can diminish the importance of this threshold. For this threshold, it would be unreasonable to give up the word "scientific," simply because crossing it, in the present case, will have consequences totally unforeseen by people like Freud himself and incompatible with the narrow scientistic ideology still associated in many minds with the project of man as an object of science. Here, once again, the past offers examples of this unexpected turn of events.

Diacritics: Against all the current claims on behalf of polysemousness, overdetermination, and the heterogeneity of microstructures, you appear to have erected a system that seeks to posit a universal explanatory matrix purporting to totalize all cultural phenomena around a historically real crisis at the origin. That origin—the historical reality of which we have already questioned—at times appears to acquire a philosophical function in your work, that of a transcendental signified that guarantees the truth of your hermeneutic procedures, which grounds the sense of history and culture and which ultimately serves to found self-consciousness—the Hegelian dialectic of desire. Is not the meaning of that origin that it is the origin of meaning in your system? that it is, therefore, in some sense the inaccessible or "uninterrogatable" *given* that predetermines the meanings or interpretations susceptible to articulation in your work?

R.G.: As my answers obviously show, unanimous victimage, for me, far from being an "uninterrogatable given," has become the primary object of investigation. There is nothing metaphysical or mystical about its relative inaccessibility. The only "real" scapegoats are those we are unable to acknowledge as such. Instead of relegating this commonsense evidence to some obscure corner of our minds, we should acknowledge its preeminence. We should regard it not as a minor specification of such modern notions as "transference," "repression," the "unconscious," "méconnaissance," etc., but as the most powerful definition for the submerged portion of the Freudian iceberg, the one mechanism truly able to supplant and supersede all the earlier solutions to the paradoxes of human culture and the human subject.

Even the most banal scapegoat effect is an unconscious structuring process. The growing ability to demystify these effects must coincide, historically, with a decrease in their power to delude. In spite of their still partly mythical nature, the texts of persecution already testify to that decreased efficacy: the victims are still perceived as omnipotent for evil but not for good anymore. They are no longer truly divinized in other words. Of the two collective transferences earlier defined, only the first one remains because it must be the least fragile. We still hate our victims, if you will, but we no longer worship them. This diminished mythical transfiguration certainly accounts for the readability of persecution in our world and the unreadability of myth *stricto sensu.* We can read persecution because it is objectively easier and we still cannot read myth even though or rather because it amounts to nothing else, in the end, than a more extreme transfiguration of the persecuted victim.

If our perception of scapegoat phenomena is inversely proportional to their effect, we can well understand why they would continue to elude our grasp, at least up to a point, even if they are in the process of losing their effectiveness. As these dynamics would unfold, victimage effects would come under our grasp, no doubt, but there would remain less and less to be grasped. This may well be the situation we are now confronting. All we can observe are, on the one hand, more or less residual and culturally marginal phenomena of the "lynching" category and, on the other, the infinite multiplication of victims, at the core of the civilized world, with little or no power to reconcile a community that tends more and more to coincide with the whole of mankind.

These developments must be characteristic of a sacrificial disintegration that for the first time in history seems irreversible. There must be several reasons for this, but they must all go back ultimately to the unforgettable knowledge we have acquired and are still acquiring of our violence and all its works, of our propensity to victimize other human beings.

Diacritics: Your work at times seems very close on the one hand to Sartre's analysis of anti-Semitism and the dialectics of desire and on the other to Derrida's treatment of the *pharmakos*. Could you sketch the outlines of your divergences from these two poles?

R.G.: In recent years, I have used the text of persecution as the "missing link" between mythology properly speaking and a reading of mythology entirely based on the structuring power of victimage. This is what I did once more in my answer to your question concerning the historical actualization of scapegoating. Anti-Semitism must be viewed first as one possible example of persecution among many others, in a process of cultural revelation that Sartre did not anticipate. There is no serious demythologizing of religion in Sartre. His remains the pre-Durkheimian and basically Voltairian view of the religious cult as parasitic of institutions that did not originate in religion. This view still prevails almost everywhere.

Could other examples of persecution play the same epistemological role as anti-Semitism? Yes, in the sense that the structure of persecution does not depend on the individual or collective identity of the victims. No, in the sense that a singular relationship does exist between the Jews and the text historically responsible in our world for the revelation of victimage as the structuring force behind the essential "idolatry" of all human culture: the Bible (see the last two questions of this interview). Anti-Semitism may be rooted ultimately in a defense reaction against the demythologizing power of the Bible. To deny the uniqueness of the Bible, as Sartre does, is to deny the uniqueness of Judaism. My own views are different.

As far as Derrida is concerned, I still view his *Pharmacie de Platon* as an important contribution to the deconstruction of sacrificial thought. In *La Double Séance*, there is a long footnote on the impossibility of a consistent theory of mimesis in Plato that is by far the best thing on the subject and it is of great importance to me. Later texts, such as *Glas*, are also of interest as witnesses to the decomposition of the primitive sacred in our world. The fact that Derrida does not distinguish the Judeo-Christian text from its theological and philosophical readings, the Hegelian one, for instance, more sacrificial than ever before, does constitute a serious limitation from my particular perspective, one, however, that does not interfere with my appreciation of his work.

Diacritics: We have a number of questions concerning your view on modern literary criticism, toward which you have adopted—in speaking of structuralists, poststructuralists, and the like—a relatively antagonistic attitude.

a. A number of American critics—Northrop Frye, for example, or Kenneth Burke, in *The Rhetoric of Motives*—have been concerned with the relations between sacrifice and the structure of literary works. Where would you situate yourself in relation to them?

R.G.: I find some analyses by Northrop Frye admirable, notably the *pharmakos* passages in *The Anatomy of Criticism*. The classificatory tendencies of the author made it predictable, however, that the threat and promise of further contamination would be too easily contained. Frye rightly feels that football and literary criticism are an improvement over sacrifice. Only the demagogues disagree. I cannot share Frye's apparent conviction, though, that in our part of the world at least, the nastier forms of violence have been decisively routed by football and literary criticism.

Kenneth Burke acknowledges a "principle of victimage" that is at work in human culture and, to me at least, this is an extraordinary achievement. This principle, unfortunately, rates no higher than a "codicil" in his definition of man (*Language as Symbolic Action* [Berkeley and Los Angeles: University of California Press, 1966]). Burke sees victimage as a product of language rather than language as a product of victimage (indirectly at least, through the mediation of ritual and prohibitions). He shares to some extent in what I would call the linguistic idealism of much recent French theory, but he does not push this idealism to the same heights of absurdity. The problem with many French developments is that you only have to stick the "radical" label on whatever heights of absurdity become visible at any given moment to intimidate vast crowds of people, at least for a few months.

I believe that Burke has never been translated into French and it cannot be a mere oversight. There must be reasons for this scandal. I regard the current "intertextual" school as a generally positive phenomenon. It has liberated American criticism from the fetish of the single work; it has made the antiphilosophical stance unfashionable. It has popularized a somewhat romantic but interesting notion of the (mimetic) "anxiety of influence," etc. In many instances, however, under a liberal sprinkling of "deconstructive" terminology, the old neocritical or thematic cake is still there and the taste is not as uncanny as one might wish.

The best work of Derrida makes one feel that deeply ingrained intellectual habits are endangered. The literary followers try to reproduce this sense of danger as a purely literary thrill, but failure is inevitable because their exclusive concentration on the literary text is intrinsically reassuring. To the intertextual corpus of Derrida, I try to add texts that I regard as even more "dangerous" than Nietzsche, Heidegger, and the pre-Socratics, those of mythology and ritual. "Deconstruction," I believe, has even more of a future than can be surmised from a perspective still dependent, if only "negatively," on the text of philosophy and of Saussurian linguistics.

In some respects at least, Kenneth Burke points the way toward more rather than less "danger." That may be the reason he remains as marginal today as he was during the long reign of New Criticism. I am all for French influence, obviously, but I would like to see it sprout vigorous and truly independent offshoots on American soil. The day this happens, Kenneth Burke will be acknowledged as the great man he really is.

b. How would you respond to traditional formalist or thematic critics who would charge you with finally reducing all literary texts to the disguised repetition of a single extratextual phenomenon, the scapegoat mechanism?

R.G.: I am sorry my work can be interpreted in this fashion. Far from being all alike, literary texts are so different from each other, in my eyes, that I am uninterested in "*littérarité*" or other concepts applicable to literature as such. The fact that a text, literary or theoretical, may simply reflect or, on the contrary, become aware of the mimetic effects on which it is founded and reveal these effects, to a greater or a lesser extent, makes an enormous difference. There is a first and essential diversity of literary texts, therefore, distributed along something like an axis of dissimulation/revelation. I cannot give a precise account of that difference and I do not claim that it can be fully mastered. The opposition between *romantique* and *romanesque* does not do full justice to the complexity of the problem.

There are other kinds of diversity that I am quite willing to acknowledge even though they do not play an important role in my work. I do believe that all human thinking ultimately goes back to the mimetic mechanisms I try to explore. This does not mean that I subscribe to the cognitive nihilism that is currently popular. Discrimination is the only instrument we have for the exploration of reality. This instrument is reliable insofar as it can be disentangled from human interaction. The first science to achieve spectacular results, I observed, was astronomy. From this great distance, trustworthy knowledge has been gradually advancing back toward human interaction; the elaboration of a real science of man is a most difficult but in my view not an impossible task. The mechanism of discrimination can turn back against itself and discover its own violent origin. The traditional objections of subjective idealism can be reformulated as "blindness and insight" or as *doublet empirico-transcendantal*, but they are philosophical objections and against the possibility of hypothetical knowledge in the science of man they will no more prevail than the excommunications of the popes against the first advances of physical science.

Because of the antiscientific temper of the times, especially in Europe, a basically sound exegetic principle, the principle of textual immanence now reinforced by Saussurian linguistics, or, more paradoxically still, by the theoretical sophistication of the hard sciences totally inapplicable to our own fields, has served as a catalyst for a new cristallization of the worst philosophical aberrations. Sooner or later critics will have to face the obvious. The interrelationship of textual elements does not authorize them to exclude or even minimize "referentiality," or to treat it as part of the text, etc.

All this, of course, would demand much more elaboration. My only purpose now is to show that there is nothing in my conception of the text that precludes multiple orders of diversity, including the slippery and unmanageable *différance* of poststructuralism that cannot be regarded, however, as the ineluctable law of all textuality.

c. Your reading of literary texts seems to alternate between an extreme literalness and an extreme hermeticism. For example: the arbitrariness of Oedipus's guilt can only be demonstrated by the most ingenious attention to textual hints and runs counter to all the traditional interpretations of the myth, notably to the Freudian one;

conversely, Hamlet's vacillation appears as the explicit manifestation of the arbitrariness of the decision either to kill or to forgive. Are these studied procedures of reading in some sense complementary? Can you specify an analytic principle that, in terms of such literary phenomena as themes, style, character, architecture, rhetorical figures, etc., governs your approach to the text?

R.G.: I hope the principal reason lies in the texts themselves. Shakespeare is playing quite explicitly with the mimetic phenomena to which most human beings want to remain blind and to which they are addicted in proportion to that blindness, at least up to a point. Hamlet is both revolted against the mimetic contagion of revenge, eroticism, fashion, philosophy, etc., and eager to become its victim in order finally to become what other men think he already is or ought to be. The presumed obscurity of the text stems from our refusal to take even the most explicit treatment of the mimetic cycle into account (the actor, the army, the imitation of Laertes . . .). Shakespeare, of course, anticipates this refusal, and craftily takes it into account to increase both the dramatic power of his play and the intellectual scandal of our own—the public's—lack of intelligence.

In the case of Oedipus, the situation looks somewhat different to me. I do not find the position of Sophocles as clear as I do that of Shakespeare, perhaps because of the greater cultural distance. I may be mistaken. Sandor Goodhart thinks that Sophocles is as fully in charge as Shakespeare. He may be right.[3] I could be influenced by the role Sophocles' tragedy played in my own discovery of structuration by victimage. In *Violence and the Sacred*, this mechanism is first reached at the end and through the means of an analysis of *Oedipus Rex*. This does not mean I grant the Oedipus myth as myth the same privilege as Freud. To me it is only one myth like any other.

d. In your reading of literary masterworks, the apparent specificity or idiosyncracies of characters tend to be overlooked in favor of uncovering the arbitrariness of their functions on the secret stage of violence. Are all protagonists interchangeable? What is the point of emphasizing the undifferentiation of the characters when it is their differences that seem to motivate their struggles?

R.G.: I say that mimetic violence *makes* the antagonists more and more interchangeable as they try and succeed in destroying each other, as they *are* less and less in other words. I do not have to say, therefore, that they ever *are* completely interchangeable.

The main point here is not what I personally think, but the efficacy of the real doubles in regard to certain texts, Shakespeare, for instance. Can we deny that the problematic of the real doubles reveals something about *Troilus and Cressida* no semiologist or semiotician will ever perceive?

The writers who interest me are obsessed with conflict as a subtle destroyer of the differential meaning it seems to inflate. I must share somewhat in that obsession. Many critics obviously do not and, fortunately for them, many writers do not either. Some of the things that interest these critics also interest me, but to a lesser degree. I do not claim to be a complete critic, or even a critic at all. I am not really interested in a text unless I feel it understands something I cannot yet understand myself. The distinction between "theoretical" and "literary" texts appears spurious to me, but few critics are ready to challenge it, perhaps because it justifies their existence as critics.

Thus, the "theory of literature" approach is alien to me. If you can write the "definitive" theory, in your own eyes, it means that literature, to you, is really a dead object. Not literature as such, I believe, but certain literary texts are vital to my whole "enterprise" as a researcher, much more vital than contemporary theory. Mine is a very selfish and pragmatic use of literary texts. If they cannot serve me, I leave them alone.

It would be disingenuous, of course, to deny that I am critical of other attitudes. An exclusive preoccupation with such things as beauty, form, classification, *"littérarité,"* etc., hides a secret contempt, I feel, for the literary text, which is regarded as incapable of truth. This, once more, is an a priori decision and under the appearance of genteel skepticism and universal tolerance it is the most oppressive form of censorship ever conceived. Literature for its own sake begins to resemble sex for its own sake and everything else for its own sake, every other kind of idolatry, in other words. The impasse is always the same.

e. The clarity and unerring sureness of your style are in marked contrast to the writing being practiced today by many poststructuralists, who justify the density and complexity of their styles with programmatic references to the materiality of the signifier—the insistence of the letter. How do you warrant writing with such clarity and limpidity, with the conceptual mastery and adherence to classical unity that have become suspect in some quarters? Do you envisage an account of the play of the signifier within your system?

R.G.: I thank you for the compliment. My answer to this question is implicit in my previous answers. I believe that the maze can be mapped out; we do not have to describe the same spirals interminably. A more economical and fruitful form of rigor is available to us. From the standpoint of mimetic systematization, the *valse hésitation* of intertextuality will look more and more superfluous, another form of *préciosité*, perhaps, that should ultimately give way to a new "classicism."

Judging from the almost universal misunderstanding of my project and its results so far, I am not sure that I am quite as clear as you kindly assume.

It seems to me, anyway, that a new style of simplicity is in the air, or a new air of simplicity is in the style. I do not know which is which but I welcome the change, and I will try to become more clear than ever myself, in docile emulation of everybody else. This is the direction in which Paris, at least, is going, including some of our most fascinating models of the recent obscurity. Could it signify that the signifier for the signifier's sake is not fulfilling its promise? I will leave the question to those competent to answer it.

f. You have played a variety of important roles in the organization of graduate studies at Buffalo, Johns Hopkins, and elsewhere. If you were forced to do so, how would you conceive of a cogent program in literary studies at the present time? What would be its bases and its goals? Is there still something to be said for the traditional notion of a "canon" of texts? How should a student—or teacher—attempt to orient himself or herself vis-à-vis the controversies in contemporary criticism?

R.G.: If one does not believe that certain texts, at least, can help us, not only esthetically but intellectually and ethically, especially at a time such as ours, which is no ordinary time, then literature is an empty and dying cult. A few may be fanaticized by the very emptiness of the cult—the last dregs of the Mallarmé phenomenon—but the many will see through this same emptiness and turn away from it.

The works I always turn to, the mimetic works in my special sense, usually belong to the traditional canon. Is it not strange that, in order to justify the existence and composition of that canon, critics have always used the same word, *mimesis*, imitation? Throughout its long history, the word has meant or appeared to mean many different things, and I would like to believe I mean it myself in a sense that is different and even unique and that can make sense out of all previous senses. This is the one problem of "literary theory" that really interests me at this time. I would like to study all literary acceptations of the word from the standpoint of mimetic anthropology. The word *mimesis* and its translations, into Latin first, then the modern languages, are the main signifiers of a literary criticism whose earlier signified may not always appear as insignificant as it does at the present time.

Vis-à-vis the current controversies, a degree of fascination is inevitable, perhaps, and even desirable in the younger people, as they enter the field, but it cannot produce anything important in the long run. If it persists into middle age it results in the world of intensely mimetic fashion that is now all around us. It gives an appearance of health, like the flushed cheeks of the consumptive heroine in romantic novels, but it is gradually emptied of life.

Diacritics: How does a theory of the relations between sacrifice and violence address itself to our contemporary situation? How is the situation like and unlike the primitive situation when, for example, the myth is anti-Semitism and the expulsion is the holocaust?

Clearly, certain texts of Judeo-Christianity—texts of the Hebrew prophets and of the synoptic Gospels—have a privileged status in your work in that they reveal in full the sacrificial foundations of the primitive universe. In the wake of this revelation, what precisely is the nature of our modern inheritance? What are the advantages of an antisacrificial system and what are its dangers?

R.G.: In his work on ancient Judaism, Max Weber perceives that the biblical texts usually side with the victims and it is a great singularity. This singularity, however, he attributes to the historical misfortunes of the Jewish nation, in a characteristic reconciliation of German imperial complacency with Nietzschean and Marxist influences. He can see the biblical concern for the victim only as a distortion inspired by psychosocial resentment. As we become aware of the structuring force behind victimage we must reexamine this simplistic dismissal. We must reexamine the universal belief in an inevitable divorce between the ethical and the epistemological.

From the perspective of unanimous victimage finally revealed, even the more archaic biblical texts look like reinterpretations of earlier myths powerful enough to undermine the mythical products of victimage *because* they side with the scapegoat and turn back this demonic figure into an innocent victim. Behind the story told by the eleven brothers to Joseph's father, Jacob, there is the vengeful consensus of this violent community and later on, in Egypt, this vengeful consensus reappears once more when Joseph is imprisoned. Everybody believes Joseph has betrayed his adoptive father, Potiphar, and committed with the latter's wife something analogous—lo and behold!—to the "incest" of Oedipus. Like the Egyptians of Potiphar, we, in the modern world, still take the incestuous business quite seriously, whereas the biblical writers, twenty-five hundred years ago, had already denounced it as the nonsense it really is.

Scapegoat demythologization alone is real, and only the biblical text carries it to its extreme conclusion. This is a harsh doctrine, no doubt, and it will take more time, more cultural disintegration for *la modernité* to take it seriously at all. The signifier is visibly playing against all of us this time, and the irony is unbearable. Our most cherished beliefs are threatened. As the evidence of what I say becomes compelling, attempts will be made to rearrange it in a manner more compatible with the self-esteem of an intelligentsia, whose sole common ground and binding theme—*religio*—has become the systematic expulsion of everything biblical, our last sacrificial operation in the grand manner.

In a world threatened with total annihilation, sacrificial resources, like fossil fuel, become a nonrenewable commodity. It would be sheer madness to expect from now on that the escalation of mimetic strife will bring back some tolerable order. We know only too well that our destructive power already exceeds or will soon exceed the ecological tolerance of the terrestrial milieu. On such conditions, ignorance of cultural foundations is becoming an impossibility. The dynamics of destructive power in our world must coincide with the dynamics of cultural awareness, as demanded by the very nature of the foundation now emerging into the light not so much in our books as in that absolute technological threat we are busy creating with our own hands.

At the highest level of political power it is already an obvious fact of contemporary life that violence must be renounced, unilaterally if need be, or universal destruction will ensue. The late prophetic and evangelical replacement of all primitive law by the sole renunciation of violence is no longer a utopian or arcadian dream. It is the scientific *sine qua non* of bare survival. It is a mere coincidence or should we suspect that far from being as hopelessly irrelevant to contemporary problems as the intelligentsia believes, the biblical text is much more relevant than the Oedipus of Freud or the Dionysos of Nietzsche?

The apocalyptic thread that runs through the prophetic writings of the Bible has less and less to do with a divine vengeance, and nothing anymore in the apocalypse of the gospels. It is articulated on a revelation of cultural origins—"the murders your fathers have committed since the foundation of the world"—that is supposed to shake the (sacrificial) powers of this world, making the abandonment of violence in all its forms the only alternative to a purely human self-annihilation.

The sacrificial misreading of Judeo-Christian scriptures, common to Christian and anti-Christian thinkers alike has only retarded, we may believe, both the arrival of the ultimate *emergency* and the correct nonsacrificial reading of the biblical text.

It is probably unwise to summarize in a few lines problems too complex and answers too startling not to appear simply aberrant in the present context. I did not want to leave your question completely unanswered. There is a more extensive treatment in the book published in March 1978 by Grasset: *Des Choses cachées depuis la fondation du monde* (kekrumména àpò kataboles, Matt. 13, 35).

Diacritics: Politically you seem inevitably to come down on the side of order and law against all forms of violent excess. Where would you situate your work and its political/ethical implications in relation to Marx or to Bataille?

R.G.: The expression "order and law" is reminiscent of "law and order." To American readers, at least, it suggests some recent alignments in American domestic politics. These alignments mean little more than the distribution of good and bad political grades to those who come down "for" or "against" law and order. Since everybody resorts to the same simplistic dichotomies, the thinking is the same on both sides. This is as it should be. "Violent excess" on the one hand, "law and order" on the other have always fed on each other. What else could they feed upon? If they did not, we would be rid, by now, of both of them.

If our readers recall the questions you asked me, and the answers I gave, they may be a little surprised, wouldn't you think, to find that I am the one who inevitably comes down on the side of order and law. All you have to do, apparently, to make that verdict inevitable is to maintain that the victims are real behind the texts that seem to allude to them. Does it inevitably follow that the impeccable revolutionary credentials go to those for whom the victims are not real? This would be a great paradox indeed! There are signs, I am afraid, that this paradox is not merely intertextual. It may well be the major fact of twentieth-century life. The ideologies with the greatest power to fascinate the modern mind are also responsible for the greatest massacres in human history, but many intellectuals have been especially reluctant to acknowledge the fact, as if ideology reinforced in them the old capacity not to see that all victims are equally real behind the ideological as well as the mythical text.

In his poem "Vespers," of *Horae Canonicae*, W. H. Auden portrays a silently hostile encounter between our ideological doubles:

> Both simultaneously recognize his Anti-type; that I am an Arcadian, that he is a Utopian.

I thank Ed Mendelson of Yale for bringing this poem to my attention. The last few lines can be regarded as an answer to your question, more eloquent than anything I could say:

> Was it (as it must look to any god of cross-roads) simply a fortuitous intersection of life-paths, loyal to different fibs?

Or also a rendez-vous between two accomplices who, in spite of themselves, cannot resist meeting

to remind the other (do both, at bottom, desire truth?) of that half of their secret which he would most like to forget,

forcing us both, for a fraction of a second, to remember our victim (but for him I could forget the blood, but for me he could forget the innocence),

on whose immolation (call him Abel, Remus, whom you will, it is one Sin Offering) arcadias, utopias, our dear old bag of a democracy are alike founded:

For without a cement of blood (it must be human, it must be innocent) no secular wall will safely stand.

NOTES

1. See Chapter 9 of this volume.
2. See *Des Choses cachées depuis la fondation du monde*, pt. 1.
3. See the essay by Sandor Goodhart on *Oedipus Rex* in the same issue of *Diacritics* as the original version of this interview (March 1978).

THE JOHNS HOPKINS UNIVERSITY PRESS

This book was composed in Linotype Caledonia text and Bernard Modern Roman display type by Maryland Linotype Composition Company, Inc., from a design by Alan Carter. It was printed on a 50-lb. Publishers Eggshell Wove and bound in a pyroxyline impregnated cloth by the Maple Press Company.

Library of Congress Cataloging in Publication Data

Girard, René, 1923-
  "To double business bound."
    1.   Mimesis in literature—Addresses, essays,
lectures.   2.   Rites and ceremonies—Addresses, essays,
lectures.   3.   Structural anthropology—Addresses,
essays, lectures.   I.   Title.
PN47.G5   809   78-8418
ISBN 0-8018-2114-2